The Legacy

A Memoir

Jean Barr

The Book Guild Ltd

First published in Great Britain in 2022 by
The Book Guild Ltd
Unit E2 Airfield Business Park,
Harrison Road, Market Harborough,
Leicestershire. LE16 7UL
Tel: 0116 2792299
www.bookguild.co.uk
Email: info@bookguild.co.uk
Twitter: @bookguild

Typeset in 11pt Minion Pro

Printed and bound in the UK by TJ Books LTD, Padstow, Cornwall

ISBN 978 1915352 392

British Library Cataloguing in Publication Data.
A catalogue record for this book is available from the British Library.

For Laurie and Stevie

Contents

Acknowledgements

I am indebted to numerous friends and fellow writers for their generous support, advice and encouragement in writing this book, sometimes intentionally, as in reading drafts of chapters and offering suggestions and fresh ideas, sometimes unknowingly by not shutting me up when I was obsessing about the unlikely family connections I kept uncovering. Special thanks are due to Annette Kuhn for her company, forbearance and help, especially during lockdown; to Mary-Jane Holmes for her invaluable judgment and Jane Harris of janealogy for ensuring the accuracy of my family trees – showing, for instance, that I am NOT, as I thought for one deluded moment, related to Sarah Churchill, Duchess of Marlborough who, as Queen Anne's favourite, was recently played by Rachel Weisz alongside Olivia Colman's Queen, in Yorgos Lanthimos's glorious film The Favourite.

I am deeply grateful to Bridget Fowler for her unstinting support and advice, often whilst out walking and talking, followed by tea and excellent homemade ginger biscuits. Special thanks to Alison Miller, Liam Stewart, Les and Usha Brown, Eileen Aird, Lynda Haddock, Carol Craig, Mae Shaw, Ian Martin, Tom Steele and Lynne Gostick for reading and commenting on sections of the book and encouraging me to keep going. Thanks, too, to the excellent archivist Gabriella Ballesio of the Waldensian Church's administrative centre in Torre Pellice, Piedmont, and to librarians at the Universities of Glasgow and Edinburgh Special Collections, Orkney's Kirkwall Public Library, the National Library of Scotland, British Library, and Bedfordshire County Council Record Office.

To Colin, Wendy and my beloved grandchildren Laurie and Stevie, thank you for everything.

Photograph by Annette Kuhn.

One

The Quest

The idea of the quest fascinates, implying a journey, overcoming obstacles, following clues towards some goal or mission, and, frequently, the disclosure of hitherto hidden secrets or treasure. When I set out on the fairly straightforward quest animating this book, I could not have known then that there would be a deeper puzzle to solve.

It all began with the chest; my most treasured possession and the thing I most loved as a child because of its secret compartment. I have lived close to the carved seventeenth-century Venetian cassone all of my life; first in my grandparents' house round the corner, and then at home with my parents and brother when my grandma came to stay. The 'secret' compartment – a deep inner box with its own flat lid, hidden in plain sight almost flush with the top of the chest – was not hard to find for anyone who opened it. Kept polished to a high chestnut sheen with Mansion lavender-scented furniture polish, it smelled delicious. I knew it had been a gift, perhaps a wedding present, to my grandparents, from an uncle who was a minister in Venice. When my mother died, it passed to me.

I also inherited a book, bound in pale green linen, with its title, *Fra Paolo Sarpi*, and the author's name, Alexander Robertson DD, and publisher, George Allen, embossed in gold on the cover. Inside, a tattered photograph – a newspaper clipping from the time of Alexander's death – bears the caption 'Notable Scots Divine'. It shows a stocky figure, snow-white-bearded, bushy-browed and bespectacled, resplendent in dog collar

1

and tam-o'-shanter. He looks relaxed, standing on a sun-drenched wooden deck dotted with pots of flowers in front of a tree laden with blossom, hands clasped behind his back, looking straight at the camera. The book – just another object, like the chest – has also followed me all my life. Only recently have I had the time or inclination to read it, although I was still not encouraged by its subject matter: a sixteenth-century radical friar.

I grew up believing that both objects came from my maternal grandmother's uncle, but soon realised that my grandfather's uncle was the donor. I should have guessed this from my grandpa's full name, James Robertson Montgomery, his middle name being the surname of his mother Elizabeth (Alexander Robertson's sister), as was the Scottish custom. I also realised that the beautiful Venetian-glass sundae dishes, once kept in my parents' display cabinet and now on my window ledge, must have come from my great-great-uncle too. Despite living in Florence with my husband and baby son for a year between 1972 and 1973, we never visited Venice or San Remo, the two places where Alexander lived and preached for most of his life – a fact I only discovered later. During subsequent visits to both cities I still knew nothing about my great-great-uncle's connection to them.

I signed up to the family history website ancestry.co.uk specifically to find out more about Alexander, knowing only that he had lived in Italy and that the lovely Venetian chest and embossed book that I had inherited through my mother had originally come from him. As an Italophile, I think I hoped that by researching Alexander's life I might find some long-lost Italian relations. As an added bonus, by following in his footsteps through Italy I could revisit some favourite works of Renaissance art featured in the Open University art history course that I had just embarked upon. More than anything else, I was curious. At the start of my family history project, Alexander Robertson (1846–1933) presented a puzzle. Why would a Presbyterian minister, born and educated in Edinburgh, spend most of his life in Italy, an overwhelmingly Catholic country?

Notwithstanding these motives, my curiosity and decision to delve into a hitherto unknown corner of my family's past had unexpected consequences, requiring a sudden swerve in direction in light of an extraordinary turn of events. One evening in late 2017, about a year into researching Alexander's life, and having signed up to ancestry.co.uk, I settled down to watch the first episode of a new BBC Two drama-documentary miniseries, entitled *Elizabeth I's Secret Agents*. I noticed that another historical miniseries was being broadcast around the same time on BBC One; a three-part drama called *Gunpowder*. Both series featured a man whose name rang a bell, though not because of my knowledge of British history. I had spotted the name in the family tree that I was constructing around my great-great-uncle. Everything changed when the name became that of a historical figure: Robert Cecil, Earl of Salisbury (1563–1612).

Until that moment I had had scant interest in the British aristocracy. As a one-time sociology lecturer I did have a strong interest in the role of class and elites in society, but the kind of history I was drawn to was the 'history from below' promoted by the History Workshop movement since the 1960s, which views history from the perspective of ordinary people rather than elites. Despite myself, however, I now found myself fascinated by and poring over the lives of statesmen, Dukes and Duchesses, Lords and Ladies – people I had scarcely heard of, and far less had any interest in, until then. My curiosity about the life of an obscure Scottish minister turned into something entirely different – a pursuit that might be described, crudely, as 'following the money'.

From the two BBC miniseries I learned that Sir Robert Cecil was chief spymaster of King James I of England and VI of Scotland, and the son of Queen Elizabeth I's original spymaster, William Cecil, Lord Burghley. *Gunpowder* focuses on how Robert Cecil foiled the Gunpowder Plot of 1605 and oversaw the torture and execution of its Catholic ringleaders. *Elizabeth I's Secret Agents* spotlights his father, who built up a spy network during Elizabeth's reign, aimed at preventing the Catholic Mary, Queen of Scots from ascending the English throne. William Cecil regarded Mary as 'the greatest threat to Elizabeth's throne, to religion and to the security of the Tudor state' (Alford, 2008, p. 154). He succeeded in his mission, eventually securing Mary's head on the block.

Robert inherited his father's network and, according to historians of the period whose books I quickly devoured, it was he who, on Elizabeth's death, more or less single-handedly secured succession to the English Crown for Mary, Queen of Scots' son, the Protestant James VI of Scotland. The Tudor dynasty ended when Elizabeth died in 1603. As far as Protestants were concerned, there were few places for her crown to go other than to James. Since James was the great-great-grandson of the first Tudor monarch, Henry VII, he could come peaceably to the throne of England and Ireland. Yet, claims Stephen Alford, the most extraordinary fact about his accession is that every detail was arranged before the Queen's death and without her knowledge. Robert, 'so accomplished in secret matters', had been quietly negotiating James's succession at the English and Scottish courts since 1601 (Alford, 2012, p. 323).

The connection to Robert Cecil that I spotted in my family tree stemmed from my great-great-uncle Alexander's second marriage to Julia Braddon (née Dawson), and seemed to hinge on a man called John Foster Barham, Julia's second cousin once removed. It came about as follows: when John Foster Barham (1799–1838) died, his widow, Lady Katherine Grimston, remarried. Her second husband was George William Frederick Villiers (1810–70), 4th Earl of Clarendon, whose '6th great-grandfather' was 'Sir Robert Cecil, 1st Earl of Salisbury'. My family tree also shows that Robert was the father-in-law of Catherine Howard (1595–1673), daughter of Thomas Howard, 1st Earl of Suffolk.

This means that I can track my family connection to Sir Robert Cecil through a series of marriages involving some of England's preeminent aristocratic families, notably the Villiers and Howard dynasties (see Appendix, Table 1). Neil Cuddy claims that, as the family (and heads) of Howards fell from royal favour during the Jacobean reign in the seventeenth century, affiliation to the Villiers family became the key connection for the English elite. This was because James I insisted that his favourites should be willing to marry into the family of his reputed lover George Villiers, 1st Duke of Buckingham, ancestor of Robert Cecil's sixth great-grandson George William Frederick Villiers, husband of John Foster Barham's widow. As a result of this rise in royal favour, says Cuddy, by the 1630s, 'the Villiers were the equivalent of Elizabeth Tudor's cousinage, the Howards, which had been so central to her regime' (Cuddy, 2000, p. 73).

A portrait of George Villiers, 1st Duke of Buckingham, previously thought to be a copy of a portrait by Peter Paul Rubens, featured in a BBC Four TV series, *Britain's Lost Masterpieces*, first broadcast in 2017. The *Radio Times* previewed the programme, stating that it involved a 'visit [to] Pollok House in Glasgow to investigate a long-lost picture of one of the most famous gay men in history, possibly painted by one of the most famous artists in history'. I saw the painting, now regarded as a genuine 1625 portrait by Rubens, at an exhibition in Glasgow University's Hunterian Gallery. At that time I did not know what I know now: that I am related to the man whom James I referred to as 'my husband'.

As with the Cecils, the appearance of the Villiers and Howard family lines in my tree boils down to the fact that my great-great-uncle Alexander's second marriage was to a woman (Julia) whose second cousin once removed was married briefly to someone who, when widowed, went on to marry the 4th Earl of Clarendon, George Villiers. I knew little or nothing about the Villiers or the Howards, or indeed the Cecils, before uncovering my many-arms'-length family relationships to them. A crash course in British dynastic history ensued, soon to be followed by forays into other fields about which I knew little, as revelations of connections to other luminaries came thick and fast. All of them derived from my great-great-uncle's marriage to Julia Braddon, and most, though not all, stemmed from her ancestral relationship to John Foster Barham.

Julia, like Alexander, had been married before. Through ancestry.co.uk I learned that her first husband was called John Clode Braddon; a discovery that sparked a flurry of incoming online information about his much more famous cousin, Mary Elizabeth Braddon. I soon learned from an English studies friend that she was a renowned nineteenth-century author of so-called 'sensation fiction'. I had never heard of her before, though I now know that her best-known novel, *Lady Audley's Secret* (1862), is today regarded as a forerunner of the detective novel, and has been adapted for the stage and made into a film three times: in 1915, 1920 and 2000. I soon found the book, a Penguin Classic, in a second-hand bookshop (see Appendix, Table 2).

Of far greater interest to me as a philosophy graduate was spotting Bertrand Russell (1872–1970), the philosopher grandson of Lord John Russell, third son of the 6th Duke of Bedford and twice Liberal Prime Minister, in my tree. He too is on the same branch of my tree as John Foster Barham (see Appendix, Table 3). One grandee I am delighted to find there is Robert Boyle FRS (1627–91), inventor of the air pump and author of *The Sceptical Chemist*, which inaugurated a new age of scientific experimentation. Another is Margaret Cavendish, Duchess of Newcastle (1624–73), the first female scientist to attend a meeting of the Royal Society, and author of *The Blazing World* (1666), which has been hailed as an early feminist science fiction classic and a forgotten masterpiece. Her husband William Cavendish, Duke of Newcastle, was the fifth great-uncle of George William Frederick Villiers, second husband of John Foster Barham's widow.

To my astonishment, I am also related to the branch of the Cavendish family that includes the Dukes of Devonshire of Chatsworth House; again because of family links to John Foster Barham (see Appendix, Table 1). Chatsworth House, built by Elizabeth Hardwick ('Bess of Hardwick'), second wife of William Cavendish (1505–57), is still occupied by the Dukes of Devonshire. Chatsworth is where Bess and her fourth husband, George Talbot, 6th Earl of Shrewsbury (who was appointed custodian of Mary, Queen of Scots by Elizabeth I), held Mary prisoner between 1569 and 1584. On her husband's death at Sheffield Castle, Bess rebuilt Hardwick Hall. To my dismay, George Granville Leveson-Gower, 1st Duke of Sutherland, whose role in the Highland Clearances involved the eviction of thousands of tenants in favour of sheep, is there too. His aunt, Anne Egerton, was the wife of William Villiers, great-uncle of George William Frederick Villiers, 4th Earl of Clarendon.

But of all the luminaries in my lineage, none were more powerful than the Cecils, whose role in the formation of the British state was fundamental. The forty-year partnership between Elizabeth I and William Cecil (1520– 98) has been described by A. L. Rowse as 'the most remarkable in English history... [and] the most fruitful in effect'. William's son, Robert, 'raised to the peerage' as the Earl of Salisbury by James I and VI, 'prolonged the family's influence until his own death in 1612, by which time the union of the kingdoms of Scotland and England was safely established... *the* secular objective of English policy brought about by that fortunate family' (Rowse, 1950, p. 275).

The Cecils, whose beginnings were neither rich nor aristocratic, benefited from one of two early land grabs. The first, during Henry VIII's reign when the monasteries were disestablished, released large tracts of land to the rising gentry and made fortunes for the King and his elites. The second, during James I's rule, bestowed lavish gifts on favourites such as Robert Cecil, whose father had already profited from his time in office during Elizabeth I's reign. One lucrative source of wealth for William was his investment in privateering during the Anglo–Spanish War. Privateers were legally licensed to attack enemy ships in the manner of pirates, but in the ostensible service of the English Crown. Privateering 'blurred the line between state interest and private wealth accumulation', or, as Lawrence Stone puts it, 'the distinction between legitimate privateering and indiscriminate piracy was hard to draw' (Mabee, 2009, p. 149; Stone, 1973, p. 7). William Cecil, as Secretary of State, and his friend Charles Howard, as Lord Admiral, were especially well placed to collaborate in this legalised piracy, using ships belonging to the Admiralty to seize goods from foreign ships. By the time he died, William had acquired a huge estate stretching from the Home Counties into Yorkshire. He also owned properties in London and other parts of England, including Burghley House in Lincolnshire, set in a park later laid out by Lancelot 'Capability' Brown and now housing one of the finest collections of early Italian Renaissance art in the UK. His descendants are still major landowners in Britain, as are descendants of other long lineages newly present in my ancestry, who also continue to hold high political office in Parliament (see Chapter 10).

John Foster Barham's pivotal position in my tree, linking backwards to the Cecils and forwards to Julia (and hence Alexander), demanded an explanation. Why did his presence have such startling consequences for my family? What in Julia's family background accounted for my family's implication in such networks of wealth and power? My revelations about distant aristocratic family links occurred in the aftermath of the 2014 Scottish Independence Referendum, in which I had cast my 'No' vote. All forms of nationalism were anathema to me. In an issue of the weekly current affairs magazine *Scottish Review*, I even wrote about the consequences of the union being dissolved, arguing that the referendum had catalysed a resurgence of the sectarianism that dogged the left in the 1970s. I predicted that the Scottish pro-independence left would split the progressive vote and deliver victory to the Tories in the forthcoming UK general election. In light of the state-building skulduggery I unearthed in the months following the independence referendum, especially regarding the Cecils' role in the union of the Crowns of England and Scotland, I had to ask myself if I might have cast my vote differently had I known all of this beforehand. Subsequent events, including Brexit and the resurgence of the radical right in the British government, have only added to my growing unease and sense that were there to be a second referendum on Scottish independence, I might well vote 'Yes', which, for me, would be a radical turnaround, given my political background and commitments.

Whilst unearthing these astonishing facts about my family background, I was reading a recently published book called *Family Values* by Melinda Cooper, which focuses on the role of the family and inheritance in contemporary capitalism. It resonated with what I was learning about the new-found cast of characters in my tree. Cooper maintains that contemporary capitalism is especially well geared to providing mechanisms for the hoarding and passing on of advantage, and that the family remains central to this. Reading Cooper's book brought to mind *The Leopard* (Lampedusa, 1960). Set in Sicily during the island's invasion by Garibaldi, hero of Italian unification, the novel's hero, the Prince of Salina, Don Fabrizio, wants to preserve his family's influence after Italy has become a single state. The novel's main theme – that everything has to change so that everything can stay the same – is voiced by the Prince's nephew, Tancredi, who has joined Garibaldi: 'If we want things to stay as they are, things will have to change'. Cooper echoes this paradox when she proposes, counter-intuitively, that rather than seeing the legal history of the modern family as a process of progressive liberalisation, it should be seen, more accurately, as a process of *preservation* through transformation. From this point of view, for example, gay marriage, by making more inclusive rather than challenging the institution of marriage and inheritance, shores up the family as an economic institution for passing on advantage. The shifting role of private inherited wealth is pivotal in Cooper's analysis. She points out that the people who benefited most from rising inflation in the 1970s were middle-income homeowners (such as myself) who, with fixed mortgage repayments and interest rates, saw their mortgage debt decrease as prices including that of housing rose. Those renting homes were not overburdened either, because wages kept up with rent rises (Cooper, 2017, p. 126).

The people whose wealth *was* eroded by inflation were the top 10%, whose money was invested in financial assets or real estate and whose incomes were derived from interest, dividends or rent rather than salaries or wages. This means that between 1972 and 1976 the falling value of stocks and shares owned by the wealthiest resulted in a reduction in wealth concentration. By thus acting like a redistributive tax, inflation enhanced the progressive tendencies of the post-war era – but only briefly. By the end of the decade, free market economists were claiming that inflation was a covert tax to extort wealth from the rich to give to the poor. In consequence, neoliberal policies rehabilitated the value of financial assets that had depreciated briefly in the 1970s, as a result of which, the past few decades have seen a resurgence of large family fortunes accompanied by a thriving of family trusts; a legal instrument traditionally used by the very rich.

Thomas Piketty is one of several theorists to note the re-emergence of private inherited wealth as decisive in shaping social class after a relative decline in the post-war era, when redistributive trends reduced wealth and income inequalities (Piketty, 2014). Cooper explains, 'When the price of assets appreciates against stagnant wages and welfare, then it is almost inevitable that family wealth will assume a decisive role in shaping and restricting social mobility' (Cooper, 2017, p. 125). Cooper's book is based on empirical data relating mainly to the US economy, but it applies equally to the UK, which has followed a similar path.

OECD data show that the UK, where social mobility has been slowing down for the past forty years, now has one of the lowest levels of social mobility in the developed world. There is, especially in the UK, a widening gap between those who own property and those who do not (Ryan-Collins et al., 2017, p. 178). When I was reading Cooper's book, friends were opening trust funds for grandchildren for inheritance tax reasons. Their wealth, in the form of property in housing, had increased massively since they had first entered the housing market, as I did in the 1970s. I even flirted briefly with the idea myself. But as I pursued my quest into Alexander's life in Italy, and as the task of joining the dots between him, John Foster Barham and the Cecils intensified, questions of inheritance took on added significance. And as my focus on one man shifted into a wider frame, the pandemic was spotlighting the stark inequalities that define Britain today.

I was born in Glasgow, forty or so miles west of Alexander's birthplace of Edinburgh, the younger child of a pharmacist father and a shorthand typist mother. Both were Christian socialists with a strong sense of social justice and the belief that 'There but for the grace of God...' I have lived and continue to live elsewhere, but unlike Alexander always return, my roots having as much to do with my political formation as with personal connections. Throughout my childhood, my father Adam Cruickshank worked for a chain of chemist shops, Cockburn & Co., and for most of that period he managed their shop in the Gorbals, an area notorious for its slums and gang violence. His father, another Adam, had settled in Glasgow with his new wife Isabella at the turn of the twentieth century. Both from farming families in Aberdeenshire, the 1901 census finds them living at the Officers' Quarters, Barlinnie, where Adam was a warden.

By the time of my father's birth in 1906, my paternal grandfather was a stationmaster on the ten-year-old Glasgow Subway, the third-oldest underground metro in the world. My parents' 1937 marriage certificate describes him as an 'electrical engineer (retired)'. The eldest of seven sons and one daughter, he should have inherited the farm but it was his brother James who did so, remaining there, unmarried, with his mother and youngest brother Harry, who had a condition known as dwarfism, until his death in 1951. Family legend has it that his horse and cart brought James home drunk every night. His brothers George and Duncan opened chemist and cycle shops in Turriff, the chemist's only recently sold to the Boots chain. George earlier worked for Cockburn's in its St Enoch branch in Glasgow, where his nephew Adam, my father, did locum work.

My parents were staunch Labour Party voters, and firm believers in the welfare state and the power of education to change lives. My brother and I were brought up in a two-bedroomed rented flat in a typical red-sandstone Glasgow tenement, a few miles from my dad's shop and close to a similar flat rented by my maternal grandparents, James Montgomery (Alexander Robertson's nephew), a travelling drapery salesman, and Jeanie Ferguson, known, I am told, as 'the belle of Rutherglen', whose father was a railway brakesman. My paternal grandparents died before I was born, but as well as my maternal grandparents, aunts, uncles and cousins from both sides of the family lived nearby.

The local 'non-denominational' state primary school, Battlefield, and senior secondary school, Queen's Park, that I attended, and the district where I lived, Langside, were so called because all were close to the site of Mary, Queen of Scots' defeat by Protestant forces in 1568 at the Battle of Langside. After the battle she fled to England where she was incarcerated by Elizabeth I and then beheaded – thanks, I now know, to William Cecil's assiduous spying endeavours. Even my local church was called Battlefield West Church. I am now an atheist, but still miss the singing of hymns, which was so much a part of my childhood. My primary and (senior) secondary schools had a mixed intake of working-class and (mainly lower-) middle-class children. Catholic kids went to separate schools nearby. I was separated from my best friend, the daughter of a single mother (although we didn't use that term then), when she failed the 'Qualie' (the eleven-plus exam). As a result, she went to the junior secondary school attached to our primary school, while I went up the road to Queen's Park senior secondary school; the Scottish equivalent of an English grammar school. I can still recall the devastation I felt at the separation, and my sense of unfairness.

When I was twelve my family moved to a bigger house a couple of miles away so that my grandma could come to stay. A beautiful woman who became obese and diabetic, she could scarcely walk when she came to live with us after my grandpa died. It was the first house my parents owned, and our first home with a garden rather than a shared 'back green'. I had a bedroom of my own for the first time, having until then slept in a bed recess in the kitchen/living room. My brother and I belonged to Selina Todd's 'golden generation', as defined in her book on social mobility in Britain, *Snakes and Ladders* (2021). The term refers to children born between the mid 1930s and mid 1950s, and particularly the decade from the mid 1940s (as we were), since they were more likely to be upwardly mobile than any generation before or since. A substantial number of people of the 'golden generation' went into the professions on which the (still very new) welfare state depended: teaching, nursing, social work and technical work. Todd's book, which draws on hundreds of personal stories, shows that many in this grouping were critical of the meritocratic rhetoric of the welfare state, aiming instead for political and economic equality: 'They helped ensure that the 1970s was the decade when Britain became more equal than at any point in modern history, thanks to significant improvements in ordinary people's daily lives, education and future prospects' (Todd, 2021, p. 217). The direction of change seemed set on ever-increasing political and economic equality.

In 1973 I returned to a lectureship in sociology after what turned out to be a 'year out' in Italy with my husband and two-year-old son. I had started teaching sociology at Strathclyde University in 1969, a year after completing an honours degree in philosophy at Glasgow University (having already trained for three years as a primary-school teacher) and getting married to a fellow philosophy graduate (who had previously trained in law). In those days it was possible to secure a post in sociology, a growing field, without a PhD, which I gained later. I experienced the 1970s as a decade of exhilaration and exhaustion. In Florence we had marched with striking factory workers and been introduced to the writings of Marxist philosopher-journalist Antonio Gramsci by our friends Mario, an English teacher, and Orietta, a trades union activist and artist, who later married. Their gift to us of Gramsci's *Prison Notebooks*, written whilst he was imprisoned under Mussolini's fascist regime, and only translated into English in the 1970s, is still one of my most prized possessions.

I came to teaching sociology indirectly from philosophy, finding in C. Wright Mills' 'sociological imagination' something that had so far been missing from my studies. The idea of a kind of imagination based on understanding the invisible social forces that influence people's lives offered a useful counter to the abstractions of philosophy. In addition to my teaching job, I helped my husband (then a journalist on the *Glasgow Herald*, and later for the BBC) with the production of a so-called 'alternative' weekly newspaper, the *Glasgow News*, which he edited in our flat. Set up in the spirit of the community journalism movement to challenge the powerful and give voice to marginalised groups, the paper had a strong social justice/civil liberties focus. For a few years we scarcely slept between Friday and Sunday nights, distributing the paper to pubs and shops on Fridays, editing and typing the next issue over the weekend, then soliciting copy for the issue after that. Housing was a major area of interest. I recall one particularly sleepless weekend finalising copy, when George Pottinger, a senior civil servant in the Scottish Office, was jailed for corruption and conspiracy during the infamous Poulson Scandal. John Poulson was a British businessman and unqualified architect whose use of political bribery to secure building contracts was disclosed in 1972. His architectural practice, which stretched across Yorkshire to Tyneside, became the largest in Europe. Both men were convicted of fraud and jailed in 1974. Pottinger was in charge of the redevelopment of Aviemore as a winter sports complex and had received gifts worth £30,000 from Poulson, who was appointed architect for the project. My recollection is that the *Glasgow News* played a key role in breaking the story. I may be wrong, of course.

Throughout much of the decade I was an active and fully paid-up member of the women's liberation movement. In Glasgow, as (mainly) socialist feminists with links to trades unions and immigrant groups, we emphasised the connection between sexism, racism, class, imperialism and consumer culture. The list was long. Labels abounded, and fine distinctions: we saw ourselves as different from our more 'separatist' or 'radical' feminist sisters in Edinburgh. We were sure that things could only get better, and that we would help make them so. I would later write, 'In the 1970s, I did not doubt that I knew the right (socialist feminist) theories and that if enough people knew them too, then, together, we could – indeed, would – change the world' (Barr, 1999, p. 30). I can still see myself in an exchange between a mother and daughter recorded in a memoir that I was then reading. The author, a sociologist, describes how her mother, Poppy (the title of the book), would gently chide her for her literal-mindedness and reliance on 'thinking' to the exclusion of imagining: 'As if,' protests the author-daughter, 'our lives are lived outside things like poverty and unemployment and patriarchy and Thatcherism and Nato?' 'It depends how you look at it,' Poppy replies, pointing out that when her daughter was unhappy, 'it was not because Nato was to blame' (Modjeska, 1990, p. 292).

Family history draws scorn from academic historians. For me it has been revelatory, disrupting assumptions and revealing facts about my background that I had been insufficiently curious to question. I soon found myself stitching together a tale akin to the old British nursery rhyme 'This is the House that Jack Built'. Sometimes referred to as a cumulative tale, the rhyme doesn't really tell the story of Jack's house, or even Jack. Instead, it shows how the house is indirectly linked to other things and people, such as 'the maiden all forlorn' and 'the cow with a crumpled horn', telling a story of how these are all interlinked. The final verse would be incomprehensible were the previous ones not there. So, too, with Alexander, who for me became a way into a narrative of interlinked historical events and people across an empire; a narrative in the absence of which his life in Italy as a writer and minister would be imperfectly understood.

On the 30th September 1885, Alexander Robertson, a widower, married Julia Braddon (née Dawson), a widow, at the British Embassy in Berne, Switzerland. The marriage was announced on page 1 of *The Times* on the 3rd October 1885. Alexander was thirty-nine and recently widowed. Julia, aged forty-three, had been a widow for twenty-three years, having been just eighteen when she first married. Nine years later, Alexander received an honorary doctorate of divinity from Montreal's McGill College (now University) in recognition of the book that set me off on my quest, the recently published *Fra Paolo Sarpi* (1893). McGill College was generally understood to be a Protestant institution. Established in 1821, its founder James McGill, a rich merchant and slave owner who was born in Glasgow and studied at Glasgow University, was a committed Presbyterian.

When *Fra Paolo Sarpi* was first published in 1893, Italy was a popular destination for Protestant visitors from North America and Britain, many of whom greatly admired the sixteenth-century radical Venetian friar who opposed papal power. Alexander was one of those 'resolutely anti-papist fans of Paolo Sarpi' so vividly depicted by Mary McCarthy in her guide to Venice (McCarthy, 2006 [1956], p. 218). That his anti-popery brought

Alexander critics as well as fans became clear to me when I found him playing a supporting role in a semi-autobiographical novel by Frederick Rolfe (1860–1913), which I located at Glasgow University's library. Written whilst Alexander was a minister in Venice, but published a year after Alexander's death, *The Desire and Pursuit of the Whole* (1934) is rooted in Rolfe's extended visit to Venice in 1908. Intending to stay just a month, he remained there until his death in 1913. Rolfe, who styled himself 'Baron Corvo', had converted to Catholicism at the age of twenty-five. In one passage in the novel, he captures his hero's thought processes as he walks from one beautiful Venetian church to another: 'He understood why polemical acatholic swashbucklers like the lying prophet of Ca' Struan fought against fact, sinned against light, by alleging that Italy has lost her faith – that, of her thirty millions, not more than two ever cross a church's threshold' (Rolfe, 2002 [1934], p. 296). An editor's note explains that the 'lying prophet' who is spreading false tales about Italy's emptying Catholic churches is the Reverend Alexander Robertson. Ca' Struan was the name of the house near the Basilica di Santa Maria della Salute in Venice, where Alexander lived and preached for many years.

In an *Appreciation* in *The Scotsman* on the 21st March 1933, on the occasion of Alexander's death, the Reverend Albert G. Mackinnon writes:

Venice gave the Presbyterian pastor a world pulpit, while Dr. Robertson in return made that city attractive to millions of visitors. The man and the place responded to each other… It was when he was at San Remo, to which he went in 1882, that he became widely known through his articles appearing in the *Scotsman*… When he was transferred to Venice, he found there his true *métier*. To build up a congregation was an impossibility, for there were few Scottish residents in the city; but to fill the church was a different matter, and the name of Dr. Robertson soon became so well known to tourists that it was a recognized part of the visitor's programme to attend his service.

Though his house 'la Casa Struan' was hidden in a side street, people of all degrees and from all countries sought him out… His circle of friends ever widened. He was received by Queen Victoria at Windsor Castle, and by King Umberto and by King Emmanuel III at Rome. He had met with King Frederick of Prussia, and Sir Morell Mackenzie was a valued friend. In that circle were also included Cecil

Rhodes, Dr. Jameson, Gladstone and Chamberlain... His hospitable home, adorned on Sundays with the Union Jack which helped to guide strangers to its 'Church in the House', will long be missed in Venice.

A few years later, the same author would again recall Alexander's house and hospitality: 'There will always remain in my memory his study which was a veritable museum of mementos from distinguished people who thus showed their appreciation' (Mackinnon, 1937, p. 133).

Alexander is buried alongside Julia in Quarter XV, Grave Numbers 20 and 21, in the English Cemetery on the island of San Michele, Venice. The dedication on his gravestone reads:

Rev Alexander Robertson DD
Commendatore Della Corona d'Italia
Cavaliere of S.S. Maurizio and Lazzaro
45 years Minister of the Church of Scotland Venice
Born Edinburgh Scotland 30 November 1846
Died Venice 17 March 1933

Underneath is an inscription:

Father I will that also when thou has Me Where I am that they may behold thy glory. For our citizenship is in heaven, from whence also we look for the Saviour the Lord Jesus Christ who shall change the body of our humiliation that it might be fashioned like unto the body of his glory.

Julia predeceased him. Her gravestone reads:

Julia Dawson
Beloved Wife of Reverend Cav. Dr Alexander Robertson
Minister of the Church of Scotland Venice
Born Flitwick England Jan 1842
Died Venice 7 March 1922

Julia had no obituaries written about her. Bringing her out of the shadows to recover her from the 'hidden history' of women's lives became an important part of my quest and story (Rowbotham, 1973). Nonetheless, I am conscious of what Joseph Brodsky describes as the most crucial lesson in composition: what makes a narrative good is not the story itself but what follows what (Brodsky, 1992, p. 38). In deciding to use my own research 'journey' as the scaffold on which to hang various subject matters, characters and events, I take my cue from Richard Holmes, who writes, '"Biography" meant a book about someone's life. Only, for me, it was to become a kind of pursuit, a tracking of… someone's path through the past, a following of footsteps. You would never catch them… But maybe, if you were lucky, you might write about the pursuit of that fleeting figure in such a way as to bring it alive in the present' (Holmes, 2011 [1985], p. 27).

Having offered glimpses of my great-great-uncle viewed from the perspective of contemporary writers, I return to his beginnings in Scotland, following in his footsteps through the past before widening the frame. Widening my frame became necessary because, early on in the course of my research, it became clear that, by marrying Julia, Alexander connected himself (and hence me) to some of the most powerful families in Britain. Unravelling how this came about is one of the main stories I seek to tell here. The details of my family tree are, for others, largely insignificant. Of far greater significance is what they say, albeit indirectly, about how the British class system persists, and more particularly, how the landed aristocracy continually renews itself with new blood, new sources of money, and frequently multiple marriages.

The order in which I recount things is shaped to an extent by *what* I learned *when* in my pursuit of Alexander. I already knew certain things about Julia's family before I learned about its Cecil connection, and I knew certain things about Alexander's life and work before I learned those things about Julia's family. On discovering the Cecil connection, joining the dots between these different areas of knowledge and different stories acquired a new urgency. I needed to know why Julia was linked to Robert Cecil through her 'second cousin once removed'. It was not long before I began to see that for 'things to stay as they are, things have to change'. How, then, did things begin?

Two

Beginnings: Edinburgh A Lad O'Pairts?

I have a photograph of Alexander with his first wife Helen; the only one I have of the couple. I saw the original on a visit to Alexander's first ministry, St Margaret's United Presbyterian Church (UPC) in Orkney, where it is housed in the church archive. A formally composed studio portrait, probably taken just after their marriage in 1876, it shows a very serious-looking couple framed within a bower of artificial flowers. Helen sits upright, facing left, her hands folded on her lap. She looks very young and rather uncomfortable in her tightly corseted dress, her light hair braided in a loose chignon. Alexander stands behind, arms folded, peering at the camera through small round spectacles; a stocky, dark-haired, shaggily bearded figure in a single-breasted suit. It is a poignant image, made more so by foreknowledge, and knowing too how hard Alexander had struggled to get to this point in his life.

Towards the end of 1926, Alexander, now eighty, reminisced about his schooldays 'when a boy, attending Moray House Normal School, before being sent to the High School'. He recalled the collapse of a local Edinburgh mansion, reported in a current issue of *The Scotsman* to have taken place in 1840. Casting doubt on the date, he wrote, 'Well, I was not born then but recall the awful tragedy perfectly. We heard of it as we left the Church of Dr Hetherington (St Paul's) at the close of the morning service. I do not think I was allowed to see the ruins that day, as I had to attend the afternoon service, and then the Sunday school. But I went, very likely on the Monday. I remember… the plucky little chap who was buried in the debris heard the men with pick and shovel working above him and cried out "Heave awa' lads. I'm no deid yet!" I cannot give the exact date of the tragedy but it must have been in the fifties' (NLS: MS 9146(1), fol. 261).

Before the BBC stopped me in my tracks, I had been scouring *The Scotsman* online to track down the many column inches that Alexander Robertson supplied to the paper over the years. I had visited the National Records of Scotland (NRS) at the east end of Princes Street in Edinburgh, and made frequent visits to the National Library of Scotland (NLS) not far away on George IV Bridge. At the NLS I was tracing Alexander's activities in Italy through reams of minutes produced by the UPC's Continental Committee and Mission Board. Who knew that Protestants had missionary outposts in Europe in the nineteenth century? I certainly didn't. The NLS's Special Collections, housing the private papers of Scotland's great and good, form a key part of Scotland's national memory. Amongst them, as many before me have discovered, it is the scrappy notes and hastily scribbled letters that are as revealing as the most important documents of state. After sampling the many letters and cards Alexander sent to architects, publishers, friends and acquaintances during his time in Italy, his small, rounded black script would become as familiar to me as my own parents' handwriting. There is a definite thrill in such tangible connections to the past (NLS: MS 2640, fol. 123).

At the same time as I was seeking clues to Alexander's life in Italy, I was tracking his earlier winding trail through Edinburgh's education system, starting with Moray House College Library, then visiting the Edinburgh City Chambers to view his Royal High School records, followed by the University of Edinburgh's Centre for Research Collections and New College Library's Special Collections in Theological Education. The *Scotsman* article about the boy in the rubble provides some facts about Alexander's upbringing and education: where and how often he attended church; the school he went to at the time of the accident; the name of the school he was about to be sent to. It also displays a taste for anecdote and tall tales.

Alexander Robertson was born in Edinburgh on the 30th November 1846 to James Robertson (1816–79) and Elizabeth Fairley (1812–68). James, the son of a joiner-undertaker, was a railway clerk and stationmaster who became a 'coal agent' after Elizabeth's death. The 1871 census records twenty-four-year-old Alexander, a 'Theology Student', still living at 28 St Leonard's Street in the St Cuthbert's parish of Edinburgh with his fifty-four-year-old widower father, twenty-one-year-old sister Elizabeth (my great-grandmother), and eighteen-year-old brother James, an agricultural labourer. The same census records Alexander's soon-to-be wife Helen Stevenson living down the road at Number 16 (see Appendix, Table 4).

Alexander's formal education began with his attendance as a day pupil at Edinburgh's Moray House Normal School, before 'being sent to' the Royal High School. Moray House Normal School (or, to give it its full title, Moray House Free Church of Scotland Normal and Sessional School) opened on the 13th September 1848 in its Canongate premises on the Royal Mile, close to Alexander's home in the Old Town. Established by the Free Church of Scotland after the 'Disruption' of 1843, it followed the usual pattern of the time, with a large 'model' (or sessional) day school and an associated 'normal' school (in the sense of 'setting norms') for students training to be teachers. The Disruption was a schism within the established Church of Scotland when 450 ministers broke away, over the issue of patronage and the Church's relationship to the state, to form the Free Church.

In 1846, the year Alexander was born, state aid to education was reorganised to give annual grants to schools that followed the state's curricular regulations, and to encourage the professional training of teachers through a 'pupil-teacher' scheme of apprenticeship of up to five years' duration (Anderson, 2018, p. 208). Linked to the normal schools (later, teacher-training colleges), which were run by the Churches, the scheme involved schools selecting promising thirteen-year-olds to receive instruction on teaching methods, outside school hours and from specialist staff. The most able boys and girls were selected through an exam to receive a Queen's Scholarship for maintenance costs during their apprenticeship.

By 1850, there were 719 Free Church schools, compared with the Church of Scotland's 914. The fledgling UPC, founded in 1847, had only sixty-one schools by 1851, around the time that Alexander began his formal education as a day-school pupil at Moray House Free Church School, before moving in 1856 to the Royal High School in its splendid neoclassical building on Calton Hill. He was back at Moray House two decades later as a trainee teacher, by which time it had been renamed Moray House Free Church Training College. So Alexander began and ended his educational career at the same institution. Student teachers were usually recommended and certificated by a local minister, and had to be able to pay their own fees.

By the time he finished his two-year teacher-education course in December 1872, Alexander was twenty-six, and had already completed a three-year general arts degree at Edinburgh University, worked as a commercial clerk, and fitted in training for the ministry along the way. Such multitasking, including qualifying for two professions, was possible because the UPC trained its ministers through summer schools, which were held at its Divinity Hall in Edinburgh. Attendance at five two-month-long summer schools was required to qualify. There is documentary evidence, backed up by the 1871 census, that Alexander attended at least one of these divinity summer schools in the academic year 1870–1. Since he also began his teacher training in January 1871, he may have been hedging his bets between teaching and preaching.

Piecing together Alexander's educational career has been tricky because 'Alexander Robertson' was Edinburgh's 'John Smith' at the time. After several false leads, I realised that my difficulty in pinning him down was not just because of the dearth of documentary evidence, but was also due to the seemingly haphazard nature of his route through education. I could find no record of his early years as a day pupil at Moray House. The closest I came to these years was in the form of dusty school logbooks dating from the 1860s, which are held at Edinburgh University's Centre for Research Collections. Discipline and cleanliness are all-important. Thus, new headmaster 'GG''s brief first entry on the 1st February 1864 reads, 'This day I entered upon the discharge of my duties… visited all the classes… pointed out the dirty state of rooms to the janitor.' Just a week later GG could report, 'I have every class always under the Master's eye.' Another common theme running through the logbooks during the 1860s and into the 1870s is the integration of day- and normal-school activities. Thus, on the 30th January 1871 the entry reads, 'The student teaching commenced today… A class of forty set aside.' I like to think that Alexander was one of these novice student teachers, as he had enrolled at the college that very month.

The 1860s and 1870s were decades of intense inquiry and legislation in Scottish education. As the work of training colleges expanded, the relationship between them and the universities became controversial. Nominally controlled by the Churches (in Moray House's case, the Free

Church), but dependent on government grants and regulations, they drew most of their students from elementary schools through the pupil-teacher system, though this does not appear to have been Alexander's route into teacher training. College training was directed at elementary-school teaching, whilst university-educated men (and only men) staffed the burgh schools in the towns and some parish schools in the country. When the 1864 Argyll Commission investigated schools, respondents described college graduates as mere 'teaching machines rather than intelligent educators of youth'. Since the training colleges were in the university towns, an obvious solution was to allow college students to attend some university classes during their training. This was introduced in 1873 – too late for Alexander, who had in any case just finished his professional teacher training of two years *and* already completed a three-year general arts degree.

The period between 1862 and 1872, when Alexander was in higher education, was dubbed the 'dark ages' by Moray House rector Maurice Paterson, because in that decade the possibility for a senior student at Moray House to study a subject in depth (which had been possible before) was dropped. When Alexander eventually returned to Moray House in 1871, aged twenty-five, he was an exemplary trainee teacher, according to Moray House's 'Progress Register'. His college certificate, dated the 31st December 1872 and signed by the rector, records him as 'having completed the full course of Training prescribed by the Committee of Council on Education and the Education Committee of the Free Church of Scotland'. It lists his 'Qualifications and Character as reported by the teachers of the respective classes' as follows:

> *Attendance: Quite regular*
> *Punctuality: Uniform*
> *Attention to Home Studies: Satisfactory*
> *Attainment in Religious Knowledge: Excellent*
> *Attainment in English viz. Reading: Good*
> *Grammar: Excellent*
> *Composition: Very Good*

Attainment in Geography and History, Excellent; in Penmanship, Very Good; Arithmetic, Excellent; Vocal Music, Very Good; Drawing, (A separate Certificate is granted for proficiency in this branch); Algebra and

Geometry, Very Good; Latin, Good; Greek, Excellent; School Management, Very Good; Political Economy, Very Good; Mental Arithmetic, Good; Physics, Very Good; French, Very Good.

Place in Class determined by Written Examinations: Very Good
Skill in Teaching: Very Well
General Conduct: Exemplary

Alexander may have missed the boat as far as educational policy and innovation were concerned but his prolonged education meant he could choose between teaching and preaching. A pragmatic quality, coupled with an eye for the main chance, is detectable in his life and character. Nothing that came his way was handed to him on a plate. He had to duck and weave to get on.

When he arrived at university in 1866, before returning to Moray House as a trainee teacher, he was nearly twenty. He had left the Royal High School three years before in 1863 and, according to the 1861 census, was already working as a commercial clerk; that is, two years *before* leaving school. I found a partial explanation for this in the Royal High School's Matriculation Book, held at Edinburgh's City Chambers, which shows that Alexander's school career was a stop-and-start affair. His name first appears in 1856–7, roll number 321, with '5/–' written against it. He was ten years old. His name does not appear again for a further five years, in September 1861–2 (roll number 188), and again the following year, in September 1862–3 (roll number 294). Since all censuses are taken in April we can safely assume that he was still working as a clerk in 1861 (as recorded in the census), and had been clerking throughout the previous four years until returning to school in September that year, just shy of fifteen.

Alexander's school record can be read against a contemporary educational campaign. The National Education Association of Scotland was established in 1850 to promote a national system of state-funded education, freely available to everyone, run by local boards instead of presbyteries, and staffed by teachers appointed irrespective of religion. The Edinburgh Royal High School, a so-called 'burgh' (as distinct from 'parochial', or parish) school, was seen as an exemplar of this kind of non-sectarian national education system. William Maxwell Hetherington, Alexander's local minister at Free St Paul's Church between 1848 and 1857, was a vigorous supporter of the association and a staunch critic of the Church of Scotland's monopoly of running parish schools.

It was common for a local minister to encourage, and even sponsor, through education bright working- or lower-middle-class boys in their congregation. Hetherington may have played such a role in Alexander's life, perhaps easing his transition to the prestigious school, which was attended by boys from all over Scotland and from as far away as Bengal. The school stressed the mix of social classes within it, although unlike Alexander, most pupils, including illuminati such as Sir Walter Scott, had middle- and upper-middle-class backgrounds. Since Hetherington left Edinburgh for Glasgow in 1857, just after Alexander's first year at the school, he would no longer be around to assist the clever schoolboy. This is, of course, conjecture based on the circumstantial evidence that Alexander's home was next door to Hetherington's church, which he attended, at 30 St Leonard's Street.

In any case, Alexander left school with just three years of secondary schooling under his belt, his first year separated from his second and third by five years. Unlike fellow student Alexander Graham Bell, the Scottish-born American inventor of the telephone, who diligently attended classes at the Royal High from 1857 until 1862 according to signed class registers, Alexander's name does not appear in any of the class registers I consulted. This is so even for those years for which he had registered and paid his 5/- fee. On this evidence, Alexander seldom if ever attended school, presumably because he was working to support his family. That he nonetheless completed a university degree and a teacher-training qualification *and* pursued enough theological study to be ordained as a United Presbyterian minister speaks volumes about his perseverance and hard work, establishing a pattern of ceaseless activity that would endure a lifetime.

Most Presbyterian churches in Scotland expected candidates for their ministry to take a university arts curriculum followed by a theological course. Since he had completed his arts degree in 1869 and teacher training in 1872, and wasn't ordained until 1875, Alexander had ample time to attend the prescribed five years of two-month-long summer schools at Edinburgh's United Presbyterian Divinity Hall, perhaps overlapping with his teacher training. Yet the only record I could find of his time there was in the *Annals and Statistics of the United Presbyterian Church* for 1870, which lists him as one of twenty-eight students admitted that year to the hall, 'under Professors Harper, McMichael, Eadie and Cairns' (MacKelvie, 1873,

p. 704). Alexander's entry reads, 'Robertson, Alexander, from Edinburgh (South College Street).' College Street was the address of one of Edinburgh's United Presbyterian congregations (ibid., pp. 192–4). It is clear that the entry does refer to my great-great-uncle, because it is confirmed in Small's *History of the Congregations of the United Presbyterian Church, 1733–1900*, which I consulted in the Orkney Room of Kirkwall Library. Small's *History* contains a reference to Alexander's address prior to taking up his first ministry, which reads, 'St Margaret Hope's fifth minister was Alexander Robertson from College Street, Edinburgh, Ordained 7 December 1875' (Small, 1904, pp. 499–501). He may have done some school teaching after graduating from Moray House, but I could find no record of this.

The UPC to which Alexander was ordained in 1875 sided with the secular lobby for a state-funded national education system to replace the old system of parochial schools controlled by the Church of Scotland. Although the Church of Scotland resisted, pressure for a non-denominational national education system in Scotland grew, and in 1872 the Education (Scotland) Act made education compulsory from age five to thirteen (raised to fourteen in 1883). This created a 'state' system that gave control of most schools to an elected school board in each burgh and parish. The 1872 Act did little or nothing for secondary education, however, and it was not until 1892 that state grants for secondary education appeared, albeit ten years before they did in England.

By 1912 there were 249 public secondary schools; some providing five years of schooling, the rest three years, and many charging no fees (Anderson, 2018). This timeline puts Alexander's three (albeit interrupted) years at the Royal High in a very different light, since it was not until 1912 that secondary schools began serving a wide social range. Alexander was a fairly rare exception in mid-Victorian Scotland as a working-/lower-middle-class boy who received at least some secondary education *at school*, even if, on the evidence presented above, he seldom attended classes.

An important consequence of the chronic underdevelopment of secondary education in Scottish schools was that Scottish universities admitted boys aged fifteen or even younger. As a result, observes George Kerevan, 'Scotland's traditional universities... were originally hybrids of secondary school, adult education class and university. Adult, male skilled artisans routinely took non-graduating classes, diffusing what was essentially secondary school education much wider than in England' (Kerevan, 2008,

p. 682). Alexander's secondary-school education was patchy and sporadic at best. For boys of talent but few resources, bursaries for university entrance were fairly widely available. Of far greater consequence for Alexander, a significant number of university entrants were older because universities were open to any male who had a little Latin.

Some adults took single courses; others, like Alexander, a full degree. There is no evidence that he graduated, but few students did, and even matriculation was not mandatory at the time. Signed class lists show that Alexander did indeed matriculate, charting his attendance from 1866 until 1869; from age twenty to twenty-three. Since in the 1860s the typical age of entry to full-time study at university was still fifteen or sixteen, Alexander was what is now termed a mature student. Robert Louis Stevenson, a contemporary fellow student of Alexander's at the University of Edinburgh, was a more typical young entrant, matriculating in 1867 to study engineering at the age of sixteen. Formal learning was of no interest to him, however. Unlike Alexander, who (as distinct from his schooldays) assiduously attended his university classes, 'RLS' seldom attended classes, preferring to 'walk, talk and drink', according to Jenni Calder's biography of the writer (Calder, 1980). Stevenson's cavalier attitude to learning would not have endeared him to Alexander, who came from the Old Town, long since abandoned by Edinburgh's well heeled for the generous space and handsome white-sandstone buildings of the New Town, where Stevenson's family lived, far away from the cobbled lanes with their tottering tenements and reeking chimneys of the Old Town ('Auld Reekie'): 'He [Stevenson] was all right, with his well-off father and his comfortable home. He did not have to work himself up' (ibid., p. 16). For the likes of Alexander, in contrast, a university education was a serious business, providing opportunities few sons of similar families in England could have dreamt of.

It is because the 1860s and 1870s were years of such intense inquiry and legislation in education in Scotland that there exists more information on the social background of students for these years than for any others before or since. The key reports of the period – the 1864 Argyll Commission on schools and the 1872 Education Act – were both too late to make any difference to Alexander. His school education ended in 1863 and his post-school education was over by 1872. Nonetheless, the statistics gathered for these years illuminate his educational career because they show that most males of working-class origin who accessed higher education at this time did so as adults (Anderson, 1983, 2018).

English education was based on privilege, its universities exclusive, expensive, and increasingly closely linked to the expanding 'public' – that is, private or 'independent' – school system. In Scotland, most schools were expected to serve the whole community. In addition, whilst universities in Scotland took sons of the local middle class and the occasional poor boy, since no formal entrance exam was required until 1892, open entry encouraged older men into university education too. In the 1860s, when Alexander was a mature student, 33% of the student body in Scottish universities were the sons of professional men, 16% came from the commercial and industrial middle class, 15% were the sons of farmers, 6% were the sons of shopkeepers and white-collar workers, and 23% were from the mainly skilled working class (Anderson, 1985).

Historically, the Scottish landed class, and increasingly the wealthy professional and business class, patronised the English public schools and a few expensive schools in Glasgow and Edinburgh. On the other hand, the inaccessibility to the English of the English independent ('public') schools and the Universities of Oxford and Cambridge favoured Scotland. In the nineteenth century after 1860, Scotland virtually filled the posts of England and Empire with its graduates. The corollary was that between 1860 and 1955 only half of Scottish-born male graduates of Scottish universities found employment in Scotland: 'The Imperial Frontier (at home and abroad) has done for Scotland what the West may have done for America… For as long as the British Empire flourished and the English system of higher education remained unexpanded external conditions have favoured the ancient Scottish universities' (McPherson, 1973, p. 172).

Robert Anderson concludes that the so-called Scottish 'democratic intellect' tradition, made famous by George Davie in his book of that title, was 'really a meritocratic one which laid great emphasis on the right of individuals to climb the social ladder; but it showed much less interest in those who failed to make this upward journey, and there was little impulse to move on to a wider definition of educational democracy' (Anderson, 1985, p. 478; Davie, 1961). For academically able men like Alexander, it was the accessibility of the universities and the absence of an entrance exam that mattered. And just as Alexander did not go straight to university from school, his route into the ministry was equally circuitous, and enabled by part-time provision. To sum up, it was the openness of the universities, their links with the training colleges *and* theological summer schools, that made Alexander's social mobility possible. It was what is now referred to as adult continuing education.

Towards the end of 2017, just before my Robert Cecil revelation, I took the train, bus and boat to Orkney where Alexander held his first post as a minister. Following his lengthy educational career, he was ordained in 1875 at St Margaret's UPC, St Margaret's Hope. A photograph in the church archive shows the new minister seated in a chair, legs crossed, and dressed in the same suit that he is wearing in the photograph with Helen, which was described earlier. Here his jacket is open, revealing a buttoned-up waistcoat, and the same spectacles are perched on his nose.

St Margaret's Hope (named after Princess Margaret of Norway, who died there in 1290) nestles in a sheltered bay on the northern coast of South Ronaldsay, where a herring fishery was established in the early 1800s. St Margaret's Church, which opened in 1856, became the main place of worship for the parish of South Ronaldsay and Burray. When Alexander took up his ministry, the congregation's membership was 235 and his stipend was £120 plus manse (Small, 1904). On the 11th January 1876, soon after his ordination, Alexander married Helen Stevenson, the second youngest of ten children born to James Stevenson and Janet Mitchell of Falkirk. Helen's father was a 'pattern maker' according to her and Alexander's marriage certificate, and a 'turner cabinet-maker' according to the 1851 census.

Alexander and Helen had been neighbours in Edinburgh. The 1871 census lists Helen (aged twenty) as a 'shopwoman' living with her brothers Robert (thirty-four) and James (twenty-three) and sister Isabella (seventeen) at 16 St Leonard's Street, just along from Alexander's family home at Number 28, having moved to the city from the small town of Falkirk, presumably to find work. It is likely, too, that the siblings attended Free St Paul's Church, and that Helen and Alexander may have met there. They also married close to home, at Gibraltar Villa on St Leonard's Hill, moving to Orkney and into the manse on a wintry January day in 1876. The 1870s were the wettest decade on record. If snow was not falling when the Robertsons moved in, it was no doubt raining.

According to the *Dictionary of Scottish Church History & Theology*, the UPC was distinguished by its voluntary principles, its promotion of overseas mission and its openness to 'enlightenment' and contemporary science. This positive depiction occludes a feature to which historian Elaine McFarland has drawn attention, which she describes as the 'unique configuration of religion and politics in Scotland'; a country where, she says, with just the right degree of tartness, 'the schismatic tendency of Protestantism was particularly well developed' (McFarland, 1990, p. 115). In the eighteenth and nineteenth centuries the dissenting churches in Orkney were in the majority, and by the middle of the nineteenth century most were United Presbyterian.

In addition to opposing any interference from the state in Church affairs, the UPC championed better education, extension of the franchise and land reform. Yet, as Jocelyn Rendall says in her history of Orkney's churches, the 'stern censoriousness' of the Kirk Sessions was very unattractive (Rendall, 2009, p. 6). Until the inauguration of the welfare state in Britain, the Church provided the only assistance that the poor, sick and needy could hope to receive. During Alexander's period as a minister in Orkney, the Church operated as a kind of local police force, applying its heavy Calvinist emphasis on discipline by punishing moral lapses and admonishing culprits. That people had to toe the line is made crystal clear in Church records held at the public library in Kirkwall. The 'sins' chastised are predictable. For instance, minutes of the Kirk Session meeting on the 26th December 1875 record that John Tulloch of St Margaret's Hope, having been 'guilty of the Sin of Fornication and suspended in consequence', has applied to be restored. On the 2nd February 1876, John appears before the session and 'having expressed his penitence... the session agrees he should be restored to privileges'. Jessie Park is less fortunate, as her readmission is delayed because, on the 11th April 1877, whilst 'glad to hear her expression of penitence for her sin', elders rule that she must wait until January before her rights are restored. And, whilst on the 10th October 1878 'Helen McIvor who has been suspended from privileges on account of the sin of ante nuptial fornication, having expressed her penitence... should be restored *sine die*', a near namesake guilty of the same infraction must wait. Thus, on the 13th August 1880, Elizabeth McIvor (now 'Mrs. Osmond'), found guilty of the sin of 'ante-nuptial fornication', has her appeal delayed until the 24th October, when the moderator (i.e. Alexander) informs the meeting that he has met Mrs Osmond several times and she has 'expressed penitence': 'Having been asked to appear at this meeting she had appeared and after having been suitably admonished by the Moderator and some of the other brethren on the Session she was restored to Church fellowship.' Her now-husband has also applied to be received: 'The moderator stated that he had conversed with him several times and after due consideration the Session agreed to receive him.'

The weather in Orkney could be equally fierce, and the winter days long and dark. If Helen had a weak chest when she joined Alexander there, it would have been made worse by the cold, wet climate. Smells from the herring fishery would not have helped. In the June of 1881 there was snow and frost in Scotland, and in October a 'great storm' caused extensive damage and loss of fishing boats. This may have been the last straw for Helen, as Alexander demitted his post that October because of his wife's ill health, having been offered a temporary appointment in charge of the United Presbyterian 'station' at San Remo in Italy. He took up the appointment in 1882 (Picken, 1972).

St Margaret's Hope Church minutes indicate that Helen suffered from a 'chest infection'. It was probably tuberculosis; a major killer in Britain at the time. At the Kirk Session meeting on the 13th October 1881, members regretfully agree to Alexander's demission and record their esteem for their departing minister, describing him as 'a Christian Minister of high toned piety and large hearted Christian sympathies... with whom their intercourse in the Session these six years have been characterised by unbroken harmony'. Alexander's departure is also covered in a lengthy article in the local newspaper, *The Orkney Herald*, which makes reference to the congregation's wish that 'a short residence in a warm climate may restore to health his beloved partner'.

There are parallels between Frederick Rolfe and Alexander Robertson, though they were faced with different pressures and dilemmas when they emigrated. Both came as strangers to Italy, though they adapted to their adopted home in diametrically opposed ways. Rolfe, attracted to Venice because of its beauty and his conversion to Catholicism, became an insider in terms of religious faith but remained an outsider in terms of his homosexuality; an orientation hinted at in his writing, such as in *Three Tales of Venice* (1950 [1913]), where he recounts boating with gondolier Bacciolo, 'the hugest, strongest, fairest Venetian torso you can imagine'. The copy of *Three Tales* which I consulted at Glasgow University Library's Special Collections room is inscribed by Scotland's first Makar (Poet Laureate) Edwin Morgan, who was also gay. His signature appears on the flyleaf back to front; perfectly legible on the reverse of the page, and a neat joke. Rolfe had fled to Venice in the wake of losing a lawsuit, living on credit, seeking a benefactor to pay off the lawyer to whom he had pledged his book royalties as security. No publisher would touch his work, which 'seethed with entertaining libels and lampoons' (Symons, 1955 [1934], p. 287). When *The Desire and Pursuit of the Whole* was eventually published after his death, several of Rolfe's expatriate friends and benefactors besides my great-great-uncle were well and truly skewered. Yet it was probably easier for Rolfe to live the life he wanted away from home. The same may have been true for Alexander, coming to Italy in 1875 to preach to its English-speaking Protestant community, bringing with him the missionary zeal of his calling and escaping the battles within Protestantism back home. There he gained access to a class from which he would have been excluded in Scotland, and found a kind of benefactor. He knew none of this when he left Orkney, faced with Helen's ill health and the promise of San Remo's climate. As things turned out, despite the Orkney elders' hopes, it was not to be a short stay in Italy. Like Frederick Rolfe, Alexander would spend the rest of his life there.

Three

Missionary Positions

Family secrets are the other side of the family's public face, of the stories families tell themselves, and the world, about themselves. Characters and happenings that do not slot neatly into the family narrative are ruthlessly edited out.
(Annette Kuhn, *Family Secrets*, 1995, p. 2)

I am looking at a framed photograph in the kitchen of my Glasgow flat, which is on the same wall as the window that looks out onto the Campsie Fells in the distance. Each time I look through the window to the hills beyond, I catch a glimpse of the street scene in the delicately hand-painted photograph. It shows an attractive church, set back on the left-hand side of a wide street, along which stroll women in long dresses holding parasols, and men in straw hats sporting canes, all bathed in golden sunlight. It is San Remo. The church is named after Scotland's patron saint. Postcards from the period show the lovely St Andrew's Church nestling beside the Hotel de Paris on San Remo's Corso Imperatrice. I bought one online and had it framed in gold. It is headed, in faint script, '*Un saluto da San Remo*' ('Greetings from San Remo').

By the closing decades of the nineteenth century the popularity of San Remo with British and American visitors had brought a large Protestant community to the town. Alexander Robertson, under the auspices of the UPC, commissioned the eminent architect Pio Soli to design a church to cater for this community, which included a substantial number of permanent residents as well as many seasonal visitors. Legal documents and architectural drawings for the church are filed at the National Library of Scotland, alongside other papers relating to the UPC's missionary work in Europe. Letters from Alexander written throughout the spring of 1883 urge Pio Soli to hurry up with the construction, possibly in view of Helen's failing health. Within months she would be dead from the lung disease that had brought the pair to San Remo in the first place, just two years before. Alexander remained in Italy and would remarry the following year.

Now I am looking at another photograph. It is of a beautiful lithograph that I located at the Bedfordshire County Council Record Office on a visit there in the autumn of 2017. It bears the caption 'The Late Residence of G. P. Livius Drawn & Lithd by B. Rudge.' Bradford Rudge was a lithographer and printer who lived and worked in Bedford. Some of his prints, including one of Burghley House, the Cecil family home, are held at the British Museum. George Peter Livius's elegant many-roomed mansion is skilfully drawn. Flanked on either side by two perfectly balanced wings and four tall chimneys, it stands in formally laid-out gardens, set against mature woods. In the foreground, a slender woman in a long dress and a large hat strolls on the lawn, her black dog ahead, tail up. A smaller figure – a gardener, perhaps – stands at the foot of steps leading up to the front door, lending a sense of scale to the garden, which extends a long way back from the woman. It is a calm scene, exuding a sense of order and established wealth.

Flipping through photographs on my phone, another catches my eye. Captioned 'Flora and Emily Foster from a water-colour by Henry Deffel, copied by Flora M. E. Wilson, 1891', it is taken from the frontispiece of a published memoir, *The Journal of Emily Foster*, which I read at the National Library of Scotland in the summer of 2017. In the painting the two girls are seated: Emily in the foreground facing left, her arms resting on the arms of her chair; Flora slightly behind facing forward. Both are dressed in elaborate, off-the-shoulder, full-skirted dresses, their hair pinned up in combs, Spanish style. It is a poorly painted copy of an original painting, probably intended as a calling card to show off the girls' sophistication and beauty. The date of the original is unclear, though Flora and Emily look about fifteen and seventeen.

Both photographs are connected to Alexander's second wife, Julia Braddon (née Dawson), an English widow who was already living in San Remo when the Scottish minister arrived in town. Flora and Emily Foster, the subjects of the painting, are Julia's mother and aunt respectively. The house in the lithograph is the Bedford home of George Livius and Mary Foster Barham, Julia's cousin-in-law and cousin twice removed. The two images hint at Julia's prosperous, cosmopolitan family background and the social and economic gulf that separated her from my great-great-uncle. Julia's first marriage, when she was just eighteen, had been to a wealthy merchant in the East India Company (EIC); her second, to Alexander, though following family tradition by marrying a clergyman, broke with it radically in terms of social class.

Alexander and Julia would live together in Italy for the rest of their lives; first in San Remo for the remainder of the 1880s, and then in Venice until Julia's death in 1922 and Alexander's in 1933. In both places, as obituaries and appreciations note, Alexander encountered a 'large and influential Protestant community of British and American people who constituted his congregation'. Such sources emphasise that it was his work as a minister and writer that brought him within the orbit of an ever-widening social circle, embracing John Ruskin, William Gladstone, Count Campello (founder of the Italian Reformed Church), Ezra Pound and Benito Mussolini, 'as well as Royalty'. 'Royalty' included Queen Victoria, who 'received him' at Windsor Castle; King Humbert and King Emmanuel III, who received him at Rome; and King Frederick III of Prussia. The last-mentioned meeting must have taken place in 1888, because when his father Wilhelm died early that year, Frederick, 'the great hope of the liberals', was already very ill with cancer and would be dead within the year. His brother, the 'military-loving young Kaiser Wilhelm II', succeeded him, and reigned until his abdication in November 1918, just before Germany's defeat in the First World War. He was the last German Emperor and the last King of Prussia (Hawes, 2017, p. 125). But it was not his work as a minister that accounted for Alexander's audience with the mortally ill King, who had spent the winter of 1887–8 in San Remo; it was Julia's family background on her mother Flora Foster's side. The Foster family had strong connections with the Prussian province of Saxony; connections that led to Julia's mother living in Dresden for three years in the early nineteenth century with her mother Amelia, older sister Emily, and three younger brothers.

If I have judged the girls' ages in the portrait correctly, it must have been painted whilst Emily and Flora were living in the Saxon capital. *The Journal of Emily Foster* (1938), the publication in which I first came across the photograph of the painting, is sometimes referred to as 'Emily Foster's Dresden Journal'. Flora was fourteen and Emily sixteen when they arrived there in 1820, soon to be 'caught up in' the Saxon court of King Frederick Augustus I, who had invited the family to visit. Frederick Augustus was the grandfather of Frederick III, with whom Alexander would have an audience more than half a century later. Amelia Foster's sister-in-law, Sarah Foster, was married to Baron Frederic Christlieb von Zezschwitz, a Moravian and well known at court.

John and Amelia Foster, the girls' parents, also belonged to the Moravian (United Brethren) Church, and the two girls were born and brought up in Bedford's Moravian community where many members of the wider Foster family lived, including the owners of the fine house in the lithograph. I had never heard of the small Protestant sect before encountering Julia's family, and when I visited its British headquarters in London's Muswell Hill, and shortly afterwards trawled the records of Bedford's Moravian community at Bedfordshire County Council's offices, I had not yet spotted the Cecil family connection. But after making the short train journey from London to Bedford, I was soon to learn that in Julia's family, religious mission went with the acquisition of substantial wealth.

The Moravian Church had a 'particular enthusiasm for mission,' says Alec Ryrie; an enthusiasm later (almost) matched by Scotland's UPC. Consecrated in 1457, sixty years before Luther began the Reformation in Germany, the Church had even earlier beginnings in Prague, then the capital of Bohemia, one of Czechoslovakia's three kingdoms of Moravia, Bohemia and Slovakia. There, Catholic priest Jan Hus built a church to preach in the Czech language, which the reimposition of Catholic rituals had proscribed. As a lecturer at the city's Charles University, Hus was an eloquent advocate of the English theologian John Wycliffe's claim that the Bible alone was the sole guide to salvation. The Lollards, Wycliffe's followers in England, resisted the wealth and land-tax exemptions of the established Church in England (Stephens, 2015).

Hus was burned at the stake for heresy on the 6th July 1415. Some years later, on the 1st March 1457, his followers took episcopal orders from the Waldensian Church, Italy's oldest Protestant Church, to form their own ministry. The new Church grew clandestinely because of Protestant persecution but eventually found sanctuary in Saxony, where a settlement called Herrnhut was established in 1722 on the estate of a Lutheran Count,

Nikolaus Ludwig von Zinzendorf. At the coronation of King Christian of Denmark in 1731, it is said that the Count met a slave from St Thomas, a Danish island in the West Indies, and invited him to Herrnhut. Shortly afterwards, two Moravian missionaries sailed to the island to preach to the slaves, thereby 'initiating the Protestant Missionary Movement of the eighteenth century' (Hastings and MacLeavy, 1979, p. 7). Zinzendorf visited St Thomas himself in 1739, and in his address to converts admonished the slaves to accept their status: 'You must know that the Lord has made everything Himself – kings, masters, servants and slaves… everyone must gladly endure the state into which God has placed him' (Mason, 2001, pp. 101–2).

Moravians were known as 'the least dissenting of Dissenters,' comments J. C. S. Mason, 'renowned for the very discreet conduct of their missions' (ibid., p. 177). Alec Ryrie describes them as 'freewheeling tolerationists [whose] emotional anti-theological and anti-hierarchical Protestantism found fertile soil wherever it fell' (Ryrie, 2017, p. 169). Their 'practice of piety' and emphasis on faith, prayer and Bible-reading spread fast. Like all evangelicals they stressed moral living, conversion, and a personal relationship with God. By the 1760s there were over two hundred Moravian missionaries in Jamaica, Labrador, Guinea and South Africa. Jamaica became the second location of Moravian mission in the Caribbean; this time sent by brothers William Foster and Joseph Foster Barham. William and Joseph were Julia's great-grandfather and great-great-uncle respectively.

John Wesley became the Moravians' English contact and even opened a meeting place for them in London's Fetter Lane, where Protestants of 'all shades' could gather. Wesley rejected the Calvinist doctrine of predestination; the belief that God had already chosen who would be saved and who would be damned. Unlike Moravians, he believed that faithful Christians could achieve moral perfection in *this* world. The result was Methodism as an evangelical movement within the Church of England, where it remained until his death in 1791 (ibid., p. 173). The eighteenth-century waves of evangelical 'enthusiasm' that swept across England are usually described as the 'Methodist Revival', implying that it was solely the work of John Wesley. Yet it was as much a grassroots movement of people who, believing that they had found personal salvation, felt compelled to try to convert others so that they too could be saved.

The Moravian practice of circulating *Periodical Accounts*, the first journal devoted solely to missionary news, became a blueprint for others to follow, greatly assisted by the new printing presses (Welch, 1989). Despite their original intent to be a movement for reinvigorating existing Christian Churches from within, Moravians eventually developed their own complex organisation, consisting of societies, congregations and settlements ruled over by committees (Pestana, 2009). Their first settlement in Britain was established in Bedford in 1745, followed by Fulneck in Yorkshire, Fairfield near Manchester, and Ockbrook in Derbyshire. Because of the importance Moravians attached to the idea of community, family allegiances were replaced by 'choirs' of married men, married women, widows, widowers, single brothers and single sisters, organised according to gender, age and marital status. Not everyone lived in a choir house, however. Julia's grandparents, John and Amelia Foster, stayed with their children at Brickhill House in Bedford, which had a farm attached. We know, too, that George and Mary Livius lived with their children in their own grand house. I like to think that Mary is the one walking her dog in the lithograph.

During Zinzendorf's time, women choir leaders played key roles in the governing structures of Moravian villages, and the Church promoted women in various leadership roles such as elders, deaconesses and, occasionally, secretly ordained priests. But all of this changed with Zinzendorf's death in 1760, when women were excluded from the committees that managed the Church; their ordination ceased, and the Church became more conservative and sexist. Women continued to be pioneers in women's education, however, and wherever a congregation was established, separate schools for girls and boys were set up (Atwood, 2015). This was to prove an important legacy for Julia.

The Bedford records show that admission to the Church could be a long process as candidates had to be approved by the 'lot', which was designed to produce one of three answers: yes, no, or blank. Another peculiar feature was the Moravian emphasis on the Lamb of God, especially his blood, and on Jesus's side wound, which was regarded as a mystical opening where believers could shelter. This strange fixation is vividly expressed on the front cover of the 1747 Labourers' Conference minutes, which bears the mantra:

> Dearest Sidehole! dearest Sidehole! dearest Sidehole!
> Thou art mine, Charming Sidehole! sweetest Sidehole!
> Loveliest Sidehole…
> (Welch, 1989)

The lamb remains the Church's symbol and marks the entrance to Church House, its London headquarters in Muswell Hill. The obsession with blood, which made Moravians unpopular in the early eighteenth century, disappeared, though the preoccupation with death took longer to dispel. Most biographies produced by the 'Brothers' are detailed accounts of their deaths rather than their lives. In 1748 Count Zinzendorf obtained an Act of Parliament to counteract the Church's negative press, acknowledging it to be 'an ancient protestant episcopal church' and encouraging settlements in the colonies. But soon after the Act's passing, John Wesley, who had come to distrust Moravians as 'a kind of Protestant Jesuits', accused the Church of misconduct (Griffin, 1988, p. 64).

There was worse yet to come. In 1753 a Lutheran Prussian diplomat published *A Candid Narrative of the Rise and Progress of the Herrnhuters*, an exposé of Moravian teaching about sex, which claimed that Moravians practised communal sex, Church elders watched newly married couples engage in sex, and the Church's organisation into choirs, segregated according to age and gender, encouraged homosexuality. Teachings on sexuality included the idea of the 'mystical marriage': intercourse was sacred, blessed by God, and religious conversion was as much erotic as spiritual. Some challenged God's maleness and regarded Jesus as 'ambiguously gendered' (Pestana, 2009, p. 188). The celebration of sex as a sacrament was sung in graphic hymns like the following:

> *O bring us, our marriage friend*
> *thy blood speckled member,*
> *which is needed for the union*
> *with our innocence once again*
> (Hymn 2121)

> *When I can eat him,*
> *so it is best for me,*
> *and when my dear husband*
> *lets his oil sizzle in me;*
> *since this grace is a sacrament*
> *that one cannot always have*
> *my body is turned toward (him)*
> (Hymn 2085)

Since many married Moravian couples did not live together but in choirs, sexual intercourse had to be highly regulated and strictly timetabled, with a room set aside for the purpose. Detailed teaching guidelines on sex were drawn up for community leaders to instruct soon-to-be-married couples, in order to ensure the sacredness of the act and the couple's comfort. An English Moravian sex manual offers detailed instructions: 'The most convenient position for the performance of the marriage union for the wife is lay down on her back having the middle part of her body raised by a pillow, to make room for the husband to kneel between them and… admit the genital of the husband into her matrix, in which she is to assist by applying her hand to the said member directing the same into the virgin-aperture.' After the act, the sex instructors are to give thanks to God with the couple, and the next day all should eat breakfast together 'to discuss any questions of concern' (Wilkening, 2018, pp. 47–8).

This period in Moravian history, when there was a deep interest in Christ's wounds and in sexuality, is known as 'the sifting time'. It led Anglicans to abandon their connections with Zinzendorf and virtually destroyed the Church's viability in England (Gibson and Begiato, 2017). It scarcely surfaces in the Bedford records, whereas the community's reliance on its wealthy members is a frequent topic, as in the congregation diary for 1801, which reveals that when George Livius mentions leaving Bedford, members worry that 'if Br Livius should move from Bedford and it should please our Saviour to take our dear Sister Foster [his wife, Mary Foster Barham] to himself, the Congregation would not be able to support itself' (Griffin, 1988, p. 41). By the time of this diary entry, George Livius was seldom attending any church services or meetings. Yet, eleven years later in 1812, he bequeathed a cottage to poor members of the community; a donation probably not unrelated to the fact that, in April that year, another member of the Foster clan, George's brother-in-law, was censured at an elders' meeting: 'The worldly proceedings of Br Joseph Foster [Barham] at Brickhill give us much uneasiness, and a public ball lately given by Mrs Foster has given much offence; we cannot but highly disapprove of this, when considering him… as a Communicant member of our Congregation but also a Preacher' (ibid., p. 41). Such censoriousness would not have been out of place at a United Presbyterian Kirk Session in Orkney. The Livius family eventually fulfilled the elders' fears, as revealed in the 1891 census, which lists George's widowed daughter-in-law living with her grown-up children in London's Berkeley Square.

Julia's grandparents John and Amelia Foster were equally wealthy members of Bedford's Moravian community whose children also gravitated to London. Their daughters Flora and Emily both married Anglican ministers. Flora Foster (1806–76) and her husband William Alfred Dawson (1809–92) initially settled in Bedford where Julia was born, but they soon moved to London. There is little on record about William, who was also born in Bedford. A letter in the Bedfordshire Archives dated the 19th June 1846 describes him as 'a most eccentric character... not noticed by any neighbouring clergy'. The reason for this reclusiveness would be clear to anyone who knew the family. William and Flora were doubly bereaved parents, their daughter Eleanor Mary having died soon after birth in October 1845, just a few months before the malicious letter was written and four years after their son Alfred died, aged three.

On a bright, sunny day, three autumns ago, I found my way to Church Road, Flitwick, near Bedford, the quiet cul-de-sac where Julia's father's church, St Peter and St Paul, is located, and where she was baptised. Inside the well-tended graveyard, close by the church's entrance, a small stone cross, engraved simply 'A. and E. Dawson', marks the spot where the two infants are buried together. Inside the church to the left of the altar, a marble wall plaque commemorates their brief lives. When Julia was born in February 1842, the third of five children, Alfred had just died. In 1845, when she was herself three years old, her baby sister Eleanor Mary also died. Julia thus spent her early childhood in a grief-stricken family, which must have left its mark.

Nevertheless, by 1848, when Julia was six years old, life seems to have improved for the family; enough, at least, for her parents to host a dinner party. We know this because the event is noted in a book about the Cavendish-Bentinck family, who are described on the book's flyleaf as 'ancestors of the British royal family'. *A Right Royal Scandal*, which I came across by accident during a web search, and immediately ordered, sets out to show how Lord Charles Bentinck's eldest son, Charley, 'fell in love with a beautiful gypsy girl, and secretly married her' – a union kept hidden from Charley's family, and especially from his uncle, William Cavendish-Scott-Bentinck, 4th Duke of Portland, 'upon whose patronage he relied' (Major and Murden, 2016, p. 107). Charley and Sinnetta (the 'beautiful gypsy girl') took a house in Ampthill in Bedfordshire in 1847, and became friends of John Thomas Brooks, 'squire of Flitwick Manor' and a distant relation of

Flora Foster. The 7th Duke of Bedford, we are told, became Charley's patron, obtaining 'livings' for him as a curate when the Duke of Portland turned his back on him because of his scandalous marriage (ibid., p. 127). One such lucrative living was as the vicar at Ridgmont; a ministry later occupied by William Charles Ellis, the said Duke of Portland's grandson and (though this is not mentioned in the book) a descendant of Charles Rose Ellis, 1st Lord Seaford, about whom there is much more to be said (see Chapters 4 and 5 of this book).

John Brooks kept a diary. In February 1848 he notes that he and his daughter were guests, along with his friends Charley and Sinnetta, 'at an evening party given by the neighbouring Dawsons at their vicarage in Flitwick'. He recalls 'dancing from half-past nine until the early hours of the morning, and the assembled guests waltzed and danced polkas'. The authors of *A Right Royal Scandal* gush, '[I]t is heartwarming to know that Sinnetta was invited, without prejudice, to join the local gentry at their dinner parties and evening entertainments, and they in turn happily took their place in her drawing room' (Major and Murden, 2016, p. 107). Of far greater interest to me than the open-mindedness here attributed to the 'local gentry' is the description of the party, because it indicates that when Julia was a child her home life was not entirely bereft of sociability and liveliness.

Another item of interest in the Bedfordshire Archives is a deed relating to Brickhill House, the Foster family home in Bedford. Dated 1862–4, the deed refers to Flora's father John Foster's will and to the 'Rev William Alfred Dawson… of Leighton Grove, Kentish Town, London… and wife Flora', noting that by signing over to John Foster's main heir the right to a proportion of the property that he acquired on marrying Flora, William received a sum of money. This means that Flora came to her marriage with a dowry. By 1851 the Dawson family had moved from Bedford to Kennington, south of the River Thames in London, where nine-year-old Julia is described in the census as a 'scholar at house'. By 1861 they had relocated north of the river to 10 Leighton Grove, Kentish Town, a street named after Sir David Leighton, a major general in the East India Company's private army, who owned a large part of Kentish Town estate.

I saw the Dawsons' fine town house on a recent visit to London. Leighton Grove is a quiet, attractive terrace off Kentish Town Road, near Kentish Town Tube Station. As chance would have it, the street is just a stone's throw away from where my son and his family now live, in a slightly less grand Kentish Town street. In the 1861 census, Julia's father has been redesignated a 'Landed Proprietor', her mother Flora is still 'Wife', and eighteen-year-old Julia, now married, has left home.

Three years later, Flora is a published author and Julia has been a widow for two years. Describing her two-volume book, *Princes, Public Men, and Pretty Women* (Dawson, 1864), as a 'kind of memoir' based on anecdotes about the Foster family, in the preface Flora explains why she feels competent to write such a book: 'Having passed many years at foreign courts, and mingled with men whose names are famous… and being connected by ties of friendship with several leaders… and actors in the stirring events which convulsed Europe for more than fifty years – I have been able to gather from eye witnesses, a number of curious and interesting incidents.' A contemporary review in *The Spectator* praises the memoir, somewhat backhandedly, as a 'very clever book whose object is to show how very amusing work may be made by making it perfectly silly' – a put-down which gives Flora no credit for any more serious intent, which is hinted at in the opening lines of her first story: 'How often have the memoirs of a woman… rendered clear the more obscure portions of history?… It is not for me to moralize, in these brief sketches, upon the great results that follow trifling causes, or to point out how even a few passing words from the lips of women, whose very existence is unacknowledged in history, have made and unmade heroes' (Dawson, 1864, p. 3). Flora had clearly read Mary Wollstonecraft's *A Vindication of the Rights of Woman* (1792).

It is tempting to wonder if Julia's marriage in 1860 to John Clode Braddon, cousin of Mary Elizabeth Braddon of 1860s 'sensation fiction' fame, influenced her mother's writing ambitions. It is not known if Mary Braddon ever met John Clode, far less his mother-in-law, though she did meet – and much admired – his two younger sisters Annie and Maria, and his father William. They met at Skisdon Hall, the family home in Cornwall, when William returned from India, 'well-to-do and generous, with his two daughters almost grown up' (Wolff, 1979, p. 31). According to her biographer, Mary was very fond of her uncle William, a merchant and judge in India for many years, and Skisdon Hall had great emotional meaning for her. She even bought it in 1866, though she sold it soon after to John Clode's older brother William, who also worked in India (Carnell, 2000).

Mary was the most popular novelist of the period, publishing over eighty novels in her lifetime. She endured the scandal of 'living in sin', unable to marry the publisher William Maxwell until his wife, who was in an asylum, died. Mary raised ten children, that is, William's five from his first marriage, as well as their own five surviving children. Born in London in 1835, the third child of a failed Cornish solicitor father and an adored Irish Protestant mother, Mary began writing shortly before her mother died, her father having already deserted them and her older brother Edward long gone to seek his fortune in the Indian Civil Service. She became the sole provider for herself and her mother, trying her hand as a stage actor before turning to writing. The success of *Lady Audley's Secret* (1862) was phenomenal, leading to eight editions in the first three months, several theatrical adaptations, a film, a musical, and sales of more than a million copies. Mary had many literary admirers, and at the height of her fame in 1865, William Powell Frith painted her portrait. In 1891 Arnold Bennett would write that 'there are thousands of tolerably educated English people who have never heard of... Hardy, Ibsen, Kipling... but you would travel far before you would reach the zone where the name of Braddon failed of recognition' (Wolff, 1979, p. 2*)*. Charles Dickens' 'favourite Braddon novel', *The Doctor's Wife* (1864), came out in the same year that Flora's memoir was published, while *Lady Audley's Secret*, which brought Mary lasting fame, was published in the same year that her cousin, John Clode, died.

Julia was not with her husband when he was found dead in his house in Pau, Côte d'Azur, on the 8th March 1862. His death certificate, which I tracked down at Pau Town Hall, offers no cause of death. It reads, 'Two citizens of Pau... declare M. John Clode Braddon, age 38, a person of private income, born and living in London, Lady Nelson's husband, son of William Braddon and Hannah-Maria Daniell from Plympton, Devon, died on 8th March at 9.30 in the evening in his house called "Lagarde" in Bordenave Street.' The town hall archivist suggested to me that 'Lady Nelson' might sound to French ears something like 'Julia Dawson'. Perhaps so, but John's death remains a mystery.

Julia's mother was brought up with high expectations for herself and her children; expectations formed from an early age in a European, rather than narrowly English, context. In Europe she rubbed shoulders with members of the nobility, leading statesmen, and people caught up in a cosmopolitan world of literature and the arts. Long before her daughter married the cousin of a celebrated author, Flora had come close to an even more famous literary figure. Whilst researching Julia's family background at the British

Library and the National Library of Scotland, I came across an intriguing story; one already familiar to American studies scholars since it concerns the celebrated American author of *Rip Van Winkle* (1819), Washington Irving.

Washington Irving (1783–1859) visited Dresden in late 1822 when the Foster family was living there. He is undoubtedly one of the men Flora 'mingled with... whose names are famous', and whose acquaintance made her feel competent to write her own memoir. Amelia Foster and her five children – Emily (sixteen), Flora (fourteen), Algernon (nine), Arthur (seven) and Morgan (five) – had left their home in Bedford on the 3rd August 1820, arriving in Dresden at the end of the month. Amelia intended to spend a few months there, but stayed three years, not returning home until late July 1823. Her husband, the children's father, John Foster (1765–1831), did not accompany them and only occasionally visited whilst they were living there.

Amelia Morgan (1782–1849) was twenty when she became John Foster's third wife. She had gone to Dresden to acquire a European education for their children and to reconnect with other Moravian members of the Foster clan; especially those of the Zezschwitz family, who were well known in the court of King Augustus. John's sister Sarah's husband, Baron Frederic Christlieb von Zezschwitz, had family connections with Count Zinzendorf, the Dresden-born nobleman who had allowed persecuted Moravians to settle on his land. One of Flora's stories in her memoir, 'The Three Regents', features Joseph von Zezschwitz, one of the Regents in charge of the country when Napoleon arrived there in 1813.

In the nineteenth century, Dresden, known as 'Florence on the Elbe', attracted many rich English people who were drawn by its beauty and vibrant cultural life: 'For a city whose name became a byword for great architecture, Dresden... never counted as one of Germany's leading medieval cities... [Yet as] anyone who has walked the Elbeside meadows under the summer sun will know, something of the warmth and generosity of the Mediterranean is present there and nature has... exercised a powerful influence over the city's life, culture and thought. When the Renaissance arrived, along with the new independence of mind wrought by Lutheranism... its basic ideas of beauty, harmony and form found a receptive environment in Dresden' (Russell, 1999, p. 119).

It is believed that when Washington Irving visited Dresden he fell in love with and proposed to Flora's beautiful older sister Emily (born Mary

Amelia), who turned him down. Emily's journal of her Dresden experiences makes several references to the writer, and Irving's own journals make clear his very close relationship with the Foster family during his stay there. In 1935 Emily's journal was bequeathed to Yale University by her granddaughter. Written in black ink with parts scored out and sprinkled with little sketches and doodles, its academic editors believe that Emily made the deletions later because, now married to a minister, she regretted some of her impulsive teenaged outpourings. A few scored-out but still legible words lend credibility to this theory: 'Flora is just laughing over my outrageous animadversions in my old journal.' When he arrived in Dresden in late 1822, Irving stayed at the Hotel de Saxe for seven months; a period described by his biographer Brian Jay Jones as the 'happiest and most heartbreaking of his life', because he became an almost daily visitor to the Foster family and was soon in love (Jones, 2011). At the time, Emily was being courted by a number of eligible young men, most notably 'Gumppenberg', 'Allegri' and 'Mr Airey', who make frequent appearances in her journal. And now, says Jones, 'here was a famous American trying to catch her eye'. According to the American editors of *The Journal of Emily Foster* (1938), Washington is 'omnipresent' in it. In fact, he first appears only halfway through.

Emily's editors believe that it was her religious nature that came between her and Irving, 'this sophisticated man of 40' who had left his beliefs in New York, 'after their excessive cultivation by his Covenanter father', a strict Presbyterian from Orkney. A much more obvious incompatibility between them was age: she was eighteen when they met; he was just a year younger than Emily's mother. Any clear-eyed reading of the journal reveals Irving's adoration to have been a burden to Emily. She was preoccupied with another, much younger suitor, the unfortunately named Gumppenberg, noting in late September 1822 (just before Irving's arrival) that she has just received 'A *triste* letter from G—g' (who is out of town), then proceeding to chastise herself: 'If tempted to do wrong Emily, cast the tempting devil behind you…'

Emily's journal, published by an academic press, is edited with footnotes that are clearly directed at its presumed readers; namely American studies students. A much more interesting question than why Emily turned down the famous writer's proposal is why he and other middle-aged nineteenth-century men such as John Ruskin *wanted* to marry teenage girls. (Ruskin proposed to the eighteen-year-old Rose La Touche when he was forty-six.) Before Emily, Irving had been in love with another very young woman, Matilda Hoffman, who died when she was eighteen. Described by her brother as 'too spotless for this contaminated world', Matilda is mentioned in a letter that Irving later wrote to Emily's mother. It offers a clue: 'I idolized her. I felt at times rebuked by her superior delicacy and purity.' In her review of *The Good Bohemian: The Letters of Ida John*, edited by Rebecca John and Michael Holroyd, Rosemary Hill conjectures, 'More than the obvious attractions of youth or the anachronistic charges of paedophilia sometimes levelled against the Victorians, there was something like a desire to preserve that quality of indeterminacy, to keep a woman like a bonsai specimen, clipped at the root to be perfect and miniature for ever' (Hill, 2017, pp. 3–5). Such a desire for unsullied perfection can be seen in Irving's view of Emily. Something akin to it is expressed in a poem he sent to her on the occasion of her birthday in May 1823. The poem begins:

> *'Twas now the freshness of the year*
> *When fields were green, & groves were gay,*
> *When airs were soft, & skies were clear*
> *And all things blossomed in lovely May*

It concludes:

> *Bloom on, bloom on, frank nature's child,*
> *Her favourite flower her spotless one*
> *Still may she guard thee pure, unsoiled,*
> *Still fresh, though ever shone upon*

Brian Jones believes that Irving asked Emily to marry him at the end of March 1823, just three months after their first meeting and two months before Emily's birthday, and that he was disappointed by her response. Yet he stayed in touch with her throughout April, and danced with her on his fortieth birthday. The strain for Emily is hinted at in one of her April journal entries: 'Irving is amiable and amusing. I must not yield to capricious coldness fits.' That she failed in this is clear from the fact that for most of April she is 'unwell' or has a headache when Irving calls. A rubbed-out entry in Irving's journal on the 14th April reads, 'determined not to dine today at Mrs F. Think of leaving Dresden.'

Yet by the 27th he is planning a poem (as quoted above) for Emily's birthday on the 4th May. On the 28th April there is an angry confrontation. Rumours of his proposal have been whispered around Dresden. When it is mentioned at a party, Emily explodes, writing in her journal, 'That report that I am to marry *"certo signore autore"* – begins to annoy me.' Just over two weeks later, on the 19th May, she writes, 'Our last evening with Mr Irving… Mama suspects he meant not to return.' He does return. Back in Dresden on the 26th June from a trip to Bohemia, this time Irving plans to leave Dresden for good. The Fosters have, in any case, also decided to return home. Irving accompanies them for part of the way, which Emily records on the 24th July, en route to Paris: 'good Irving has given up the Rhine to go with us to Rotterdam.'

Washington Irving visited the Fosters at Brickhill House in Bedford the following July, and stayed with them for ten days. By then, John Foster was also present. The last time Irving saw the family was in London in 1832, by which time Emily was married to the Reverend Henry Fuller (Reichart, 1935, pp. 35–9). Years later, aged fifty-two and the mother of five children, Emily writes to the author, asking if he will see her eldest son who is travelling in America: 'Do tell me about yourself, dear Mr Irving. You do not know… how often I think of you' (Irving, 1864, p. 192). Irving's reply on the 2nd July 1856 is fulsome: 'My Dear Mrs Fuller, You can scarcely imagine my delight on opening your letter… A thousand recollections broke at once upon my mind of Emily Foster as I had known her at Dresden, young and fair and bright and beautiful… who had painted the head of Herodias… and… was more beautiful than the head which she had painted… I treasure it as a precious memorial' (ibid., p. 194).

Irving's diaries record another meeting with Emily and her mother, which took place in Paris in 1825. Shortly after, he wrote Emily a letter, which took two or three days to write. That he wanted to marry her is disputed, though his biographer Brian Jones is convinced that he did, noting that 'Emily's younger sister' (Flora) later recalled of Irving, 'He has confessed to my mother, as to a true and dear friend, his love for Emily, and his conviction of its utter hopelessness… Poor Irving!' (ibid., p. 213). Flora also refers to his 'blasted hopes' in her own memoir. Irving's first biographer, his nephew Pierre Irving, disagrees, portraying Irving's first romance with Matilda Hoffman as unique, and dismissing Flora's memoir as 'a collection of ephemerae' in which she 'indulged her love of titles, wealth and notoriety' (Kime, W. R. 2006 [1977]).

Whatever the truth about Irving's eight months in Dresden, Amelia and her children spent most of their three-year sojourn there living in three different houses, including the sumptuous Courland Palace, described by Alan Russell as a 'mini-masterpiece of baroque styling' (Russell, 1999, p. 121). Their activities included balls at the Saxon court, royal boar hunts, trips to the mountains, visits to the theatre, and domestic life, 'like a quiet English island set down in the sea of diplomats and courtiers' (Foster, 1938, p. ix). They spent a lot of time with Irving's writer-dramatist friend John Barham Livius, who was in Dresden trying to adapt foreign plays for the London stage. John was the son of George Livius and Mary Foster Barham, whose Bedford mansion featured earlier. Courland Palace became a venue for plays, mounted by Livius for the Foster girls. Emily's journal offers glimpses of these performances, soon to be joined by Livius's famous friend.

The Fosters were in Dresden at a time of dramatic change for Saxony and its capital. Napoleon's last military success had taken place just a few years earlier, at the Battle of Dresden in 1813, and the Napoleonic Wars had roused new ideas of political liberation, which were resisted by conservative rulers (Clayton, 1999, p. 21). The 1814–5 Congress of Vienna secured Saxony's survival, though as a much smaller kingdom, with the traditional Elector now made King. Frederick Augustus I, at whose invitation the Fosters had come to Dresden, was the first Elector to receive this post-Napoleonic title. Despite political turmoil, Dresden's cultural life flourished in the 1820s, with 'amateur scribbling' much in vogue as well as amateur and professional theatre (Purver, 1999, p. 205).

For the Fosters there was also personal tragedy. In September 1821, a year before Irving's arrival, Emily's much-loved little brother Algernon died. As his health worsens, Emily's grief is palpable in her journal, where she also records how keenly she anticipates her father's infrequent visits. On the 22nd April 1821, Flora's fifteenth birthday and a few months before her brother's death, Emily writes, 'Mama proposed a little plan to amuse papa when he arrives: each to write an Italian play to act to him.' Soon after, she writes, 'I sometimes think this life is worse than insensibility for one cannot be happy, and one can suffer very much – I cannot expect to be happier than I now am yet I am far from it – discouraging thought! The fear and love of God alone can protect the mind from sin. We talked of the independance [sic] of women and regretted that we had not more.'

The two sisters would have been aware of post-revolutionary ideas about liberty and equality circulating throughout Europe, and would have known about and probably read Mary Wollstonecraft's *A Vindication of the Rights of Woman* (1792). They could speak several languages, and Emily's descriptions of events and reflections on life are written in a mixture of French, German and English, with the occasional Italian word thrown in. Her entries display an affectionate and serious nature, spiced with a sense of fun and flashes of self-awareness that suggest some internal conflict between desire and expectation. It is the journal of a teenager, with copious underlinings and expressions of feeling, sometimes extravagant and frequently sad: 'Dear little Al, so ill. If he ever becomes a man he will be a noble one such penetration and wit, such generosity and warmth – he looks lovely – deep purple blue eyes fair delicate skin, lovely nose.'

A few days later on the 21st June 1821, she writes, 'Thursday dear Papa's birthday. F [Flora] laid out his picture among flowers to the delight of the children but Mama came up in tears – thought it was a bad plan.' Several pages follow, written in French and expressing religious feelings. Then, heartfelt, she writes, 'I must have an aim, some activity to relieve my inner feelings I think that this restlessness from idleness must often be the cause of crime.' When her father arrives, she is overjoyed: 'Papa at last arrived. He is come, he is come and in a moment we were in his arms.' A few pages on we learn *why* John Foster has come: 'What a painful thing is illness in a house – Papa is constantly in tears – alas he cannot live – He says "God's will be done" – He is very delirious, as Mama says "why why is the sweet child so tormented".' The remainder of the entry is in French: 'Surrounded by friends though he may be, one who is dying is always alone; he no longer belongs among them.' On the 4th September 1821, Algernon dies. He is ten years old. 'As Papa came from speaking with Count Lippi he was alarmed we were all sitting round him when his dear breathing ceased – How lovely did he look – Nobody knows, papa said once, how I loved Algernon – The dear little boys [Arthur and Morgan] want to know, if we should know him again in heaven – Papa read that beautiful part in the bible where David loses his child – the funeral.'

There is a gap in the journal of several months. When Emily resumes her writing, it is with a number of entries about her favourite suitor 'Gumppenberg' (underscored). The sisters' resumption of social activities after a period of grieving coincides with the reappearance of the young

Bavarian soldier who has been absent from Dresden for a while. On the 5th February 1822 she dances with him, on the 10th February she is presented at court, and on the 12th February they attend a masked ball. By the 10th July, Emily is in a self-critical mood again: 'I think too much of the defects of those I love. Mama has a letter… asking me in marriage for a friend. [Gumppenberg?] Wrote a dismal letter in response to his joyful one. In the evening I met Mme A – who laughed because G—g *m'avoit fait la cour*. He never made *la cour* [sic] to me – I should not have liked him so well if he had.'

By the 2nd September, Emily has returned to her reflections on the comforts of a pious life: 'I believe nothing in the world as happy as a domestic, very religious life, the most exalting, the most above odious commonplace… one need seldom be unhappy with piety – it is least from misfortune that one suffers. Religion alone can make the prosperous man a happy man, the unfortunate resigned.' (She will eventually adhere to this script by marrying a clergyman and settling down to a life of motherhood and domesticity.) Two pages later, stirred by thoughts of the now-departed Gumppenberg, she is pondering the temptations of the flesh: 'A *triste* letter from G—g. If tempted to do wrong Emily, cast the tempting devil behind you… Why do we say "Lord, lead us not into temptation", who would taste poison to be able to blame the taste?' (Several lines are scored out here.) And Washington Irving is about to arrive in town. Recounting a night out at the theatre in December, she writes, 'How exceedingly strange that G—g does not write. At the play Mr Irving, the author of the *Sketch Book* was introduced to us.'

Later in the nineteenth century, the Fosters moved away from Bedford to London and lived in 'various grand houses in Regent's Park and Pall Mall'. Brickhill House was let to tenants and eventually sold. An article entitled 'Historical Images, Brickhill and the Foster Family', published in the *Bedfordshire Times and Standard* on the 3rd January 1947, laments the loss of Brickhill House, which had burned down on Boxing Day the previous year. Describing it as a 'mansion', the article mentions that the ruined house had a date of 1668 over a fireplace, and that by the time it burned down few people remembered it. The house stood on what was then called Foster's Hill and is now Foster Hill Road.

At no point in Emily's journal is there any mention of *why* her father is so seldom with the family in Dresden, or how they can afford such an extended and luxurious sojourn away from home. My most important discovery prior to spotting the name Cecil in my tree offered up a clue. I had been spending hours trawling through an online database compiled by University College London (UCL), alerted to it by the Jamaican addresses of a number of Julia's ancestors, revealed to me through ancestry.co.uk. UCL's *Legacies of British Slave-Ownership* (LBS) project is groundbreaking, its online database of British slave owners in the Caribbean providing the most illuminating picture of British slaveholding to date. In light of what I learned from its records about the Foster family, it was not difficult to explain John Foster's long absences. And reading *The Journal of Emily Foster* in light of this knowledge, I was immediately aware of the diary's gaps and silences – a form of concealment akin to bad faith that would be revealed again and again in the course of my research.

Four

Jamaica: Blood Legacy

[T]hey will have work – work – work, night and day, sick or well, till we are quite
done up; and we must not speak up nor look amiss, however much we be abused.
And then when we are quite done up, who cares for us, more than for a lame horse?
This is slavery.
(Mary Prince, *The History of Mary Prince*, 1831)

Silence is violence.
(Poster at a Black Lives Matter rally at Holyrood Park,
Edinburgh, June 2020)

Like most white Britons of my age, I grew up ignorant of Britain's history of slavery and its role in the formation of modern Britain, despite coming from Glasgow, Britain's 'second city of Empire', where that history is written in stone, visible everywhere from shipyards like Kingston Dock to street names like Jamaica Street. Until the summer of 2020 when the British media gave proper coverage to the Black Lives Matter movement, few people had thought much about Britain's colonial history. Many people learned more about it in a few months of toppling statues than during their entire schooling. Besides a re-evaluation of imperial monuments, the Black Lives Matter campaign encouraged debate about the economic legacies of Empire.

Yet despite this recent surge of interest in Britain's colonial history, the enduring effects of that history are still poorly understood, and some of

Britain's wealthiest and most powerful citizens still downplay, even deny, its continuing legacy in many people's lives today (Sanghera, 2021). In June 2020, Britain's Prime Minister Boris Johnson called for a 'change of narrative', and for black people to give up their 'sense of discrimination and victimisation'. He made this statement just as the Office for National Statistics (ONS) revealed that four times as many black Britons were dying of Covid-19 as white ones; some of them infected while doing their jobs as bus drivers, nurses and doctors, but most because of poor health or lack of resources – indicators of structural racism (no genetic factor having yet been identified). Alex Renton maintains that the ignorance and cover-up of racism today are as notable as slavery itself, and their effects just as pernicious (Renton, 2021, pp. 6–7). The most shocking discovery in my family history relates to this elided history of slavery. Nobody in my family knew anything about the connection between that history and the Venetian chest that inspired my research.

In the early 1820s, when Alexander's second wife (Julia's mother) was a teenager, enjoying a rich cultural life in Dresden far from her Bedford home near London, it would have taken several weeks to travel from London to Spanish Town, the colonial capital of Jamaica. It was a journey of 4,700 miles which the family's absent father must have made frequently as the owner of several slave plantations and hundreds of slaves in the Caribbean. Born in Jamaica in 1765 on his father William's sugar estate in the parish of St Elizabeth, John Foster also died there. It may well have been from there that he set out on the long sea voyage in 1822 that would take him to his dying son Algernon in Dresden.

The 1833 Slavery Abolition Act is remembered as a triumph of British liberalism. Yet at its heart was a multi-million-pound compensation payout – not for the slaves, but for the slave owners. A huge archive containing forty-six thousand entries details the amounts of money paid out to slave owners in compensation for their loss of human 'property' in the Caribbean. Research by University College London (UCL) which houses the archive sheds light on a decades-long battle by slave owners against abolition, and a fierce propaganda war by supporters of slavery. As a result of this battle, slave owners received the largest bailout in British history. The Slave Compensation Commission Archive names everyone who submitted a claim. Of the forty thousand owners spread across the British Empire who made claims, three thousand of those who lived in Britain owned 50% of the total number of slaves (Olusoga, 2015). These were the slave owners who went on to transform Britain, and they included several members of the Foster family. Julia's grandfather, the absent father in Dresden, is listed as slave owner 'John Foster of Bedford (c.1765–1831)'. He owned jointly with his brother Frederick the Dawkins estate (comprising the Bogue and New Eden plantations) in St Elizabeth parish, which they had inherited from their father. John also owned Two Mile Wood estate in St Elizabeth and its 215 slaves, as listed in the 1824 *Jamaica Almanac*.

The early 1820s were years of rebellion and unrest in the British Caribbean; there was a slump in the price of sugar in Britain, and falling profits. During these years John Foster would have had to attend to his affairs on the island. His absence from the family when they were in Dresden, and from most of Emily's journal during the period 1820–3, can be readily accounted for in these terms (see UCL's *Legacies of British Slave-Ownership* database). Before discovering my connection to the Cecil family, I had already uncovered a long history of slave ownership in Julia's maternal family background through the UCL database, which records British slave ownership in the West Indies stretching back to the seventeenth century. Its records of compensation payments to slave owners after the Slavery Abolition Act took effect on the 1st August 1834 lists several Fosters, including John Foster Barham, as beneficiaries. It will be recalled that John is the 'hinge' person in my tree, linking me back to the sixteenth-/seventeenth-century Cecils and forward to Julia and Alexander in the nineteenth and twentieth centuries.

Catherine Hall has pointed up the significance of the family, including aunts and uncles, cousins, in-laws and stepchildren, as key to the transmission of plantation wealth and as the bedrock of British economic organisation in the late eighteenth and early nineteenth centuries. Marriage and inheritance were central to the intergenerational transmission of wealth; hence cousins marrying each other was commonplace. To recap briefly, Julia's grandparents were 'John Foster of Bedford' and Amelia Morgan, his third wife. John's second wife, Flora Foster (not to be confused with Julia's mother), was also his cousin. Overlapping kinships were also important in the accumulation, consolidation and hoarding of wealth. Repeated marriages contracted among a small circle of families resulted in kinship networks stretching over generations (Hall, 2014, pp. 20ff.).

The Foster family's slave plantations in Jamaica were based mainly in the parish of St Elizabeth, in the county of Cornwall. They included the sugar estates of Elim and Lancaster as well as Two Mile Wood and the Bogue and New Eden plantations. The family was part of a small elite of plantation owners on the island, which stretched back to the middle of the seventeenth century. Yet Emily's teenage journal and her sister Flora's book of anecdotes, written in her middle age, are totally silent on the source of the family's wealth. It is worth sketching in here the longevity and extent of the Fosters' slave-owning history so as to fully appreciate the scale of these evasions.

The UCL database shows that the planters who succeeded most in Jamaica and acquired substantial wealth arrived within the first decade of settlement. Three-quarters of the eighty-eight biggest Jamaican patentees – that is, those who acquired two thousand acres or more during the seventeenth century – had taken out their first grants by 1670. The Fosters were in that first group of settlers. Land in Jamaica soon began to concentrate in fewer and fewer hands, as it did in England. In Barbados, '[a]s early as 1680, a mere 175 English planters collectively owned more than half of the island and claimed nearly half of the enslaved population' (Scanlan, 2020, p. 29).

John Foster of Bedford's great-great-grandfather, Captain John Foster (1618–76), took part in Admiral William Penn's expedition to the West Indies in 1655, sent there by Oliver Cromwell to wrest control of Jamaica from Spain and make the island an English colony. It was a conquest inspired by anti-Spanish and anti-Catholic sentiment, 'framed in part [by its leaders] as a war against the popery and cruelty of the Spanish in the Americas' (Pestana, 2009, p. 89). The division of Europe into Protestants and Catholics was one of the motivations that propelled Europe into the wider Atlantic world, says Carla Pestana, who maintains that when the English entered into colonisation of the Caribbean and the Americas, they were fuelled by a 'sense of... superiority [arising from their] Protestantism... with its emphasis on literacy and individual faith' (ibid., p. 65).

Captain John Foster and his son Thomas were among the first recipients of land that was handed out when Jamaica became an English colony. Many members of the Jamaica Assembly were also major slaveholders, as were most of the island's judges and magistrates (Dunn, 1972). A list of judges and magistrates in the 1776 *Jamaica Almanac* includes several descendants of Colonel John Foster, John Foster of Bedford's grandfather (1681–1731). When the colonel died, he left five Jamaican sugar plantations, staffed by 768 slaves and valued at £33,958, to his family. His will, dated the 27th August 1731, is chilling in its casual treatment of slaves as items of property: 'Elizabeth Smith of Barbados', Colonel John Foster's wife, is bequeathed £1,500 yearly, and 'the following negro slaves named Pompey, Cordon, Jean, Abigail, Black Sarah, Little Sarah, Silver and Clarissa and ten other negroes such as she shall chuse fit for raising stock... I give to my daughter Margaret £4000 to be paid to her at age 18 or on marriage... and a negro wench named Jenny... I give to my daughter Sarah £4000... to my son Thomas... when 21 and to his heirs all my estate known as Elim plantation. To William I give Dawkins Estate. To John I give Lancaster. To Samuel I give Two Mile Wood. To Joseph half of Island that is with me and my son-in-law Florentius Vassall... To Samuel and Joseph when 21 I give my land in Cape Boneta about 1000 acres.'

Multiple marriages contracted between and within plantation-owning families were the norm, consolidating wealth and political power across centuries. For example, Colonel John Foster's widow Elizabeth (née Smith) remarried twice. Her third husband, Henry Barham, owner of the vast Mesopotamia estate and sugar plantation in Westmoreland parish adjacent to St Elizabeth, had been a trustee and witness to John's will. On marrying his widow, Henry became stepfather to the Fosters' seven children. Having no children of his own, he left Mesopotamia to the Fosters' youngest son Joseph, on condition that he append the name Barham to his (see Appendix, Table 5).

The UCL entry on Henry Barham MD notes that his father (another Henry, and a fellow of the Royal Society) appears in the *Oxford Dictionary of National Biography* (*ODNB*) as a descendant of Nicholas Barham of Barham Court, Kent. The 'Barhams of Barham Court' included yet another Henry. *That* Henry Barham's wife was Elizabeth Culpeper, who was the maternal aunt of Katherine Howard (c. 1521–42), Henry VIII's unfortunate fifth wife. When a girl, Katherine frequently visited her aunt Elizabeth and uncle Henry at Teston (later named Barham) Court. Henry died before his niece's royal marriage in 1540, so he was at least spared the knowledge of her beheading two years later for having sex with her cousin, Thomas Culpeper, who makes a fleeting appearance in Hilary Mantel's *The Mirror and the Light* (Russell, 2017; Mantel, 2020).

The *ODNB* note on Henry Barham MD points to another strange twist, in light of his slave-owning interests: Barham Court (also known as Teston House) played a key part in the early history of abolitionism. For it was here that, in the mid 1780s, a small group of wealthy Anglican evangelicals – including Hannah More, Reverend James Ramsay, and Lord Charles and Lady Margaret Middleton – met. The 'Teston Clan' of abolitionists otherwise shared the same priorities of evangelicals and social reformers in England at the time, comments Christopher Brown: 'They assumed the poor should remain poor, but suffer less, worship more, and behave better' (Brown, 2006, p. 346).

Regarding Julia's more recent ancestors, the UCL entry on her grandfather John Foster of Bedford notes that, as co-heir with his brother Frederick to the Bogue and New Eden estates (together known as Dawkins estate), he left his half-share of the estate(s), 'together with the people and land since bought jointly' with his brother, in trust to Arthur Fitz John, his eldest son by his present wife Amelia. John's estate at Bedford, which included a farm as well as Brickhill House, was committed under his marriage settlement to Amelia, and thereafter to Arthur. Land known as Knott's Corner, bought from the corporation of Bedford, was bequeathed to his youngest son, Hugh Morgan. When John's main heir Arthur (1813–42) died unmarried in Jamaica, his estates there and in Bedford passed to his younger brother Hugh, their middle brother Algernon having died in Dresden as a young boy. Little from the estates was bequeathed directly to John's daughters Emily and Flora (Julia's aunt and mother), though the deed quoted in the previous chapter indicates that his will made provision for dowries in the form of land or property to pass to their husbands on marriage. Another estate, Shelton Hall, went to John's daughter Margaret by his first marriage to Margaret Place, with whom he had had three sons who had died young. Another son from this marriage was Edward Place Foster (1798–1862), who was written out of the family history. Born in Bedford and died in Porto Bello, Jamaica, Edward married a Jamaican woman of mixed race, Margaret Macfarlane (1821–1903), who was born in Porto Bello and died in Montego Bay. Probably a slave, she may have been a descendant of Alex Macfarlane (1703–55), a Scottish astronomer who made a fortune as a planter in Jamaica. He left his astronomical instruments to Glasgow University, which named its observatory after him. The couple had nine children.

John Foster died at the Bogue estate in St Elizabeth on the 30th June 1831, and is buried in St James parish, Montego Bay. There had been growing unrest among Jamaica's slave population throughout that year, as there had been in the early 1820s; another period when John absented himself from his family. A rumour was circulating that Parliament had agreed that the slaves would be freed by Christmas, but the planters were blocking it. The biggest slave revolt occurred in December 1831 across north-western Jamaica, including the parishes of Westmoreland, St James, and St Elizabeth where most of the Fosters' plantations were located. Known to Britons as the 'Baptist War', it was led by the Baptist deacon Samuel Sharpe, who told potential recruits that 'the King and English people wished the negroes to be emancipated... the only obstacles... were the obstinacy and selfishness of the planters' (Taylor, 2020, p. 202). The Baptist War, says Padraic Scanlan, 'helped convince a wavering Parliament to move forward with the 1833 Slavery Abolition Act' (Scanlan, 2020, p. 14).

Another event that year was the Scottish poet and abolitionist Thomas Pringle's publication of *The History of Mary Prince* (1831), one of the first books in the British Empire to be substantially produced, if not written, by a slave woman. Mary Prince, a baptised Moravian, was taught to read by missionary women. Her book was one of the most famous publications of the Anti-Slavery Society. Yet she is now almost completely forgotten; more so even than another freed slave whose band of freed black men, the 'Sons of Africa', campaigned to end Britain's slave trade, and whose autobiography, *The Interesting Narrative of the Life of Olaudah Equiano* (1789), helped lead to the 1807 British Slave Trade Act. The South African-Scottish writer Zoë Wicomb remembers Mary Prince in her novel *Still Life*, resurrecting her spirit and reimagining Pringle's life in a time-shifting narrative that is as illuminating as it is playful (Wicomb, 2020).

When slavery was eventually abolished in 1834, John Foster's benefactors received compensation from the Slave Compensation Commission for his remaining six hundred slaves. In addition, in 1835 his widow Amelia received £30 5s 5d for the one slave she owned in her own right, and his daughter Emily, author of the Dresden journal, was awarded £112 16s for her six slaves. As a slave owner herself, Emily cannot possibly have been blind to her father's occupation, even as a teenager. The amounts paid out by the commission to members of the Foster family were £7,467 for the Bogue estate and its remaining 363 slaves, £4,232 for Two Mile Wood and its 209 slaves, £7,252 for Elim and its 385 slaves, and £3,127 for Lancaster and its 167 slaves, totalling £22,078, a sum worth nearly £18 million today.

Translating historical amounts of money into modern equivalents is fraught with difficulty and has to be hedged around with all sorts of caveats. Comparisons are especially difficult when they involve long-run inflation calculations. I have decided not to fret too long over this. Later in this chapter I provide a brief justification for using the Relative Wealth Index (RWI) for my comparisons. This calculates change in prices according to change in purchasing power, using data on average earnings for all workers (Renton, 2021, p. x). In *An Economic History of the English Garden*, for example, Roderick Floud uses this measure of 'average nominal earnings' to calculate the gardener and landscape architect Capability Brown's salary in current terms (Sanghera, 2021, p. 265; Floud, 2019).

The extraordinary wealth acquired by one branch of the Foster family, the Foster Barhams, affords a telling example of how it was families rather than individuals who fostered the Caribbean plantation system. Charting the course of the Foster Barhams' accumulation and consolidation of their astonishing wealth over successive generations and through multiple marriages helped me solve the mystery of my family connection to the Cecil family. I was greatly assisted in this by Richard S. Dunn's *A Tale of Two Plantations*, which contains an extended case study of the Foster Barhams and of the Jamaican slave economy they oversaw for generations as both planters and politicians.

Dunn's book contrasts two systems of slavery: the British West Indies system, which existed from about 1640 until 1834, and the North American system, which lasted from about 1680 until 1865. Whilst by 1700 over 310,000 black slaves had been imported into the British West Indies through forced migration, only fifteen thousand had been brought into British North America by the same date. By 1750, the Atlantic slave trade, focused on the Caribbean, had landed 850,000 Africans, and by the close of the British slave trade in 1807, it had landed 2.3 million slaves. By these same dates, 150,000 and 388,000 African slaves respectively had been sold into North America; a vastly smaller number. Yet by 1807, the end of the Atlantic slave trade, the 2.3 million slaves imported into the British sugar islands had generated a slave population of just 775,000, whereas by the same date the 388,000 Africans imported into North America had generated a slave population of 1.4 million. This difference denotes that slaves brought to the Caribbean died off and had to be replaced, whereas those brought to North America expanded through natural reproduction at roughly the same rate as the white population (Dunn, 2014, p. 3). By some estimates the average lifespan of an imported slave in the Caribbean was seven years; that of a slave born in bondage, twenty-one years. Barry Higman outlines key elements of the Caribbean economic system: 'The principal features of plantation economy were found in the large scale of landholdings, dependence on enslaved and other forms of forced labour, horizontal management, monoculture, high population density, high rates of African to European people and high value per capita output' (Higman, 2008, p. 5).

As a result of this mode of production, by the middle of the eighteenth century, the sugar planters of Jamaica were among the richest people in the world. Accumulation and consolidation of properties enabled the bigger planters to take the wealth of the smaller, whilst '[t]he great wealth of the few depended on the poverty of the productive many' (ibid., p. 10). British apologists for slavery point to its ancient roots as if to excuse the fact that for nearly two hundred years Britain developed it as the motor of an economic system that devoured the lives of millions of African men, women and children. Over this extended period, which some people argue could not be racist because 'race' did not exist then as it does now, Britain was dehumanising black people on an industrial scale. To insist that race wasn't a 'thing' during this period is to engage in splitting hairs, says Sanghera: 'What Britain was *doing* at the time to most of the black people it interacted with is surely significant' (Sanghera, 2021, p. 152).

Throughout the eighteenth century, the British were the world's foremost slavers, with prosperity peaking between the 1750s and 1780s when the process of geographical expansion slowed. The second half of the century saw the beginning of the distinction between proprietor and planter, when the high rate of absentee proprietorships of Jamaica created the need for a class of intermediary managers, 'without parallel in most of the Americas' (Higman, 2008, pp. 10–11). Many of the planters had already retired to Britain, leaving plantation management to 'attorneys' (managers) and overseers. As a result, the British Caribbean islands became bases for increasingly exploitative profit-making. In North America, owners continued to live among their slaves.

To reflect this difference, Dunn structures his book around two case studies: one of a plantation in the Caribbean; the other of a North American plantation. The Caribbean case study is of Mesopotamia, a plantation in the Jamaican parish of Westmoreland, which was owned by the Foster Barhams. Mesopotamia came into the family's possession in the following way: when its original owner Ephraim Stephenson died in 1726, it passed to his wife Mary, who remarried. When her second husband also died, she took a third: the aforementioned Henry Barham (1692–1746), a Jamaican doctor who already owned a plantation called Spring, adjacent to Mesopotamia. When Mary died in 1735, Henry left Jamaica for good. Back in England, having already inherited substantial property through his first childless marriage, Henry married another wealthy widow whom he had known in Jamaica, having been witness and trustee to her first husband's will.

Henry's new wife was Elizabeth Foster (née Smith), long married to Colonel John Foster (Julia's great-great-grandfather), with whom she had a large family, and whose will was outlined earlier. When John died in 1731 Elizabeth had married another Jamaican plantation owner, who promptly also died. Returning to England, she took her third husband, the recently bereaved Henry Barham. Henry therefore attained real wealth by marrying well, not once, but twice. He was also the third husband of each of his wives *and* had no children of his own. Substantial wealth enabled him to keep a town house in London's Grosvenor Square and a country estate at Staines.

As Elizabeth's third husband, Henry, now stepfather to the five Foster boys and two Foster girls, took a special interest in his youngest stepson Joseph, whose Jamaican inheritance from his father, a sugar plantation named Island in St Elizabeth, was smaller than his brothers' inheritances. In light of this, Henry bequeathed Mesopotamia to Joseph on the condition that he adopt the Barham name and guarantee his mother a lifetime income from the property. When Henry died in 1746, his widow took over the estate, with Joseph (now legally renamed Joseph Foster Barham) becoming its owner at the age of majority and full-scale operator on his mother's death in 1756. Thereafter, Mesopotamia was owned by four generations of what was now called the Foster Barham family, mainly as absentee owners.

Elizabeth was buried with her husband at Staines. Their memorial inscription refers to Henry's descent from Nicholas Barham of Teston, Kent, and to Elizabeth's marriage to John Foster, with reference to his ancestor, 'Thomas Foster of Northumberland… who being concerned in the capture of Jamaica had large tracts of land allotted to him'. It is largely due to this Foster Barham marriage alliance and the complex path to it and beyond that the remarkable lineage in my family tree is traceable, stretching back from Alexander and Julia to the Cecils, Howards and Villiers; key players in the Elizabethan and Jacobean courts. In short, my link to the sixteenth-century Cecil family is rooted in the slavery-derived wealth, accumulated over almost two centuries, which enabled members of the Foster family to marry into the British aristocracy in the eighteenth and nineteenth centuries. Later still, this wealth would help to invisibly underpin Julia's life in Italy with Alexander (see Appendix, Table 5).

The Fosters and Foster Barhams left traces wherever they went, whether in journals such as Emily Foster's Dresden journal and her sister Flora's memoir written in middle age or, far more significantly, in the slave records compiled by the Foster Barhams, which are now lodged in Oxford's Bodleian Library as part of the 'Clarendon Papers'. How this came about is part of a long story involving multiple marriages and other strategies for accumulating wealth, which I'll come to shortly. Before leaving Jamaica in 1735, Henry Barham took an inventory of the 248 slaves on his Mesopotamia plantation. There were 124 males and 124 females, including many children, indicating a natural population increase. All of this was about to change. After 1736 the slaves seldom saw their master, who, on leaving Jamaica, had left all of his property in the hands of an overseer. The gender balance shifted from fifty-fifty in Henry's time to 116 female slaves and 152 males, meaning that Mesopotamia was no longer prepared for natural growth.

By the mid eighteenth century the expansion of sugar production had created an ever-increasing demand for more slaves, with the result that between 1736 and 1762 they were brought in from African slave ships. The slave records for the period tell a terrible story. The large number of deaths, especially of women, indicates that Mesopotamia's managers severely overworked the slaves. Contemporaries believed that a major cause of the low birth rate lay in 'planter opposition'. In 1751, a planter told John Newton, a slave trader turned abolitionist and the evangelical hymn-writer of 'Amazing Grace', that it was cheaper to work slaves to the utmost and by 'little relaxation, hard fare, and hard usage, to wear them out before they became useless, and unable to do service; and then to buy new ones, to fill up their places' (Sheridan, 1974, p. 244; see also Walvin, 2007).

Henry's heir to Mesopotamia, Joseph Foster Barham (1729–89), who took over full control of the estate in 1756 when his mother died, was the first of the slaveholders in Jamaica to compile the slave records on which

Richard Dunn's book is based. These records form the bulk of the Barham Papers, which are now housed at the Bodleian Library, providing a key resource for contemporary researchers of British slave-ownership. Henry Barham's original inventory became a baseline for measuring change over time, making the records especially useful. Joseph was a baby when his father died, and just seven when his mother married Henry. After an elite education at Eton and Trinity College, Oxford, Joseph visited Jamaica in 1750, returning to England after a year with a slave called George. As the owner of 3,788 acres in Westmoreland (Mesopotamia) and 2,708 acres in St Elizabeth (Island), with products worth £2,850 and £2,150 annually, he could easily survive well as an absentee planter.

Joseph and his older brother William (Julia's great-grandfather), who owned the nearby Dawkins estate in St Elizabeth, were received into the Moravian Church in Bedford soon after Joseph's return from Jamaica. William had been nine when his father died. He, too, benefited from an elite education in England, after which he returned to Jamaica, married (twice) and had seven children, returning to Bedford with his family in 1747 'in consequence of his wife's health', his first wife, Elizabeth Vassall (1725–c. 1743), having died shortly after their marriage. Joseph's memoir describes his brother's conversion to Moravianism. One day in 1753, Joseph testifies, William followed him into the Brethren Chapel in Fetter Lane, London. There, he writes:

> He heard from the mouth of Bishop Spangenberg exactly what he stood in need of... the simple, clear... proclamation of the gospel of grace for lost sinners... [S]cales seemed to fall from his eyes... Having found the only true consolation for his heart by... the Brethren Church, he lost no time in seeking admission to it... and he was honoured by the Lord to be the instrument of commencing the Mission in Jamaica. Since his first awakening, the thought had often occurred to him, whether, deriving as he did a large income from the labour of the negroes, it was not a Christian duty for him to care for the souls of these poor slaves... In the zeal for missionary enterprise prevailing in the Brethren's Church, he clearly saw the path marked out for him... Br. Caries, with two assistants, was sent thither in the year 1754.
>
> (Foster, 1768, p. 22).

The missionaries arrived in Kingston, Jamaica, on the 7th December 1754. Records note that 'Brothers William Foster and Joseph Foster Barham who sent the missionaries owned substantial slave estates in St Elizabeth and Westmoreland.' A Moravian chapel was built on the Mesopotamia estate in Westmoreland and the missionaries' headquarters were located at Elim in St Elizabeth, where 'about 900 slaves' worked in conditions described in the missionaries' diaries as 'more than inhuman'. By 1756 there were seventy-seven baptised slave members of the Church and four hundred under instruction. Joseph's memoir of his brother does not mention the birth in that year of William's son John Foster (Julia's grandfather), although there is a lengthy description of William's 'departure' in 1768, after which his son John, from the age of three, was brought up in Bedford along with his six siblings by his widowed mother Dorothy. Like his father and uncle, he scarcely knew his father.

According to Joseph's testimony, it was through Moravianism that William found a means to temper his guilt and justify the wealth he acquired on the backs of 'these poor slaves'. By offering the slaves a chance of salvation in another life, he salved his conscience in this one. Joseph adopted the same strategy. Whilst expressing concern for the slaves' health and souls in letters to estate agents and overseers, the Clarendon Papers also reveal that he and his friends were not convinced that the slave trade should be abolished: 'They satisfied themselves by saying that slavery had existed in all ages... admitted it to be an evil but regarded it as a divine dispensation' (Ward, 1988, p. 214). Such rationalisation belies the extreme cruelty fuelling this divinely dispensed evil.

After the American War of Independence (1775–83), sugar prices rose and Joseph Foster Barham, now in his fifties and without his wife Dorothea's influence (she, a devout Moravian, had died in 1781), became estranged from the Moravian Church. In 1785 he married Lady Mary (Pole) Hill, the widow of Sir Rowland Hill, in an Anglican ceremony, and the couple moved to Hardwick Hall in Shropshire. Despite quitting Bedford's Moravian community, Joseph continued to support the mission at his Mesopotamia estate. Sugar production expanded and income from the estate grew to £9,000 per annum, an immense sum. He died suddenly in 1789 of a paralytic stroke. He was fifty-nine.

The new master of Mesopotamia, Joseph's eldest son Joseph (1759–1832), henceforth Joseph Foster Barham II, had been brought up as a Moravian

Nonconformist. As such, he was banned from Eton and Cambridge. After attending a Moravian school in Germany, he entered Sweden's Göttingen University in 1775. A spell in the West Indies followed between 1779 and 1781, when he managed his Island estate and visited Mesopotamia. After returning to England, he never again set foot on Jamaica, and after a continental tour between 1791 and 1792 he followed in his father's footsteps by marrying into the aristocracy. Lady Caroline Tufton (1771–1832), daughter of Sackville Tufton, 8th Earl of Thanet (1733–86) and Mary Sackville (1746–78), became Joseph's wife in 1792 (see Appendix, Table 5). Since Lady Caroline was legally a minor when she married Joseph, consent had to be given by her guardians, the 'Most Notable John Frederick, Duke of Dorset & Hon John Leveson-Gower'. John Leveson-Gower's third wife, Mary Tufton, was the daughter of Thomas Tufton, 6th Earl of Thanet. His nineteenth-century descendant, George Granville Leveson-Gower, was the notorious 1st Duke of Sutherland who cleared thousands from his land during the Highland Clearances (see Chapter 10 of this book).

With a little help from ancestry.co.uk and some further reading, I discovered that Caroline's great-grandmother was Lady Anne Clifford (1590–1676), hereditary Sheriffess of Westmoreland (in the north of England) and owner of Appleby Castle, Brougham Castle, and Skipton Castle in Yorkshire. Anne was the sole surviving child of George Clifford, 3rd Earl of Cumberland and a witness at Mary, Queen of Scots' execution. In line with her father's will, the Clifford lands had to pass through the male line before going to Anne, who came into her inheritance in 1643 (see Appendix, Table 6). Anne is the author of yet another journal, *The Diaries of Lady Anne Clifford, 1603–1676* (Clifford, 2009). I managed to buy a copy when I visited Skipton Castle a couple of years ago, where there were several books about Lady Anne and 'the fabulous Cliffords'; the title of another book that I purchased from the tiny castle shop (Mitchell, 2002). At the time of my visit to the ruined castle, I had no inkling of my connection to the fabled family. Journalist Kenneth Roy, editor of the *Scottish Review* (the weekly journal for which I write), was one of her fans. I only discovered this when I read a tribute to her diary-writing skills in his own beautifully written memoir, published posthumously, and written whilst in hospital during the last few weeks of his life (Roy, 2019). I wish I had known about the diaries earlier. I would have valued Ken's astute insights.

Having acquired a large property in Wales from his mother, and joined the Church of England, a political career as the Whig MP for Stockbridge was now open to the new master of Mesopotamia (Dunn, 2014, p. 39). Like his father when *he* became a lapsed Moravian, Joseph Foster Barham II (Julia's first cousin twice removed) wanted slave owners to continue funding new missions in Jamaica, urging them to 'get hold of the minds of our negroes and correct their manners'. Joseph thought Moravians the most suitable evangelists for Jamaica because they addressed the heart, not the head, preaching passive submission rather than encouraging a spirit of inquiry among the slaves. Baptists and Methodists who were just embarking on missionary work on the island were, in his view, dangerous incendiaries, and Anglicans served only the white population.

On the 25th February 1795, as MP for Stockbridge, Joseph called for postponement of William Wilberforce's motion to abolish the slave trade in British vessels because, he said, 'local considerations' swayed him: the 'complete ruin' of the planters and the danger of rebellion. Yet, five years later, he was writing to his attorneys in Jamaica, 'I cannot approve the purchase of any negroes from the ships on any account whatsoever', thereby withdrawing from the Atlantic slave trade before the British Parliament prohibited it in 1807. A recent analysis of mortality rates on the Mesopotamia estate adds a twist to this 'early' withdrawal, showing that female slaves first observed during Joseph II's ownership faced an increased risk of death compared with those observed during his father's tenure. The work regime in operation under Joseph II after withdrawal from the slave trade is a likely explanation, as more women had to work in the cane fields, reducing their survival rate by around 30% (Forster and Smith, 2011). By 1818, eleven years after the abolition of the slave trade in Britain, slave deaths in Mesopotamia still outnumbered births, and by the 1820s Joseph had come to believe that the slaves were themselves responsible for this demographic 'failure', being naturally 'dissolute' and incapable of hard work. Reviewing population change in Jamaica between 1762 and 1833, Dunn's conclusion is different, attributing it to 'an extraordinarily abusive slave system at work' (Dunn, 2014, p. 43). A printed poll tax for March 1814 credits Joseph with 2,448 acres at Mesopotamia, 355 slaves and 466 head of livestock, managed by six white men and an overseer. Slave registers for 1814–34 show that, with deaths far outweighing births each year, his slave force shrank to 316 over the period. In 1820, fieldworkers at Mesopotamia were likely to die at the age of thirty-eight (Scanlan, 2020, p. 75). Dunn concludes from this analysis that Joseph II's claim to care about his slaves' well-being had little basis in reality.

In 1832, just before his death, Joseph produced a pamphlet, *Considerations on the Abolition of Negro Slavery*, asserting that Caribbean slaves were unfit for freedom and in need of 'moral improvement'. This was a reprise of a longer pamphlet published in 1824 in response to anti-slavery agitation at the time, and part of a decades-long anti-abolitionist campaign (Foster Barham, 1824). At probate, in August 1833, Joseph's total Jamaican estate, exclusive of land and buildings, was valued at £41,093. His remaining slaves were priced at £20,195, worth around £17 million today according to the Relative Wealth Index (RWI). The RWI uses wage growth and income 'worth' to calculate change in prices according to change in purchasing power. The other method used for calculating such change is Relative Price Worth (RPW), which uses the average price of a range of goods and services in the base year and compares with the same today. This is how we measure inflation, but as time passes RPW is less meaningful because the things we buy change (houses, say, rather than slaves), as does availability. Academic historians find the RWI more useful. It also works better for larger sums, especially in property. An Edinburgh town house costing £1,000 in 1800 equates to £81,300 using RPW, but to a more realistic £1.1 million using RWI (Renton, 2021, pp. ix–x). As such, I have generally used RWI, but by any measure, Joseph's estate represented immense wealth.

In the 1820s and 1830s large sugar plantations throughout Jamaica became dysfunctional, with 'rebellious' slaves, falling sugar prices in the British market, and shrinking profits. Joseph's eldest son John Foster Barham (1799–1838) succeeded his father to estates in Pembrokeshire, Hampshire and the West Indies, including Mesopotamia. He never visited Jamaica and had no interest in the slaves, who were, in any case, on the verge of emancipation. He was, though, very interested in receiving compensation for his loss of 'property', and so filed a claim on the 1st August 1834, the date on which all Jamaican Assemblies declared slavery abolished. A transition period – whereby slaves aged over six were to become apprenticed labourers, obliged to work for their former masters for forty-five hours a week – ended on the 1st August 1838 when the slaves were fully freed (Black, 2011, p. 198). Jamaica remained a British colony. John estimated the value of the 316 slaves in Mesopotamia on Emancipation Day at £13,538. On the 12th

October 1835, the Office of Commissioners of Compensation awarded him £5,612. Annual income from the estate was recorded as £1,509, having shrunk from £9,000 in the latter part of the previous century. Associated claims for St Elizabeth and Westmoreland brought a further £5,873 and £2,752 respectively. This was mere icing on the cake since the family had already made vast fortunes over two centuries on the backs of slaves. Like his father, John Foster Barham served as a Whig MP in Stockbridge and, from 1834 until 1837, Kendal. Four addresses are listed for him: Trecwn, Pembrokeshire, South Wales; 26 Queen Anne Street, London, England; Appleby Castle, Westmoreland, England (confusing, because of the Westmoreland estate in Jamaica); and Stockbridge House, Stockbridge, Hampshire, England.

In 1836 John was certified as being of 'unsound mind' by a commission of lunacy; perhaps unsurprising, in light of his family's history of interbreeding. He died in March 1838. In 1834, two years before being certified, he had married Lady Katherine Grimston, daughter of James Walter Grimston, 1st Earl of Verulam, thus following in his father's and grandfather's footsteps by marrying into the aristocracy. On his death, John's widow administered his estates; those in Pembrokeshire and the West Indies were entailed on his brother Charles following problems with his brother and next of kin, William, who died shortly afterwards. In 1842 *The Times* reported on subsequent litigation around compensation for the Mesopotamia and Island estates: 'Barham vs Earl of Clarendon' (see 'John Foster Barham', UCL *Legacies of British Slave-Ownership* database).

John's widow had remarried. She was now the Countess of Clarendon, having married George William Frederick Villiers, Earl of Clarendon, in 1839. Katherine's new husband had a famous ancestor: George Villiers (1592–1628), 1st Duke of Buckingham, James I's lover, whose 'lost' portrait by Rubens would later feature in a BBC documentary. 'Found' in Glasgow's Pollok House, it was bought by the Stirling-Maxwell family, whose fortune derived from *its* slave plantation, Hampden in Jamaica. John Foster Barham had died intestate, without issue. He had already directed his agents in Jamaica to stop taking inventories of slaves and to close the Moravian mission. Fortunately, when she married the Earl of Clarendon his widow brought the Foster Barham family archive with her, thereby preserving for posterity the two Joseph Foster Barhams' detailed longitudinal record of slave life at Mesopotamia in the Clarendon Papers.

Another case study in another book underlines the extreme violence permeating the entire Jamaican plantation system of wealth production. It also touches on another branch of the Foster family. In James Walvin's splendid book, *The Trader, The Owner, The Slave: Parallel Lives in the Age of Slavery* (2007), the titular owner is Thomas Thistlewood (1721–86), best known for the detailed diary he kept whilst living in Jamaica, where he had emigrated. It is a diary 'minus reflection or sustained judgment, just the facts,' says Toni Morrison. 'It is this, his divorce from moral judgment, not at all atypical, that shed light on slavery's acceptance' (Morrison, 2017, p. 8). The diary shows how quickly Thistlewood was socialised into a culture of brutality among a group of poorly paid white men, above whom overseers and managers ('attorneys') imposed their employers' will. A small owner elite were intent on making as much money as fast as possible to return home before disease killed them (Hall, 2017, p. 15).

When he arrived in Jamaica in 1750, Thistlewood was first employed by wealthy plantation owner Florentius Vassall (1709–78) as overseer of his Vineyard Cattle Pen in St Elizabeth. Florentius's wife was Mary Foster (1714–75), Julia's great-great-aunt. Mary, the daughter of Colonel John Foster and Elizabeth Smith, was Joseph Foster Barham's sister, born, like him, at Elim, St Elizabeth. Thistlewood soon learned that a culture of fear underpinned the plantation system. One of the people he learned this from was Florentius, who ordered three hundred lashes for a slave in Thistlewood's care; an event recorded in his diary. He also witnessed a man hanged from a tree at Vineyard Pen and having his hand cut off. Degraded forms of punishment invented by Thistlewood himself are recorded too. Finding a slave eating sugar cane, he 'had him well flogged and pickled, then made Hector shit in his mouth'. Another time, more elaborately, he 'put in a gag whilst his mouth was full and made him wear it 4 or 5 hours'. He called this the 'Derby dose' after the first man on whom he inflicted it (Renton, 2021, p. 153).

It was, however, the meticulous record of his sex life that made Thistlewood's diary famous. He was a serial rapist. During his thirty-seven years in Jamaica he logged 3,852 occasions of intercourse with 138 women, noting the time, place and degree of satisfactoriness of each encounter, the only distinguishing mark given to rape over other economic transactions being his use of Latin. Toni Morrison quotes from a diary entry in September 1751: 'About... 10am *Cum* Flora, a congo, *Super Terram* among the canes, above the wall head, right hand of the river, towards the Negro ground. She had been for watercress. Gave her 4 bitts' (Morrison, 2017, p. 9). After falling out with his employer, Thistlewood became overseer on a plantation whose owner later moved the slaves to 'Paradise' (Sara Collins' 2019 prize-winning novel *The Confessions of Frannie Langton* is set in a plantation called Paradise, near to a plantation called Mesopotamia).

Thistlewood possessed works by Scottish Enlightenment writers and borrowed the *Edinburgh Review* from a friend – intellectual pursuits that did nothing to temper his brutality or that of his colleagues. By improving his sense of self-worth through self-education he may even have managed to further distance himself from the 'uncivilised' slaves. Stuart Hall has noted how necessary is 'the other' to our sense of identity, and Sathnam Sanghera cautions that Thistlewood's 'cognitive dissonance, his ability to compartmentalize, his refusal to accept the brutal reality of what he was doing even as he cultivated a sophisticated demeanour, echo a psychological pattern that is common in British approaches to slavery' (Hall, 2017; Sanghera, 2021, p. 205).

Thistlewood was well aware of how *he* was viewed by the planter elite; never invited to meet visiting dignitaries or to the balls accompanying their visits, and noting in a 1767 diary entry that he has heard 'Theo Stone and Mrs Vassal, old Flor[entius]'s wife, wear the richest dres[s] of all the gentlemen and ladies at the governor's ball, on the King's birthday'. Thistlewood's first employer in Jamaica was a descendant of John Vassall, a Huguenot refugee from the Netherlands who settled in England and whose son William emigrated to Barbados, where he already owned a plantation. The capture of Jamaica from the Spanish in 1655 created another Caribbean opening for the family, and by the eighteenth century William's descendants, including Florentius Vassall, were among the leading planters in Jamaica (Smith, 2006).

In his seminal article on the early years of colonisation of the Caribbean by the English, Hilary Beckles, now vice-chancellor of the University of the West Indies, maintains that the two dominant features of agricultural history in the English West Indies were the formation of the plantation system and the importation of large numbers of servile labourers. In Barbados, which was colonised by the English in 1627, nearly three decades before Jamaica, large plantations developed within the first decade of settlement, producing tobacco, cotton and indigo, using mainly European indentured labour. Effective colonisation was made possible by this early formation of large plantations designed for the large-scale production of commodities and their distribution on a world market. *Preceding* the emergence of the sugar industry and the general use of African slave labour, early Caribbean planters like William Vassall in Barbados (who speeded up economic growth in the late 1640s and early 1650s through the production of sugar by black slave labour) already owned plantations stocked with indentured servants (Beckles, 1985).

William's descendant, Richard Vassall (1732–95), the only son of Florentius Vassall and Mary Foster, matriculated at Glasgow University in 1751, when around a quarter of the few hundreds of matriculated students at that university came from outside Scotland. Some, like Richard, were religious dissenters, because Scottish universities, unlike Oxford and Cambridge, were open to them. Many English dissenters studied there, particularly medicine, and especially at the Universities of Glasgow and Edinburgh, where students from the colonies were common (Sher, 1985). When Richard married Mary Clarke twenty years later, they had one child, Elizabeth (1771–1845), who was born and brought up in Jamaica. *This* Elizabeth Vassall (Julia's second cousin once removed) would become Lady Holland when she married Henry Richard Fox, 3rd Lord Holland (1773–1840) in 1797, thereby fulfilling the Foster Vassall family's dream of belonging unequivocally to the highest ranks of the British aristocracy.

When the pair married Henry was twenty-three and Elizabeth twenty-six, a divorcee, and the mother of five children, having first married when she was just fifteen. Henry and Elizabeth went on to have seven more children together, four of whom did not survive childhood, three from Elizabeth's first marriage having also predeceased her. Under her grandfather Florentius's will, Elizabeth inherited Friendship and Greenwich estates close to Mesopotamia, the large estate in Westmoreland owned by her maternal great-uncle Joseph Foster Barham. She was just six when her grandfather died in 1778, and with her husband she held these estates, along with Sweet River Pen, jointly until their deaths. When her father died in 1795, before her second marriage and the annulment of her first, Elizabeth noted in her diary that his death 'put me in possession of great wealth, upwards of £10,000 per annum' (Holland, 1908 [1795], p. 131). When she died in 1845, five years after the death of her second husband, Lord Holland, she was buried at Ampthill, Bedfordshire, near to her grandmother Mary Foster's family. She had become estranged from her children and almost entirely excluded them from her will. One of the people who benefited from this was Lord John Russell (1792–1878), son of the 6ᵗʰ Duke of Bedford, prime mover of the Great Reform Act of 1832 and twice UK Prime Minister. She bequeathed to him for life the income from the family's Lambeth estate. Elizabeth Vassall-Fox, Lady Holland, is listed as a 'Plantation Owner' in the UCL database. Her entry in the *ODNB* makes no mention of this fact.

Some powerful alliances were instrumental in delaying the abolition of slavery by many years. Some of the people featured in this chapter were pivotal in these alliances, which were forged over generations through family connections, friendship networks and, crucially, inheritance. Especially notable among them were Joseph Foster Barham II MP and Henry Richard Vassall-Fox, Lord Holland. Another was Charles Rose Ellis, Lord Seaford, who was mentioned briefly in the previous chapter and who will feature strongly in the next.

Slavery's history is downplayed by those who most benefited from it. Yet it still blights our entire society: 'The story is too recent, its legacy too awful, for us to accept it for what it was – an inexcusable crime, the "original sin" of the British Empire', as the historian Simon Schama puts it. The enslavement of Africans, he continues, was a necessary condition of the success of the Empire; the stain left, 'no amount of self-congratulation at its eventual abolition can altogether wash away' (Renton, 2021, p. 3; Schama, 2003, p. 324). It also left an indelible stain on my inheritance, the Venetian chest, with which my quest began.

Five

Jamaica: Lasting Legacies

I think [Churchill] would be very proud of the continuing legacy of Britain in those places around the world... a stark contrast, of course, with other less fortunate countries that haven't had the benefit of British rule.
(Boris Johnson, while Mayor of London, 2014; see Taylor, 2020, p. 297)

It was not until 2015 that British taxpayers finally paid off the government debt incurred by 'compensating' Caribbean slave owners for their 'loss' nearly two centuries earlier. The debt had to be refinanced repeatedly in the years following emancipation. The public revelation of this fact (of which most British people remain unaware) was not accompanied by any government apology to the Caribbean or to the British taxpayer for its failure to disclose the inherited debt. Instead, a Treasury 'Friday Fact', tweeted in February 2018, revealed that 'because it had taken so long to pay off the debt, millions of "living British citizens helped pay to end the slave trade" [sic]'. Besides misconstruing the 'fact' as being about the slave trade rather than slavery itself, as historian David Olusoga pointed out at the time, the government was in effect asking black Britons to celebrate paying taxes to compensate those who had enslaved their ancestors (Taylor, 2020, p. 300).

Pioneering slave owners like the Vassalls, Fosters and Foster Barhams colonised the Caribbean and inaugurated a system of wealth creation that enriched their descendants for generations, leaving behind a legacy of poverty, unemployment and disease as the occupational hazards of

Caribbean life. Having made their fortunes by the middle of the eighteenth century, these slave owners returned to Britain, where their social progress had a huge impact. Many were given peerages and others used their wealth to secure seats in the House of Commons. By the time of the slave compensation scheme in 1834, the House of Lords contained thirty-seven members who were slave owners, and of the 650 MPs at the time, eighty of them made claims under the scheme. Such penetration of the British establishment secured the interests of slave owners well beyond the end of slavery, right up until the present day.

Abolitionists had hoped that their first victory in March 1807 – abolition of the British transatlantic slave *trade* – would encourage slave owners to take better care of their slaves. Instead, the slave owners sought an alternative *source* of slaves in Guyana, where, by 1820, there were three hundred sugar plantations. Any hope of reduced brutality vanished when slave registers revealed a mortality rate of 17%. The goal of abolitionists now became slavery itself. But as Padraic Scanlan has pointed out, 'consensus around the abolition of the slave trade was possible in part because emancipation was a distant horizon' (Scanlan, 2020, p. 188).

When rumours of the anti-slavery campaign in Britain reached Guyana in the summer of 1823, thousands of slaves in the Demerara colony downed tools and torched plantations. Many of the rebels were shot and the ringleaders executed. Slave owners turned up the volume on their propaganda campaign, including Joseph Foster Barham II MP, who argued that the slaves were dissolute and responsible for their own failures, and John Gladstone, a major slaveholder in Demerara, who claimed that the slaves had no reason to rebel as they were well fed and had Sabbath rest. In turn, Gladstone's son William, elected to Parliament in 1832 on a pro-slavery ticket, believed that slavery was 'not necessarily sinful', whilst George Cruikshank's famous John Bull cartoon satirised the British public's sympathy for the slaves, implying that it made them avert their eyes from the poor in their own country (Olusoga, 2015). Major publishers John Murray and William Blackwood solicited pro-slavery articles; some for Murray's flagship journal the *Quarterly Review*, and some, by the likes of Sir Walter Scott, for *Blackwood's Magazine*, which was launched as a conservative rival to the more liberal *Edinburgh Review*. The pro-slavery campaign of the 1820s and 1830s was spearheaded by the so-called 'West India Interest': the countless merchants, civil servants, judges, writers, publicists, landowners, clergymen and politicians who were the slave owners' most powerful domestic allies (Taylor, 2020). The 'Interest' also relied on support from other sections of the British population, including working-class radicals like William Cobbett, a popular journalist and virulent racist.

Some members of the peerage were particularly active in defending slave-owning interests, notably Charles Rose Ellis, Lord Seaford (1771–1845), a regular contributor to the *Quarterly Review* who as a child had inherited his father's Jamaican estate of Montpelier and its 1,310 slaves, worth £20,000 at probate. As chair of the West India Committee, he supported 'moral improvement' of the slaves and resisted any moves towards emancipation (see 'Charles Rose Ellis, Lord Seaford', UCL *Legacies of British Slave-Ownership* database; Ward, 1988). Ellis is of special interest to me because his foster sister was Julia's ancestor, Elizabeth Vassall, with whom he was raised in Jamaica by her parents Richard and Mary Vassall, when his own parents drowned in 1782. His parents were John Ellis, Governor of Jamaica (1729–82) and Elizabeth Palmer (1750–82). Both of Charles's grandfathers, George Ellis and John Palmer, were Chief Justices of Jamaica. George's wife (Charles's grandmother) was Anne Beckford, who belonged to one of the wealthiest families in the West Indies. Charles's uncle John Palmer (his mother's brother) married Mary Ballard Beckford (1736–97). When John died, Mary married Edward Long (1734–1813), best known for his *History of Jamaica* (1774), which justifies slavery in terms of the genetic inferiority of the African. At the time of her second marriage to Edward in 1758, Mary owned an estate called Friendship, which she had inherited from her father. This is the name of the estate in Westmoreland which Elizabeth Vassall (later Elizabeth Vassall-Fox, Lady Holland) inherited from her grandfather Florentius Vassall in 1778. If this is indeed the same estate, which I am unable to establish, it would no doubt have had something to do with the fact that Mary's nephew (through her first marriage to John Palmer) was Charles Rose Ellis, Elizabeth's foster brother.

The Fosters and the Vassalls were paired in various ways with other powerful Caribbean slave-owning dynasties. Tracing the links and cross-matching them with the UCL database has been time-consuming but illuminating. For instance, the Fosters were related through marriage to the wealthy Manchester-based merchant Hibbert family. Robert Hibbert (1770–1849) owned Georgia estate in Hanover parish, close to St Elizabeth parish where Julia's grandfather John Foster of Bedford was a planter.

When Robert returned to England he became a partner in the Hibberts' West India Counting House, bought East Hyde estate in Bedfordshire, became High Sheriff of Bedfordshire in 1815, and in 1818 sent a Unitarian missionary to his Jamaican estate to 'Christianise' the slaves. In 1790 Robert had told a parliamentary select committee investigating slavery that the 'natural indolence' of black women meant that they 'took advantage' of being pregnant when in his opinion the exercise in the cane fields would be good for them. When his own wife was pregnant in 1800 he noted that she spent twenty-two days in bed to avoid miscarriage. Historians estimate that a quarter of pregnancies among enslaved women ended in miscarriage, as a result of which many planters said they had a *culture* of making themselves abort (Renton, 2021, p. 175). It is not difficult to imagine why this would be the case if true: rape, trauma, and not wanting to have a child born into slavery, for a start.

The details of the connections between the Fosters and the Hibberts, as with other wealthy slave owners, are complex and difficult to portray in words; some more so than others. Thus Robert Hibbert appears in my tree as 'husband of sister-in-law of sister-in-law of brother-in-law of maternal grandfather [John Foster of Bedford] of wife [Julia Dawson] of great granduncle [Alexander Robertson]'. The second-mentioned sister-in-law was Ann Brooks (1767–1818) who married Ballard Beckford Nembhard (1761–1821), thereby making him part-owner of Hounslow estate in St Elizabeth. Ann's sister Marianne (1763–1809) had married John Foster (1748–1840) at Elim, St Elizabeth, in 1777 when she was fourteen. *That* John Foster was John Foster of Bedford's cousin. He was also John of Bedford's brother-in-law, because John of Bedford's second wife Flora Foster (1766–1802) – not to be confused with his daughter (Julia's mother) of the same name – was also his cousin. She was, in other words, *that* John Foster's sister. To complicate matters further, John Vassall (1743–79), another cousin, married Elizabeth Brooks (b. 1757), the oldest Brooks sister, in 1776.

Convoluted connections such as these are not easy to grasp. The important point is the interconnection between, and consequent lobbying power acquired by, wealthy slave-owning families as an anti-abolitionist political bloc. Complex familial interconnections among powerful dynasties of Jamaican slave owners stretched over generations and criss-crossed the British Empire, paving the way for their absorption into the British aristocracy. A nice example of this is that much of the remainder of the Beckford family's vast wealth was absorbed into the estate of the Dukes of Hamilton through marriage. An illuminating case study of the Hibbert family describes their lasting impact on Britain through their acquisition of colonial wealth, charting the transgenerational transformation of their capital from property in commodities (as merchants) to property in people (as slave owners), and finally to investment in land, political position and cultural capital (Donington, 2014). Becoming gentlemen improvers, the Hibberts acquired land in Britain and an interest in public service and building country houses, thereby securing their assimilation into the English gentry and aristocracy.

Modern historians point out that most of the vast fortunes made out of the West Indies trade during slavery were 'hidden', because they were based in insuring, bankrolling and mortgaging the planters, merchants and shippers (Renton, 2021, p. 169). Moreover, the wealth of some of the most successful British Caribbean planters like the Vassalls and the Hibberts lay chiefly in their land, whose value (including its enslaved population) rose substantially through the second half of the eighteenth century, especially in Jamaica where there was a property boom. Despite the wealth already acquired through their Caribbean interests, the Hibberts received a further £103,000 (about £80 million today) in compensation payments as both slave owners and creditors. They had certainly lobbied hard for compensation and against emancipation. George Hibbert (1757–1837), Robert Hibbert's cousin, who entered West Indian affairs through his family's merchant firm in Manchester, is particularly notable in this respect. Elected first chairman of the City of London's West India Dock Company at its inaugural meeting in August 1799 when it was launched as a joint-stock company, George became MP for Seaford in 1806, displacing Charles Rose Ellis as leader of the West India Committee. On the 12th March 1807, a few weeks before the Abolition of the Slave Trade Act, he tabled a petition on behalf of the planters, arguing that high taxation was ruining West Indian sugar on the world market. Four years later, he supported Joseph Foster Barham II's proposal to use free labour from the East Indies in place of slaves; a type of indentured servitude that was effectively slavery by another name (Jordan, 2005, p. 159). When his term as an MP ended in 1812, he was appointed by the colony as the colonial agent for Jamaica to promote its interests in Britain (Taylor, 2020, p. 68).

Despite fierce anti-abolition agitation throughout the 1820s and into the 1830s, led by Charles Rose Ellis and Joseph Foster Barham II and supported by the likes of George Hibbert, public opinion was eventually won over by the abolitionists, who gathered 1.5 million signatures on anti-slavery petitions. Slave uprisings played a major role in this, the slaves' determination to resist despite brutal reprisals proving irresistible, bad for profit, and lending momentum to the anti-slavery movement (Wicomb, 2020, p. 248). In 1832 the government drafted plans to abolish slavery. Having lost the moral argument, the slave owners switched the grounds of their case by turning to Britain's property laws to enlist arguments around compensation. Half of the Acts passed in nineteenth-century Britain concerned private property. By arguing that the abolition of slavery amounted to confiscation of their *property*, the slavers presented compensation as a non-negotiable condition of abolition. 'Emancipation announced what generations of landowners had insisted, that the right to property was sacred, even if the "property" claimed was a human being' (Scanlan, 2020, p. 289).

One of the most insistent of these slave-owning landowners who prepared the ground for this argument was Joseph Foster Barham II, who in his 1824 pamphlet *Considerations on the Abolition of Negro Slavery and the Means of Practically Effecting It* had listed several 'impediments' to emancipation. High up on that list came the slave owners' fears that 'they will bear all the loss incurred'. For reasons of 'necessity and justice', he argued, 'compensation should be considered' (Foster Barham, 1824, p. 23). Having fought vigorously against emancipation, but seeing the writing on the wall, Foster Barham insisted that to gain the slavers' cooperation with abolishing slavery, '*Let the nation at once assume to itself all colonial property, and make moderate but just compensation to the proprietors for the whole.* Let the nation then do on its own account, what it desired the present proprietors to do. Then, if there be risk, it will be incurred *as it ought*, by the nation' (ibid., p. 35; author's own italics). Clothing his pro-slavery economics in a form of English nationalism, Foster Barham was arguing that the planters – as, essentially, British landowners – were entitled to the same protection 'in their persons and fortunes' as in Great Britain and Ireland (Taylor, 2020, p. 133). He even laid out a plan of action which included setting a specific date to fix a price on each proprietor's 'property' (Foster Barham, 1824, p. 43). Something like that plan was adopted ten years later, by which time his son John had succeeded him.

This reframing of the issue of slavery in terms of property rights was the slavers' biggest triumph and the most far-reaching in its consequences.

Abolitionists had spent decades arguing that slaves were *not* property. At the very last minute they had to abandon this most fundamental principle because by 1833 it was clear that emancipation could only be achieved if linked to compensation. To appease the slave owners, the government proposed a £20 million compensation scheme for them. This is equivalent to around £17 billion today, though some calculations put it much higher. As Sathnam Sanghera explains, quoting the *Financial Times*, 'if half the money bought corporate debt with proceeds reinvested, it would now be worth £150bn' (Sanghera, 2021, p. 138). The slaves were to receive nothing.

Britain in the 1830s was an even more indebted country than it is now. There was no income tax. Consumption (purchase) tax was all that the government could use to raise the money to meet the bill, so the main burden fell on the poor rather than the rich. A staggering 40% of total government expenditure in 1834, following the 1833 Abolition Act, was paid out to a small group of (in many cases) already very rich people. If compensation were offered in 2020 in proportion to the UK's total budget, says Padraic Scanlan, it would equal roughly £200 billion:

> Compensation was a fantastic deal for lenders, and a massive transfer of wealth from the public purse to the private sector – perhaps the largest, in proportion to the size of the government's budget, in British history. Investors could be very confident that the British government would not default... The expense of compensation could be used to justify austerity in fiscal policy while increasing the government's influence over financial markets and enriching banks and wealthy private investors.
>
> (Scanlan, 2020, pp. 288–90).

The deal set a pattern that would be followed by future governments, the closest modern equivalent being the post-2008 bank bailout, with a similar impact on the poor as against the rich. In the 1830s, the West Indian slavery system supported credit systems that were simply 'too big to fail', as the banks were said to be after 2008. As a result, the slave compensation scheme in effect bailed out a privileged minority (Olusoga, 2015). Compensation to owners was based on the slave market prices of the 1820s, which varied from colony to colony. In Jamaica, a child was valued at £6, a fieldworker at £50, 'and a valuable artisan like a sugar-boiler might be £100' (Renton, 2021, p. 249).

One of the compensation scheme's claimants was Julia's great-aunt Maria Morgan, Dowager Countess of Carhampton (1777–1857), the only sister of Julia's grandmother, Amelia Morgan. Maria's husband John Luttrell-Olmius, 3rd Earl of Carhampton (1739–1829), was sixty when he took the twenty-one-year-old Maria as his second wife. The Earl's mother Judith Maria Lawes (1720–98) had inherited substantial wealth from her father, Sir Nicholas Lawes (1652–1731), Governor of Jamaica between 1718 and 1722. She left Swallowfield estate and pen in St Andrews, Jamaica, 'together with the enslaved people on it', in trust to her grandchildren for life, and then to her son John, whose widow, in turn, claimed compensation for the estate. Maria was awarded £876 8s 2d for forty-seven slaves, equivalent to about £118,000 in today's money (see Appendix, Table 5).

The UCL historians have cross-referenced the names of slave owners who received compensation with national institutions, so as to assess how profits from slavery shaped Britain today. The rapid industrialisation of Britain in the nineteenth century largely rests on slavery, which is embedded, too, in Britain's London-based financial world. Slave owners in the 1830s diversified into financial developments such as Imperial Life Insurance (now Aviva). Slavery is also central in the formation of the nation's 'great estates' and cultural institutions such as the Royal Society and the British Museum, as well as charities such as the Royal National Lifeboat Association, one of George Hibbert's enduring legacies. Many of the fellows and trustees of these cultural and philanthropic bodies are historically linked to the slave compensation scheme.

The social and cultural capital acquired through slave-generated wealth remained even after the money was gone, reshaping British society in the nineteenth century, and was redeployed into country houses, connoisseurship and philanthropy. One intriguing trivial example of these cultural legacies, which I uncovered by joining some of the dots in my family tree, revealed a connection between the slave-owning Foster Barham family and the famous D'Oyly Carte theatre and opera company. Richard D'Oyly Carte, the company's founder, married twice. His second wife was Susan Helen Couper Black, who was born in Wigtown, Scotland in 1852. Susan's mother was Ellen Foster Barham, daughter of Dr Thomas Foster Barham, grandson of Joseph Foster Barham (1729–89), owner of the vast Mesopotamia estate in Westmoreland, Jamaica.

There were European cultural legacies too. When I located the death certificate of Julia's first husband, John Clode Braddon, at the town hall in Pau, I mentioned to the archivist that various members of the Foster Barham family had also died there. She promptly emailed snapshots of the family at play in Pau: fox hunting, horse racing and playing golf – clubs set up by the fashionable town's rich nineteenth-century British residents. Taken from a scrapbook compiled by the Baron d'Este (a descendant of the Renaissance art patron Isabella d'Este, Marchioness of Mantua), they included a funeral card for the 'Baronne de Vaufreland', Marguerite Conine Foster-Barham (the hyphenated form of the surname was adopted later). Baron Louis de Vaufreland was the French aristocrat and Nazi double agent who recruited his lover Coco Chanel into the *Abwehr* in 1941.

In the years following abolition, the slave owners won another battle. Their racial theories, based on the 'inferiority of the negro', outlived them and seeped into British culture, minted in the propaganda wars against emancipation that are now largely forgotten. The only part of the story that *is* remembered is about abolition. As a result, men like John Gladstone are remembered as 'planters' or 'merchants', and my slave-owning ancestors through Alexander's marriage to Julia appear on censuses as 'merchants' or 'farmers'. The 1821 census lists Julia's grandfather John Foster of Bedford in the latter category, effectively erasing his occupation and main source of wealth as a slave owner.

Stuart Hall describes disavowal as a complex psychic manoeuvre that 'allows people to "know" and "not know" at the same time. It suppresses and conceals' (Hall, 2017, pp. 186–7). This is a fair description of the strategy adopted by John Foster of Bedford, who wrote a book. Published in the same year as the Abolition of the Slave Trade Act was passed, it makes not a single reference to slavery or to Jamaica. It is about farming in Bedfordshire. A very slim book, thrillingly titled *Observations on the Agriculture in the North of Bedfordshire*, it opens with a discussion of the enclosure system; the 'great change... which... has converted more than half the arable land... from an open field to a divided state' (Foster, 1807, p. 10). Outlining benefits of the arrangement, John concedes its defects: 'A great increase in rent... induced some and compelled more to force the land to a number of successive exhausting crops' (ibid., p. 11). Whilst expressing concern about labour costs, John heaps praise on the late 5th Duke of Bedford, Francis Russell (1765–1802), 'to whom we justly look up as the author and patron of all our rural improvements… in whom every moral, social, and political virtue were united, whose transcendent abilities… were the objects of admiration, not only of his friends and countrymen, but also of our national enemies' (ibid., pp. 48–9). Agriculture became the Duke's main employment in his later years. He even set up a model farm at Woburn, Bedford, and had Bedford House in London, designed by Inigo Jones, razed to the ground. Russell Square and Tavistock Square were erected on its site. On the shift in balance between farming and manufacturing, John reckons that '[t]he labouring class are in general better maintained than formerly [though] instances of depravity are every where too frequent, yet… there is more morality, sobriety, and regular industry, than where manufactories have been introduced' (ibid., p. 50).

No mention, then, of the social costs of the enclosure system, in which, between the start of the seventeenth century and the middle of the nineteenth (a period when few 'commoners' could influence Parliament's decisions), around 6.8 million acres of common land were enclosed by Acts of Parliament. As a result, common rights to use open fields and wasteland for grazing and growing food were extinguished in Britain. Reading John Foster's book, what struck me was the similarity between enclosure in Britain and the Caribbean plantation system, insofar as the large scale of landholdings through the accumulation and consolidation of smaller properties by the bigger owners was concerned. Enclosure in Britain involved the forced amalgamation of smallholdings worked by peasants into large farms, which landlords then leased to 'capitalist tenants who could afford to make capital investments' (Brenner, 1985, p. 49). Similarly, land in the colonies concentrated in fewer and fewer hands early on. John Foster of Bedford was writing about enclosure at its zenith. Yet his book is as silent about the dispossession of British peasants as it is about the sugar 'manufactories' in Jamaica that fuelled his family's comfortable life in Bedford and, for a time, Dresden.

The parallels are striking, though nothing in British history can compare with chattel slavery and the silence surrounding it. As Catherine Hall and her UCL co-authors observe, 'Slave-ownership is virtually invisible in British history… elided by strategies of euphemism and evasion originally adopted by the slave-owners themselves and subsequently reproduced widely in British culture' (Hall, 2014, p. 20). A stark example of this cultural silence is the *Oxford Dictionary of National Biography*, which includes hundreds of

Britons who owned slaves but identifies very few of them as slave owners. George Hibbert's entry lists him simply as a 'merchant'; John Foster's as a 'farmer'. The UCL project sets out to correct such omissions by showing that slave ownership permeated the British elites of the early nineteenth century and helped form those of the twentieth century. When Hall examined the writing strategies of the slave owners and their descendants post abolition, she found that some even construed themselves as victims of emancipation, so erasing the horrors of slavery through strategies of disavowal (Hall, 2014, pp. 163–202). The government's compensation scheme marked acceptance of the view that the institution of slavery had been effectively sanctioned by the state, since 'the nation' – that is, the British taxpayer – was to bear the cost of losses to slave owners, as Joseph Foster Barham II had proposed a decade earlier. As a result, slave owners felt no personal guilt. Some even went on to write history books and memoirs without mentioning slavery. The memoirs of Henry Richard Vassall-Fox, Lord Holland, leader of the Whigs, are notable in this respect, despite his marriage to Elizabeth Vassall bringing him the Jamaican estates of Sweet River and Friendship, worth around £7,000 a year.

Henry had taken the Vassall name when he married Elizabeth, so as to secure her West Indian properties for himself and his children. It was a condition of inheritance imposed by Elizabeth's grandfather Florentius that the Vassall name should come immediately after the Christian name. Before Henry, when just fifteen, Elizabeth had married thirty-eight-year-old Sir Godfrey Webster. While touring Europe, she met the 3rd Baron Holland and they started an affair. In 1797, now divorced from Webster, who had also added her surname to his in order to gain access to her fortune, Elizabeth writes in her journal, 'My wretched marriage was annulled… on 4 July. On the fifth I signed a deed by which I made over my whole fortune to Sir G. W. for our joint lives.' On the 20th July 1799, now Lady Holland, she makes a rare reference to the West Indies: 'The immense price of sugar has defeated the avarice of the proprietors of it… The revenues of the West Indians will be considerably diminished, and tho' I ultimately may suffer… I should feel very little sorrow if they had been at 0 for the last few years; then *he* would not have added another example to the many – that injustice thrives' (Holland, 1908, p. 33). The *'he'* referred to is, of course, Sir Godfrey Webster. It is *his* income from *her* sugar that will be diminished. 'Sir G. W.' did retain for life Elizabeth's West Indian income of £7,000 per annum, but 'life' was brief. Elizabeth married Henry Fox two days after the divorce and Webster committed suicide three years later (see 'Elizabeth Fox née Vassall', UCL *Legacies of British Slave-Ownership* database).

The protégé of his uncle Charles James Fox (1749–1806), Henry followed in his footsteps by opposing the slave trade despite being a West Indian slave owner himself. Charles, whose statue stands in London's Bloomsbury Square clad in the garb of a Roman senator, proposed the bill to abolish the slave trade on the 10th June 1806, just before his death. His statue, erected in 1816, stands facing another one, across Bedford Square, in Russell Square. Erected in 1809, this statue is of Francis Russell, 5th Duke of Bedford (1765–1802), the object of John Foster of Bedford's veneration. One hand rests on a plough; the other holds ears of corn. Tom Crewe sees the juxtaposition of these two statues as a 'marvellous piece of political theatre'; a reminder that 'there are bits of the city that don't actually belong to us' (Crewe, 2017, p. 7). Property is key.

Henry was a main beneficiary of Francis Russell's will when the latter died at Woburn, unmarried, in 1802. Henry's widow Elizabeth (1770–1845) reciprocated by leaving a large slice of her estate to Lord John Russell (1792–1878), the son of Francis's brother John Russell, 6th Duke of Bedford (1766–1839). According to a footnote in a recent book, when Henry died in 1840 his widow inherited Holland House as well as the 'manor of Ampthill' in Bedfordshire. But 'she was in debt and persuaded her son to agree to them being sold. The Duke of Bedford [presumably Francis Russell, 7th Duke of Bedford and Marquess of Tavistock (1788–1861)] bought them in 1842, adding them to his holdings in the area' (Major and Murden, 2016, p. 156).

Property was certainly key to Elizabeth's second husband. Whilst supporting abolition of the slave *trade*, when it came to slavery itself, Lord Holland was anxious to uphold 'the various orders of society without which property cannot subsist'. His overriding concern was to protect property rights, and he pressed to secure the maximum amount of compensation for the slave owners, working with the West India Interest throughout the 1820s (Kriegel, 1977, p. 269; Taylor, 2020). Three claims under the slave compensation scheme were made in the names of Lord and Lady Holland. Yet Lord Holland's *Memoirs of the Whig Party During My Time* (1852), published twelve years after his death, whilst saying that the abolition of the slave trade ended one of 'the greatest evils to which the human race has ever been exposed', omits to mention that he owned hundreds of slaves in

Jamaica. Memories of plantation slavery are just too troubling: 'Amnesia was a less troubling condition,' remarks Catherine Hall (Hall, 2014, p. 172).

Amnesia still dominates the fierce anti-abolitionist struggle fought by Caribbean slavers and their representatives in Parliament two centuries ago, which began even before the abolition of the slave trade in 1807. My distant forebears through Alexander Robertson's wife Julia were central to that inglorious, decades-long battle; particularly Joseph Foster Barham II, who was at the forefront of a powerful alliance to delay or otherwise thwart emancipation. An entry in Elizabeth Vassall's journal, written in Nice in February 1792 before she became Lady Holland, offers a useful reminder of the long-standing nature of some of these alliances. Charles Rose Ellis was her travelling companion; 'a very old friend of mine; we were brought up for many years absolutely together,' she notes, alluding to their time together as children in Jamaica, when her parents fostered the orphaned Charles.

Since Elizabeth would become Lady Holland when she married Henry Richard Fox, the Lords Holland and Seaford were effectively brothers-in-law (see Appendix, Table 7). They were also close friends and frequent correspondents. In 1832, shortly before sailing to Jamaica to visit his estates, Lord Seaford wrote to his fellow absentee plantation owner friend Lord Holland about the imminent emancipation of Caribbean slaves: 'What the Negroes look to, in freedom, is merely to be exempted from labour, or at least to continue to occupy their houses, and to cultivate their grounds, for their subsistence, without reckoning on having to pay rent for house or land,' he opined. Assumptions and attitudes such as these led to management policies post emancipation that made residence and access to grounds dependent on wage labour for the estate on which the worker lived, and on the payment of rent (Higman, 2008, p. 247). Lord Seaford believed that those who refused to pay rent should be ejected, so as to force the freed slaves to return as wage labourers to the plantations they had worked on before emancipation.

Robert Wedderburn, an agrarian socialist, saw the dangers in this for the freed slaves. Born in Jamaica in 1762, the free son of an enslaved woman and a slave-owner physician father, Robert's childhood among slaves had fed his belief that emancipation had to include the abolition of private property. Comparing the fates of the enslaved with those of poor landless workers in Europe, he came to believe that a gradual emancipation that allowed the slaves to keep the land they had made profitable would be better than immediate landless freedom. Provision grounds worked by slaves for generations had been held collectively; with more land, they could produce more and sell the surplus to buy both land and freedom. Even if emancipation gained in this way took generations, if freed people held land in common, 'then no missionaries could hector, no landlords could gouge' (quoted in Scanlan, 2020, p. 301).

Wedderburn's foresight proved correct. Even after 'full freedom' was granted in 1838, at the end of the so-called 'apprenticeship' system, binding freed slaves to work for their masters for a further period, the slave owners did all they could to maintain their power. The apprentices believed that the houses they lived in and the plots of land they cultivated (mainly to feed themselves) were theirs. But when apprenticeship ended, the emancipated Africans had to pay the planters rent or leave the houses and plots they had built and cultivated (Dick, 2008). In holding down wages, the planters were supported by a Jamaican House of Assembly and by imperial powers that promoted a notion of Jamaica as existing primarily to produce for the benefit of the 'mother country'. This meant a 'plantation economy with no space for peasant aspirations' (Hall, 2020, p. 12).

Some people in the 'mother country' continue to benefit disproportionately from Jamaica, especially those whose inherited wealth from their ancestors' slave plantations is now invested in parts of London with sky-high property and rental values. One such is the Howard de Walden Estate, owned by the family since 1710 and consisting of ninety-two acres of Marylebone, including Harley Street. Its current head, Mary Czernin, the 10th Baroness Howard de Walden, is worth an estimated £3.73 billion. In 1850, a shilling (£0.05) a day was the wage for men on Lord Howard de Walden's Jamaican estate of Montpelier (Renton, 2021, p. 259). It is not clear if this sum was in Jamaican currency or sterling; in 1850, a labourer's wage in rural Britain was about £1 a month. The Baroness's predecessor, Charles Augustus Ellis, 6th Baron Howard de Walden (1799–1868), also held the title of 2nd Baron Seaford. He was the son of Charles Rose Ellis, 1st Lord Seaford, and Elizabeth Hervey, whose father was Lord Frederick Hervey, 4th Earl of Bristol. Charles Augustus Ellis succeeded to the Howard de Walden barony in 1803, aged four.

Charles Rose Ellis, who had inherited the Montpelier estate from his parents when he was a child, became one of those Jamaican absentee proprietors who, in the late eighteenth century, wished to place their slaves under the care of missionaries. During the 1790s, 'prodded' by Joseph Foster Barham II, he had turned to the Moravians and, in 1797, presented a successful motion to the Commons, passing responsibility to Assemblies in the West Indies for taking steps to 'diminish the necessity' of importing slaves, whose 'moral and religious improvement' was what was needed (Mason, 2001, p. 137). As the acknowledged head of the West India Interest in Parliament at the time, Ellis's motion was merely a delaying tactic, says Barry Higman (1976, p. 158).

Joseph Foster Barham II, who had entered Parliament in 1793, four years after inheriting *his* father's Jamaican estate, seconded the motion, believing it to be the way slavery could be reformed rather than ended, and the slave trade brought to an end. The reasoning was that the need to import slaves via the slave trade would diminish gradually because immoral conduct was the reason Jamaica's slave population failed to reproduce itself. The absence of a 'natural increase of Negro slaves', Moravians like Foster Barham believed, was due to diseases consequent upon the 'promiscuous use of women' (Mason, 2001, p. 133). Almost all of the 'more vocal of the abolitionists' were committed to the principle of gradualism (Olusoga, 2017, p. 223). Even Wilberforce, who pressed for immediate abolition of the slave *trade*, was at first a gradualist concerning abolishing slavery, declaring after the abolition of the slave trade in 1807 that 'before [slaves] could be fit to receive freedom, it would be madness to attempt to give it to them'. Such gradualism (or 'ameliorism') was typical of early anti-slavery societies, and 'anti-emancipationist propaganda made much of the establishment of missions and schools by benevolent planters'. Joseph Foster Barham II mobilised planter friends in the House of Commons to back an extension of the Moravian mission into their estates, enthusiastically supported by Charles Rose Ellis, 'along with Joseph Foster Barham's Foster cousins' (Dresser, 2001, p. 204). This alliance of powerful interests against the immediate abolition of slavery, spearheaded by close friends the Lords Holland and Seaford and underpinned by the missionary position of the Fosters and Foster Barhams, worked as an effective delaying strategy. The decision of anti-abolitionists to back the Moravians provided a rationale for their stance. Following their successful Commons motion, anti-abolitionists needed the slaveholding islanders to 'give the appearance of acting positively' (ibid., p. 137). Amelioration was sold as an alternative to emancipation. It is thus likely that the Foster Barhams' Moravian initiative delayed the British abolition of slavery by several years.

The Interest, Michael Taylor's welcome new book, endorses this conclusion. Focusing on 'how the British establishment resisted the abolition of slavery', it fills in some of the details of how the anti-abolitionist alliance worked in practice. In the summer of 1823 the political atmosphere in the Caribbean was 'febrile,' he writes, 'for news of the anti-slavery campaign and the very *discussion* of emancipation had provoked the fury of the colonists', spurring the two past chairmen of the West India Committee, George Hibbert and Charles Rose Ellis, to work together that summer to allay the resident slaveholders' fears (Taylor, 2020, p. 66). Whilst they were actively collaborating to keep the planters onside with the delaying tactic of amelioration, Joseph Foster Barham II was penning his pamphlet on the same theme. According to *Considerations on the Abolition of Negro Slavery and the Means of Practically Effecting It*, which I discussed earlier in relation to its theme of compensation, the major 'impediment' to emancipation is 'readiness': 'Until the Slaves can be fitted for freedom, emancipation would be injurious even to themselves' (Foster Barham, 1824, p. 2). In any case, Foster Barham insists, 'The Slave is now… better off than the labouring class of other countries… [though] in civil and moral respects, his condition is not materially changed… Moral improvement is the hinge on which things must turn' (ibid., p. 4). The 'chief means of moral improvement are religion and education… [and] [t]he United Brethren (commonly called Moravians) have led the way' (ibid., p. 20).

In her social history of Bristol as a slave-trading port, Madge Dresser reveals that, by 1824, the publication date of Foster Barham's pamphlet, some of the town's most prominent planters were donating money to the Society for the Conversion and Religious Instruction and Education of Negro Slaves, a charity which supplied missionaries to the plantations. Michael Taylor notes that on the Society's governing board sat two 'senior members of the Interest', Charles Rose Ellis and George Hibbert (Taylor, 2020, p. 87). By then, ownership of West Indian plantations was often a facade 'concealing the reality of mortgaged property… scarcely more the property of the planters, than the planters themselves were the property of the… creditors on this side of the Atlantic'. From this perspective the colonial interest resided in London, Liverpool, Glasgow and Bristol, not the colonies (Dresser, 2001, p. 204).

In *Sugar and Slavery*, Richard B. Sheridan contrasts two eighteenth-century views on the role of the colonies in Britain's economic growth, with Adam Smith and Edmund Burke representing opposite poles of this debate (Sheridan, 1974). In *The Wealth of Nations* (1776), published before the abolition movement was founded, Smith argued that the sugar colonies were not a source of wealth but a drain on the 'mother country' in terms of government and military expense as well as private capital and credit to support the debt structure of the sugar economy (Jordan, 2005). Burke believed that they *were* important sources of wealth, infusing Britain's landed aristocracy and supporting the nascent Industrial Revolution. Slave-grown sugar undoubtedly yielded huge profits to a planter oligarchy who bought landed estates and intermarried with the aristocracy to form a bloc of parliamentarians who influenced imperial policy in their own interest for years to come (Sheridan, 1974; Higman, 2008).

Yet Smith's prescience about the debt structure of the sugar economy is borne out by history in the form of the debt inherited by the British taxpaying population centuries after the end of slavery. The delaying tactic of amelioration, followed by victory over compensation by the slave owners, had far-reaching consequences. All claims for compensation had to be made on a standard form, completed copies of which arrived in their tens of thousands at the London office allocated the task, with all claims and awards recorded in a new national archive. Within four years every claim had been paid out through an extraordinarily efficient bureaucratic scheme – a blueprint for the modern state. That the debt incurred in paying compensation to slave owners was not paid off until 2015, and that this was kept hidden from the public for a further three years and only then made public because of a Freedom of Information request, surely ranks alongside a recent claim that landownership is 'one of the clearest cases of a cover-up in English history' (Shrubsole, 2019, p. 25).

Before following up on this assertion, and as a prelude to pursuing Alexander and Julia through Italy, I want now to turn to the ventures of a different branch of the Foster family in another colonial context: India in the eighteenth century. For whilst the Fosters were extracting wealth from the bodies of slaves in the West Indies, another branch of the family was making a fortune in the East Indies. Parallels and links between the Fosters' fortune-seeking ventures in the West and East Indies, also ferociously plundered by the British, began to emerge as I delved into yet another set of archives held in London.

Six

India: Mission and Mammon

In a commercial country like England, every half-century develops some new and vast source of public wealth, which brings into national notice a new and powerful class. A couple of centuries ago, a Turkey Merchant was the great creator of wealth; the West India planter followed him. In the middle of the last century appeared the Nabob. These characters in their zenith in turn merged in the land, and became English aristocrats.

(Benjamin Disraeli, 1845)

Towards the end of 2018 I renewed my membership of the British Library so that I could access its vast archive on the British East India Company. I knew that members of Julia's family had connections with the Company, including her first husband, John Clode Braddon. I knew too that the fine Bedford house in the lithograph described at the beginning of Chapter 3 was bought with money brought home from India by George Peter Livius, whose wife was Julia's first cousin twice removed, Mary Foster Barham. Their son John Barham Livius also made a brief appearance in that chapter as Washington Irving's playwright friend, who introduced the author to the Foster family in Dresden.

There is a large painting, attributed to Johan Zoffany, which normally hangs in the India Office in London, but which I saw at the British Library when it was out on loan as the centrepiece of its exhibition on the East India Company. Dated 1785, it is titled *Major William Palmer with His Second*

Wife, the Mughal Princess Bibi Faiz Bakhsh. It shows the major, relaxed and resplendent in his uniform, seated beside his wife, a Princess of the Royal House of Delhi, on his right, and her sister on his left. Three of their children and their Indian nannies complete the picture. The British Library's accompanying note reads, 'The celebration of such relationships in paint would have been entirely unacceptable to later generations in India.'

The 'West India planter' characterised by Disraeli in this chapter's epigraph was the central figure in my previous two chapters. In this chapter, it is the 'Nabob', in the form of George Livius, whose eighteenth-century adventures in India overlapped with the Foster family's wealth-producing and missionary exploits in the West Indies. George was a wealthy member of Bedford's Moravian community who married into the Foster family. His spell in India overlapped with that of Major William Palmer, to whom I shall return below. I have no idea if the two men ever met or were aware that they were distantly related through marriage.

George Livius was born in Lisbon in 1743, his parents having fled there when driven out of their home in Lower Saxony because of the persecution of Protestants. Before settling in Bedford as a converted Moravian with his wife Mary Foster Barham, George had worked in India for the EIC from 1773 until 1783 (see Appendix, Table 5). His position there as 'Head of a Commissariat', under Governor-General Warren Hastings, made him very rich and certainly one of the richest men in Bedford's Moravian community. He returned from India with a fortune of £60,000 (Burke, 1838, p. 550).

Livius's tenure in India coincided with a period of reform and regulation of the EIC, which had been founded in 1600 with a royal charter 'granted by Queen Elizabeth to the Governor and Company of the Merchants of London, trading into the East Indies' (Lee, 2003, p. 342). Fortune-seeking merchants were among the Company's first directors who, in 1608, sent ships to India with letters from King James I seeking the Mughal Emperor's permission for the English to trade. By 1647 the EIC had twenty-three outposts in the country, called 'factories'. These became the grand port cities of Calcutta, Bombay and Madras, protected by walled forts such as Fort William in Calcutta.

Warren Hastings' presidency of Fort William and of the Supreme Council of Bengal made him the first de facto Governor-General of India; a position he held officially from 1773 until 1785, coinciding with most of George Livius's spell in Calcutta. It was a period during which British imperial rule over Bengal was solidified with the conversion of a trade area into an occupied territory under a military-civil government. Soldiers and armed mercenaries came to outnumber the EIC's merchants. George's name first appears in a volume of writers' petitions for entry into the Indian Civil Service held at the British Library, when 'Daniel Wien' recommends his appointment as a writer (clerk) with the EIC. His name next appears in 1771, in a handwritten list of appointees for Bengal; a position he took up in 1773 (Folios 374, 377 and 381, Volume J/1/8).

I was able to chart George's progress in the bureaucracy from the *Press Lists of Ancient Documents Preserved in the Imperial Record Room of the Government of India*, which are held at the library in several massive volumes (O.I.R. 354.541). Some of the entries suggest that George's time at the EIC was not friction-free. It all starts mildly enough. On the 17th March 1775, according to the 'Proceedings of the Board of Revenue', George is proposed for the office of 'Military Storekeeper'. Subsequently, on the 12th September, the new military storekeeper tables a letter enclosing an 'estimate of copper, lead, steel and iron required for his department for the ensuing year'. Further missives from Fort William in 1776 request '400 maunds of pig lead to be supplied to the military storekeeper' and such like, with similar requests throughout 1777 and 1778, including one for tents – an order that will cause the board a great deal of frustration and cost them much ink. On the 15th October 1779, a 'motion for further examination of the way in which Mr. Francis passed the accounts of Mr. George Livius' is tabled, eliciting a flurry of entries about the accounts, which concludes tersely on the 1st November: 'Accounts of cash received for disbursement of the Military Storekeeper's office from April 1775–September 1779.' On the 29th June 1780, a letter from 'Capt. G. Livius Military Storekeeper' reports that '5,859… musket barrels were delivered aboard the *Royal Charlotte* without his knowledge'. On the 25th April 1782, a letter from 'Capt. John Lewis of the ship *Valentine Barabullah*' protests that guns on board his vessel were 'lent free of charge' and yet the military storekeeper 'demands payment'. A week later, a letter enclosing two further bills is George's riposte.

Such entries, besides indicating that George's tenure was not conflict-free, also hint at some collusion between himself and 'Mr. Francis' (Philip Francis, about whom more will be said below) concerning his accounting practices. By the end of 1782, George has tendered his resignation and requested passage home on the *Lord Mulgrave*. His position as military storekeeper offered many opportunities for making money on the side and he was assiduous in claiming whatever he felt was his due. Press lists for the period between January 1785 and June 1787 demonstrate this in minute detail. For instance, in the 1785 listings, a full page is devoted entirely to a dispute and a letter of complaint concerning 'heavy losses' that he will suffer. This is because tents, made 'under order' by the board, are now being rejected as 'not up to standard'. The letter of complaint is from George's attorney, Henry Vansittart. The case had been rumbling on since 1782, gathering pace in August 1784 (after George's return to England) with 'Mr. Wheler's recommendation that the stores in question be… received by the Company… or delivered back to Mr. Livius's Attorney'. The tents are now worse than ever, says 'Captain John Murray, Commissary-General'. A few days later, 'Lieutenant-Colonel Allen MacPherson, Quartermaster-General', recommends that Livius's agents mend the tents; John McIntyre, 'Secretary of the Board of Ordnance', thinks the 'Commissary of Stores, Town Major, Quartermaster-General and Adjutant-General' should inspect them to see if they can be rendered serviceable. The case is decisively terminated when the quartermaster-general advocates the 'total rejection of the tents', hence Vansittart's 1785 letter of complaint.

A decade earlier, in 1775, when George Livius was two years into his residency in Calcutta, the city's population had reached 250,000, including around 2,500 Europeans, making Calcutta 'one of the first modern, international cities, populated by a cosmopolitan crowd all hoping to take a cut of the good times' (Baron, 2001, p. 65). Away from his duties as military storekeeper, George appears to have enjoyed himself and to have had some influential friends. This is clear from one of William Hickey's anecdotes. Hickey (1749–1830), an English lawyer sent to India by his solicitor father for embezzling money from him, is best known for his *Memoirs*, which tell vivid tales of life in late eighteenth-century London, Calcutta, Madras and Jamaica. His name was adopted years later as the nom de plume under which the *Express* newspaper's gossip column was written. One of his anecdotes concerns the fabulously rich Nabakrishna Deb, a powerful middleman of the EIC and one of Bengal's biggest magnates. Known to the English as 'Nobkissen', Deb regularly hosted glittering events called 'nautches', which were attended by the leading lights of Calcutta's high society. Hickey's description of one such event yields a glimpse of George Livius at play:

> On Monday night Rajah Nobkissen gave a nautch and magnificent entertainment to several persons of distinction in commemoration of Miss Wrangham's birthday... The surprising agility of the male dancers occasioned loud acclamations of applause... After supper there was a ball, which was opened by Mr. Livius and Miss Wrangham who were dressed in the characters of Apollo and Daphne. When the minuets were ended, country-dances struck up and continued till three in the morning.
>
> (Baron, 2001, p. 69)

'Miss Wrangham' (Emma Wrangham) had many suitors, notes H. E. Busteed in his gossipy account of 'Old Calcutta'. George Livius, nicknamed 'Idea George' by William Hickey, was one of them, if an article in the *Bengal Gazette*, entitled 'Bon Ton Intelligence', is anything to go by. As Hickey writes in the *Gazette*, 'The celebrated beauty has again, we hear, refused Idea G—. It is true there is a little disparity between the parties, yet there are few ladies in her situation who would have declined the offer on that account, or would have thought it could have counter balanced a settlement of £20,000' (Busteed, 1908, pp. 196–9). George was obviously well known as both a bon viveur and very rich.

He was also inspired by missionary zeal. In 1772, before leaving Bedford for India, he had formed a plan to send Moravian missionaries to Bengal. The plan failed but a Moravian mission was established in the Danish territory of Serampore, in the hope of later success in British territory. Penelope Carson believes that, because of the growing influence of Methodism and 'new dissent' in Britain, a successful Moravian mission to India would have been seen as a threat to the Church of England as the established Church (Carson, 2012). Undaunted, George tried again in 1777, offering his house near Calcutta for a Moravian settlement. The London board of the EIC again refused. A decade on, George's friend Charles Grant would put forward another proposal for government-sponsored missionary activity in India, by which time Lord Cornwallis would be Governor-General, with Grant his right-hand man on commercial matters.

Charles Grant (1746–1823) was one of many Scots who prospered in the service of the British Empire. Beginning in the military, having arrived in Bengal in 1768, he rose through the ranks of the EIC to become its chairman. Grant's closest friend from the early 1770s until the mid 1780s in India was George Livius (ibid., p. 28). Grant believed that Indian social life was corrupt and that Britain's conquests in India were morally justifiable because of its possession of 'a superior truth': the heathen would perish in hell if the British did not intervene (ibid., p. 52). Grant did not gain official support for Christian missions, but his characterisation of the degraded nature of Indian – especially Hindu – society profoundly influenced British attitudes to India. He returned to England after twenty-two years' service; one of those described disparagingly by Disraeli as 'nabobs' who arrived home laden with riches that enabled them to buy country estates and parliamentary seats 'above the going rate' (ibid., p. 18).

George Livius had other important friends and connections with the EIC. His brother-in-law was Edward Wheler, chairman of its board of directors in London when George took up his initial post as writer, and from 1777 until his death in 1784 a member of the Supreme Council of Bengal, the highest executive authority in British India (ibid., p. 27; Mason, 2001, p. 82). The Supreme Council was established in 1773 under the East India Regulating Act in an effort by British MPs to have some oversight of the EIC as it staggered from one financial crisis to another. These crises culminated in a dramatic collapse in 1772, when shortfalls in land revenues left the EIC with debts of £1.5 million and £1 million in unpaid tax owed to the British Crown (Dalrymple, 2019, p. xxx).

The Company only survived with the aid of Bank of England loans, granted by a massive government bailout because its demise might bring down the whole credit system. Something similar, but on a bigger scale, would occur in the following century when the British government awarded the owners of West Indian slaves £20 million in compensation for their loss of 'property'; yet again bailing out British merchants, creditors and banks who were deeply involved in the colonial credit structure through loans and mortgages (Butler, 1995). The EIC was a radically new type of business: a joint-stock company which, unlike a family business (the norm at the time), could issue shares on the open market and so raise much larger amounts of capital.

As with more recent mega-corporations, comments William Dalrymple, the EIC was both hugely powerful and extremely vulnerable to economic uncertainty. But unlike, say, Lehman Brothers, it really was too big to fail: 'So it was that in 1773, the world's first aggressive multinational corporation was saved by history's first mega-bailout – the first example of a nation state extracting, as its price for saving a failing corporation, the right to regulate and severely rein it in' (Dalrymple, 2019, p. 12). In an effort to 'rein it in', in addition to establishing a Supreme Council, the 1773 Regulating Act set up a Supreme Court in Calcutta, with a Chief Justice and three judges appointed by the Crown. The Supreme Council comprised the Governor-General Warren Hastings, supported by four councillors, three of them nominated by the British Parliament. It was 'desperately unfortunate for Warren Hastings,' comments Tristram Hunt, that among those first council appointees was 'the brilliantly destructive bureaucrat Sir Philip Francis (1740–1818), who made his primary purpose the forcing of the first Governor-General from office' (Hunt, 2014, p. 207).

Francis was appointed to the Supreme Council of Bengal in 1773 on a salary of £10,000. On his arrival in Calcutta in 1774, besides becoming Warren Hastings' most dangerous critic within the Company, Francis became one of George Livius's closest friends, sharing a house with him in the early years of his residence in India, and calling him 'an intimate of my house and my left-hand man'. In 1775 Francis bought the house known as the Lodge, and in 1780 he sold it to Livius. According to Busteed, it was also Francis who secured the post of military storekeeper for Livius (Busteed, 1908, p. 119). Two years before selling his house to Livius, Francis had come before Calcutta's new Supreme Court, charged with a serious crime. Known as the Catherine Grand case, and a huge scandal at the time, in today's climate of 'Me Too' it could have spelled the end of Francis's career. Historian Linda Colley has written about the case in a biography of Elizabeth Marsh, the first woman to explore eastern and southern India. She returns to it in another book, which contains a perceptive analysis of Francis's political ideas in the context of a wider project to make women and gender visible in world history (Colley, 2007; 2010). Colley characterises Catherine Grand as 'the formerly respectable, too-young wife of a fellow East India Company official' (Colley, 2007, pp. 276–83). The bare outline of the story is as follows.

At about 10.30pm on the 8th December 1778, a man saw an odd-looking bamboo ladder propped against the wall of a house in a fashionable part of Calcutta, and fetched the house's chief servant. They saw a tall man slipping out of the house. The servant recognised him as 'Mr. Francis', a friend of his employer George Grand. The servant knew that Grand's sixteen-year-old wife Catherine was alone in the house, and later told of how Francis pressed money on the two men to let him go, saying, 'I'll make you great men.'

In the legal action brought by George Grand against Francis, witnesses agreed that Francis (aged thirty-eight) had in the past paid 'conspicuous attention' to Catherine, reputedly the 'most beautiful woman in Calcutta'. There was no evidence presented that Catherine had agreed to, or even known of, Francis's evening visit 'for any purpose, much less for the purpose of adultery'. Francis was accused of having 'ravished, debauched, lay [sic] with, and carnally known Catherine Grand' (Colley, 2010, p. 117). He was found guilty of 'criminal conversation with another man's wife', and fined 50,000 rupees (about £5,000) on the 6th March 1779. Grand abandoned his teenaged wife, who left India and eventually became the wife of the first Prime Minister of France, Charles Talleyrand – not, then, a victim, as things turned out, says Colley, but a 'future princess of the Napoleonic Empire' (ibid., p. 148).

Philip Francis supported radical causes such as abolition of the slave trade, and the French Revolution. Yet, says Colley, '[l]ike most political revolutionaries... [he] combined an abstract commitment to extensive liberty and radical change with a belief that women were necessarily a special case... [and] his hungry, sexual aggressiveness... was given much freer vent when he arrived in Calcutta' (Colley, 2007, p. 280). Calcutta was still a 'frontier town'; a fact underlined by the 'contrast between the manner in which Philip Francis felt he could behave in Calcutta and how he normally presented himself in London' (ibid., pp. 281–3). The same was true for George Livius, Francis's friend, housemate and confidant, though George's relationship with the lovely Miss Wrangham seems innocent in comparison. Nevertheless, the fact that George lived with and bought a house from Francis suggests some shared values.

Two days before George Grand initiated the court case against him, Francis sent a letter to the British Prime Minister, Lord North: 'You will probably hear of a supposed improper connection between me and a *French* woman,' he writes, with a stress on Catherine Grand's foreignness which was 'at several levels, key,' says Colley. Other factors besides nationality allowed Catherine to seem sufficiently 'other' as to not be covered by the conventions of female virtue upon which Francis normally insisted. She was Catholic and had been born in the Danish colony of Tranquebar in southern India, so could be perceived, and was later referred to by European commentators, as 'an Indian' or 'a creole' (Colley, 2010, p. 135). Like Jean-Jacques Rousseau, Francis stressed 'the necessity for men and women to act out distinct and demarcated roles'. Marriage was indispensable to this because it confirmed women's dependent status. Political rights, Francis argued in print in 1794, belonged 'generally and collectively in all men', but could not and should not belong to those who were 'voluntarily or necessarily dependent' (ibid., p. 144). Gender and the independence born of property mattered more to Francis than ethnic origin or skin colour when it came to access to political rights. Accordingly, his schemes for a regeneration of Caribbean slave society required that male slaves marry and be given a portion of land. Colley's summation is acute: 'Francis's views are a reminder that there were brands of early liberalism that discriminated more explicitly in regard to gender than in regard to race or geography. It needs to be considered how far *this* strand of liberalism, with its stress on the civic potential of virtuous male householders... and on dependency as a largely *sex-specific* trait, constituted part of the creed's appeal... to those non-European advocates and intellectuals who by the early 1800s were beginning to adapt it and adopt it' (ibid., p. 145).

Warren Hastings made sure that Francis's embarrassing conduct was regularly discussed in Calcutta's Supreme Council. At the same time, Charles Grant, to whom George Livius had introduced Francis, became a useful ally to Francis in his attacks on Hastings' administration: 'I gave to you what I gave to very few,' Francis told Grant in 1779. 'I gave you my heart' (Embree, 1962, p. 46). Hastings is said to have admired Livius, the closest friend of his two main enemies, lamenting, 'God help me, I am ashamed of such an enemy' (ibid., p. 45).

Hastings was close to another person linked through marriage to Julia Braddon: Major (later General) William Palmer (1740–1816), Hastings' Military Secretary from 1776 until 1785, and the subject of Zoffany's painting, which was described above. Major Palmer was already married when he met his Mughal wife Bibi, who is in the painting. As a young soldier he had been sent to the West Indies, where he had married Sarah Hazell, 'a Creole beauty', in 1761 (Dalrymple, 2004, p. 266). When he was posted to India six years later, Sarah remained in St Kitts with their daughters, whilst William and their sons Samuel and John sailed to India, where he married for a second time. A century later, the separated couple's great-granddaughter (through Samuel's son George), Mary Georgiana Palmer, married Edward Nicholas Coventry Braddon, cousin of John Clode Braddon, Julia Braddon's first husband and the older brother of Mary Elizabeth Braddon, who had left home for India to seek his fortune (see Appendix, Table 2). He found it, first working in his cousin William's merchant business before joining the Indian Civil Service and holding various posts as a government magistrate. Knighted in 1891, he became Premier of Tasmania (1894–9), then an MP in the first Australian Parliament (Carnell, 2000, pp. 135–6). His cousin William (John Clode's brother), who was also born in India, had married Margaret Selina Patton in 1838 in Calcutta. Her grandfather, Colonel Robert Patton, an officer in the EIC's army, went on to become Governor of St Helena. Family residences and estates associated with the Braddons, as listed in Burke's 1891 *Genealogical and Heraldic History of the Colonial Gentry*, include Treglith, Tasmania and London. Two London gentlemen's clubs are also listed.

In the last two chapters, which dealt with the Caribbean interests of Julia's ancestors, I noted that Elizabeth Palmer (1750–82), daughter of John Palmer, Chief Justice of Jamaica (1724–73), was the mother of Charles Rose Ellis (1771–1845), who was brought up in Jamaica with Elizabeth Vassall (later Lady Holland) as her foster brother (see Appendix, Table 7). Marriages between well-off families in India and the Caribbean were common, and there were strong family connections between the Palmers in the West and East Indies in terms of investment in property. For instance, the UCL *Legacies of British Slave-Ownership* database profiles George Palmer, London East India merchant (1772–1853), noting that he and his brothers were awarded compensation for mortgages on several estates in Grenada and 240 slaves, amounting to around £6,500. *This* George Palmer (not the George Palmer of 1795–1840, who was Major William Palmer's grandson) is listed in the *Oxford Dictionary of National Biography* (*ODNB*) as a 'merchant and philanthropist' and as vice-chairman of the RNLI. There is no mention of his slave-owning interests. This George Palmer appears in my tree as the grandfather of Archdale Villiers Palmer (1832–1908), husband of Helen Hodgson Taylor, second cousin of Mary Georgiana Palmer (1840–64), great-granddaughter of Major William Palmer (1740–1816) and first wife of Edward Nicholas Braddon (1829–1904), cousin of John Clode Braddon. Helen's maternal grandfather was John Palmer, brother of Samuel, born in St Kitts in 1767 to William Palmer and his first wife, Sarah Hazell. This means that when Helen married Archdale Villiers Palmer, she was marrying her cousin (see Appendix, Table 2). It *is* complicated.

Despite the measures put in place in 1773 to rein in the EIC, oversight remained minimal. The loss of the American colonies in 1783, a sharp decline in overseas trade, and increased unemployment at home caused anxiety in Britain, whose empire seemed on the brink of collapse. Evangelical Christians seized on the crisis to argue that only the proper observance of Christianity could solve the nation's ills. Charles Grant was the key figure in extending this idea to India, bringing his religious opinions directly to the EIC boardroom with his 1787 'Proposal to Establish a Protestant Mission in Bengal and Behar' (Carson, 2012, p. 19). Unlike George Livius's earlier Moravian effort, this proposal came from Company servants who were also members of the established Church. It was initially unsuccessful, but missionaries soon began profoundly to change British perceptions of Hindus, from being inheritors of ancient wisdom, as Hastings believed, to being seen as 'poor benighted heathen… wholly corrupt… and wretched as they are depraved' (Dalrymple, 2004, p. 46).

Philip Francis took a similar view, writing with contempt of the 'ignorant and unimproved natives of Bengal' and insisting that English should be the language of government in India. Francis wanted to be Governor-General himself, and had earlier tried to persuade council members that Hastings was a corrupt despot, part of his case being that the latter had lived too long in India and been exposed to its corrosive influence. Hastings loathed Francis just as much: 'this man of levity, the vilest fetcher and carrier of tales… without one generous or manly principle' (Dalrymple, 2019, p. 240). The rivalry between the two men paralysed the Company's administration for years, before reaching its climax in a duel on the 17th August 1780. Both survived, but Francis was wounded.

The Catherine Grand scandal had undermined Francis's standing in Calcutta, and he returned to England in 1780, where he used some of his Indian wealth to buy a parliamentary seat and to seek Hastings' impeachment. In 1782, Edmund Burke, then a rising Whig star, put before Parliament twenty-two charges against Hastings, which had been drawn up by Francis. As a result, says William Dalrymple, the charges were full of fantasies, demonstrating the ignorance of the British about the 'subcontinent they had been looting for thirty years' (ibid., p. 313). After his attempted impeachment that lasted from 1788 until 1795, Hastings was acquitted. Political and financial scandal had already forced him to retire in 1785.

With Hastings' successors, Lord Cornwallis (in post 1786–93) and Richard Colley, Lord Wellesley (in post 1798–1805), the policy of respect for Indian culture that had been pursued by Hastings was totally abandoned in favour of what cultural historian Tom Steele dubs 'red-blooded Anglicisation' (Steele, 1997, p. 54). Cornwallis's other main mission was to end the EIC's past practices of 'small salaries and immense perquisites', which he tackled by raising salaries and banning Company writers from engaging in private trade on their own account. George Livius had been well placed in his storekeeper post to engage in such 'private trade' to augment his salary, as hinted at in the minutes quoted earlier. Cornwallis set about embedding the principle of property in Bengali society so that it would 'embrace the sound principles of Whig England: looking after the land and paying taxes' (Hunt, 2014, p. 208).

Cornwallis's reforms, which were implemented after 1793, drew on proposals for a settlement between the EIC and indigenous traditional landholders ('zamindars'), which had been drafted by Philip Francis. The reforms created permanent property rights for them in return for a land tax fixed by Company officials in perpetuity. If they failed to pay up, the land would be sold to someone else. As a result, income from land revenues was vastly increased, with those who bought land from the traditional landholders effectively throwing in their lot with the new Company order: 'In this way, a new class of largely Hindu, pro-British Bengali bankers and traders began to emerge as moneyed landowners to whom the Company could devolve local responsibility' (Dalrymple, 2019, p. 329). The resulting huge increase in land value had an unintended consequence: since there were now more riches to be made as landlords in country estates than as traders, 'the… agents of the eighteenth century became the rural *rentiers* of the nineteenth century' (Hunt, 2014, p. 209).

Philip Francis, mastermind of Cornwallis's reforms, far from succeeding Warren Hastings as Governor-General as he so desired, never again held salaried public office after 1780. He became MP for Yarmouth in 1794 and for Appleby in 1802, but his career never fully recovered from the Grand affair. His self-confidence remained undimmed, however, as a letter to his brother-in-law, 'Mr. Collings', on the 17th April 1796 testifies: 'Encouraged by my success in the East, I have lately turned my thoughts to the West, from Hindoos to Negroes, from Betel to Tobacco, to Sugar and Molasses.' Nor did scandal in India estrange him from polite society in England. This is clear from his boast to his daughter that he has just had 'dinner with Lady Holland and the prince there too at Holland House', as well as 'riding out at Chatsworth with Lady Georgiana, Duchess of Devonshire – the Duke of Devonshire and Duchess of Bedford were there too'. There are indeed several references to Francis in Lady Holland's (Elizabeth Vassall-Fox's) journal. On the 30th May 1799 she writes, 'Francis diverted me excessively the other morning. I got up unusually late, and… I was told he'd been in the library for some time. Ld H [Lord Holland] was still in bed, and as he [Francis] is at times amusing, I sent to say I would see him as I dressed. He came to my door, and there paused, saying, 'Are you sure the person you sent for was *me*… Will you really admit *me* into your private room?' When I repeated the invitation he was delighted. He is very vain, and any distinction quite turns his head, especially from people he rather calls great folks' (an editor's note explains that Francis was the son of a protégé of the first Lord Holland).

Julia's connection to India and to the EIC went beyond her birth family's relationship to George Livius. The Bedford property that her grandmother Amelia inherited from her husband John Foster passed down through the male line on Amelia's death, as did the Jamaican inheritance. Nevertheless, since Julia's mother Flora brought a dowry to her marriage through her father John Foster's will, there would have been pressure on her own daughters to 'marry well'. When she reached eighteen, Julia duly married the rich East India merchant John Clode Braddon, who was born in India. John's father William Braddon (1787–1858), originally of Skisdon Lodge, Cornwall, had arrived there in April 1806 aged nineteen, and a month later married sixteen-year-old Hannah Maria Daniels (or Daniell), at Fort William, Calcutta. Hannah's father John Daniell, who worked for the Bengal Civil Service, was from a Nonconformist (Baptist) family in Bristol.

After the abolition of West Indian slavery, abolitionists set their sights on forced labour in British India, securing laws in 1843 to abolish slavery in Bengal, Bombay and Madras, where enslaved Indians were claimed as property mostly by the EIC's Indian clients. At a stroke, the new laws created a body of labourers who could be hired for low wages. In the late 1830s, EIC officials had taken steps to establish tea plantations in Assam, west of Bengal, where tea planters resented the many Assam peasants who wouldn't work for low wages: 'Massive plantations were a convenient solution, as they forced peasants off their land and into the fields' (Scanlan, 2020, p. 343).

William Braddon was a director of the joint-stock Luckimpore Tea Company in Assam, whilst also holding various posts with the Bengal Civil Service. Appointed writer for the EIC in July 1805, he took up his post in Bengal the following year, three decades after George Livius made the same journey. The list of writers held at the British Library's Asian and African Studies Reading Room charts his progress from clerkly duties to various appointments as a judge and magistrate, until retiring 'on Annuity' on the 25th March 1840. His wife Hannah, who had borne him twelve children, had died in 1834 aged forty-four, when John Clode was just nine. William lived a further twenty-four years, dying reportedly from wounds sustained during a break-in at his house at Plympton in Devon. Witness to a codicil to his will on the 24th December 1858, James Henry Chowne, his son-in-law, would also witness John Clode's will four years later.

The criss-crossing of families inhabiting various sites of Empire in the eighteenth and nineteenth centuries helps explain how Julia Dawson and her first husband, John Clode Braddon, met. It also helps to account for how my great-great-uncle Alexander and Julia ended up together in San Remo. Class and religion – various forms of 'dissenting' Protestantism especially – were strong factors. British colonial expansion and ambition, which made some people very rich as well as geographically and socially mobile, was another. Various members of the Foster Barham family had connections with Pau, where Julia's first husband died: Henryson Foster Barham (b. 1843) was British vice-consul there, and Margaret Foster Barham (b. 1805), second wife of Dr Thomas Foster Barham, died there in 1884. With its beautiful weather, Pau rivalled San Remo as the place to be for wealthy Britons in the late nineteenth century.

John Clode Braddon signed his will in Pau on the 3rd March 1862, just five days before his death, bequeathing his 'real Estate in the County of Cornwall devised to me by the Will of my late father to my said brother William Clode Braddon... and all the residue of my... estate unto my brother-in-law James Henry Chowne... and Richard Strode Hewlett of Portsmouth... Commander of the Bath [his sisters' husbands]'. Whilst thus keeping the family wealth firmly within the Braddon bloodline, John gave 'unto my dear Wife Julia Braddon all my household goods, furniture plate and plated goods books prints pictures linen china glass and personal effects for her own absolute use'. Much more importantly, he covenanted 'the sum of two thousand pounds... to the Trustees of my marriage settlement to pay the annual income thereof to my said Wife for her life'. Since John died just two years after marrying Julia, and they had no children, she would have been a relatively well-off widow when she met and married Alexander Robertson many years later.

The social circles within which the Braddons moved were worlds apart from those of the Scottish minister who was living at the time in San Remo on a meagre salary with his ailing wife. When Julia met Alexander there, two decades after her first husband's death and still in receipt of the annual income bequeathed in his will, she could offer material as well as emotional support to the widower. The dual source of this wealth lay ultimately in the fortune Julia's family had made over two centuries in Caribbean slavery, and, more immediately, in a lifetime pension derived from the EIC's conquest of India. The fortunes to be made in the West and East Indies by some families were huge and interconnected. George Livius had made his fortune with the EIC. His wife was the daughter of Joseph Foster Barham, owner of the vast Mesopotamia sugar plantation in Jamaica. His descendants and Foster cousins fought tooth and nail against emancipation of the slaves who worked on their Caribbean plantations, and then, when they lost, they fought for compensation.

The story comes full circle.

Seven

San Remo, Italy:
Reforming Mission

There was an old man whose Giardino
Was always so cheerful and green O –
Every hour he could spare, – He sate in a chair
In the midst of his summer Giardino
(Edward Lear)

The Corso degli Inglesi circles up the hill in San Remo and then loops along the ridges that point down to the sea like the bent fingers of a hand. Here rich English families built villas surrounded by gardens, with turrets and balconies gazing down at the bays: by the end of the century, the curving road would be a ribbon of art nouveau 'Liberty' architecture. A narrow lane, the Via Hope, winds steeply down from the Corso to the shore. This was where Lear built his house, the Villa Emily… Below his garden lay a patch of land dotted with olives, and beyond it, across the road and the railway, the dazzle of the Mediterranean flared to the blue horizon… In particular, the thought of the garden delighted him.

(Uglow, 2017, pp. 417–8)

When Julia met Alexander in San Remo, she was on a mission; perhaps not the same as his, and perhaps fuelled by shame (conscious or otherwise) about the source of her wealth, but similar enough and compelling enough for the pair to form a lasting bond. Alexander's mission in San Remo, besides providing Protestant services and a new church for visitors and expatriates under the auspices of the 'Foreign Mission Board' of the UPC, was to save Italian Catholics from the yoke of the Roman Catholic Church. This, he insisted, was not the same thing as trying to rescue Catholics from their Catholic *faith*: the Church, not Catholicism, was the culprit. Julia had the added advantage of having powerful friends and influential connections, including Edward Lear's next-door neighbours, with whom the poet would have a massive falling-out, which I'll come to shortly. For now, Jenny Uglow sets the scene:

> What delighted Lear most was the utter quiet: only birdsong broke the silence... He paid calls on Lady Janet Kay-Shuttleworth next door and her daughter Janet Elizabeth ('Jenny' to friends, 'Puss' to her family), who was in her late twenties. Both were 'very kindly and friendly'. Lear knew Janet Kay-Shuttleworth through his friendship with her stepfather, Frederick North: she was half-sister to... Marianne North ('Pop' to the family), and had known Charlotte Brontë and Elizabeth Gaskell... Yet despite [her] connections Lear disliked her aura of 'trouble' and illness, as well as her non-stop talking... Then he sat back to enjoy his Riviera garden... [H]e thought of buying another patch of land... the empty plot below, which Thomas Hanbury had rented to the Kay-Shuttleworths, but... he wasn't worried, 'for even if Mr Hanbury builds, I look over the highest possible house'.
>
> (ibid., pp. 449–52)

Julia had been living in San Remo for some time before Alexander appeared on the scene, soon to be a widower. She was probably acquainted with the famous limerick writer who lived up the hill from her friends, the Kay-Shuttleworths, though I cannot be sure of this because her life before and after meeting Alexander is almost entirely undocumented. Since Julia, unlike her mother and aunt, did not write a memoir or keep a journal, I found myself in the virtually uncharted territory of women's networks in late nineteenth-century Europe, piecing together fragments from here and there to form a picture of my great-great-aunt. One snippet I seized upon early on was embedded in Alexander's obituary:

the brief mention of a kindergarten that Julia is said to have set up at Dovadola in 1895.

Dovadola is a small town in Emilia-Romagna, close to Predappio, Benito Mussolini's birthplace, where his father was the village blacksmith. I came across the nursery school's name, the 'Asilo Infantile Donna Giulia', in a book about the Waldensian Church, the oldest of Italy's Protestant Churches, which was founded in the twelfth century by Peter Waldo as one of several home-grown European Protestant denominations with pre-Lutheran roots. The Church survived in alpine valleys bordering Switzerland until the sixteenth-century Reformation, when it became the only Italian branch of the 'Reformed' Churches. Gabriella Ballesio, the helpful archivist at the Church's administrative centre in Torre Pellice, Piedmont, provided me with further details about the infant school. The school did open in 1895, she explained, but was not called the Asilo Infantile Donna Giulia until 1902, when Julia became its benefactor and the Protestant church in Dovadola broke away from the Old Catholic (Reformed) Church of Italy. Gabriella elaborates: 'Thanks to the help of Alexander Robertson (then pastor in Venice) and his wife Julia Robertson they became an Independent Protestant church, entirely supported by the couple. Mrs Robertson was able to rent two small buildings in the town that were used as a chapel and a small house for the pastor of the congregation. At the same time, Mrs Robertson started to finance a kindergarten/elementary school... On September 1st, 1910, Mr and Mrs Robertson signed an important agreement with the Waldensian Church. From that moment on the congregation in Dovadola would become a Waldensian church' (Gabriella Ballesio, email, 15th May 2019). This indicates that, had the church in Dovadola not broken away from the Old Catholic Church of Italy, Julia would not have become its or the infant school's benefactor. She had the means to fund such projects and was an astute negotiator as well as an innovator; in this case, by first enabling the church to become independent of the Catholic Church using her own funds, then a few years later handing it over to the Waldensian Church. The name of the infant school shows, too, that she was no shrinking violet, clearly marking it as *her* bequest.

Torre Pellice's archive revealed another intriguing piece of information, demonstrating that Julia was a patron of 'good works' *before* linking up with Alexander, and that her involvement with the Waldensian Church predated their marriage. The archive reveals that, in 1884, when still known as Mrs

Clode Braddon, Julia jointly founded an elementary school for girls in San Remo. The school first opened on the top floor of 6 Via Gaudio before relocating in September 1887 to Casa Gaglietto, 9 Via Umberto, by which time it belonged to the Waldensian Church. It continued to function as the co-educational Waldensian School of San Remo for a further fifty years. The 1885 *Annual Report on the Waldensian Churches in Italy* records the school's beginnings with a brief note from Matteo Enrico Malan, pastor of the Waldensian Church in San Remo: 'Two British women founded a small school in San Remo, and thanks to the help of several benefactors decided to donate said school to the Waldensian Church.'

Julia's project in Dovadola with Alexander would follow a similar pattern: first funding some independent provision (i.e., independent of the Catholic Church) which, once established, could then be handed over to the Waldensian Church. Missionary Board minutes for July 1885 reveal the women's names: 'Mrs. Clode Braddon and Mrs. Kay-Shuttleworth founded a school for young ladies in San Remo… They offered said school to the Waldensian Church and we accepted the offer.' Five years later, the *Waldensian Commission of Italian Evangelization* report (1890) is able to document that the school, 'though much opposed by the clerical party… has gained the esteem of the San Remese… while this year we have had sixty and had to refuse a hundred for want of space and materials'.

I came across an intriguing link to one of the characters involved in these events when I read a review of Caroline Moorehead's *A House in the Mountains: The Women Who Liberated Italy from Fascism* (2019) and immediately bought a copy. What had caught my attention was the name of one of the four freedom fighters featured in Moorehead's book: Frida Malan, a fighter with the 'fifth Alpine division of Val Pellice' and 'the only girl in a Protestant family of militant boys'. Frida was one of four women friends from Piedmont who joined the Italian resistance movement when, between September 1943 and April 1945, Italy was embroiled in a brutal civil war of partisans against fascists. My archivist informant Gabriella at Torre Pellice confirmed what I had guessed: Frida Malan, brave anti-fascist partisan, was the granddaughter of Matteo Enrico Malan, the Waldensian pastor who in 1885 recorded that 'Two British women founded a small school in San Remo' and donated it to the Waldensian Church.

One of the Waldensian School's most famous latter-day pupils was the novelist Italo Calvino. Though born in Cuba, he was brought up in San

Remo by freethinking pacifist parents who did not want their son to receive a religious education, and who loathed Mussolini's ruling National Fascist Party. According to Calvino's *Political Autobiography of a Young Man* (2003), when he was growing up in San Remo, the town differed from the rest of Italy because it was 'still populated by elderly English people, Russian grand dukes, eccentric and cosmopolitan types'. Most people around him were hostile to fascism, though his own family's sympathies lay 'not so much with liberal democracy as with all the progressive movements that were out of the ordinary', including the Russian Bolsheviks and Atatürk's secularising mission in Turkey. Calvino's parents' opposition to fascism had less to do with its violence than its 'two cardinal sins: the alliance with the monarchy and the reconciliation with the Vatican' (ibid., p. 132).

When Italo enrolled at the Waldensian School in 1929, Mussolini had just signed the conciliatory 'Lateran Accords' with the Vatican earlier that year, by which time Julia, one of the school's founders, was dead. With the signing of the treaty, the Vatican became an independent enclave (a territory of 109 acres within Rome) and its members exempt from fascist laws. At the same time, the Church was granted authority over marriage, and religious teaching in schools was made obligatory, with bishops given the right to appoint and dismiss instructors. In return, the Vatican recognised the fascist state, with Rome as its capital, and bishops had to swear an oath of loyalty to the state. Whilst Catholicism and fascism did not share common ideals, says Prescot Stephens in his history of the Waldensian Church, they did share common enemies – liberalism and socialism – which was 'enough to bring Church and state together' (Stephens, 2015, p. 310). It was this alliance between state and Church that Calvino's parents despised most and the Waldensian Church feared most. Yet Alexander applauded it, sending regular reports to *The Scotsman* which framed the Lateran pact as necessary to combat socialism. Had Julia lived, given her connection to and support for the Waldensian Church, I think it unlikely that Alexander's approval of the compromise would have been quite so enthusiastic.

Calvino explains how his perception of himself as an outsider began when he left primary school: 'At [secondary] school they asked that I be excused from religious instruction and not… attend Mass or other religious services. While I was at a Waldensian primary school… this did not cause me any problems: Protestant, Catholic, Jewish and Russian Orthodox pupils were all mixed up together… [T]he state high school… exposed me to…

isolation' (Calvino, 2003, p. 133). Joining the Italian resistance movement in 1944, Calvino became part of a clandestine communist group, fighting alongside partisans like Frida Malan in northern Italy. After the war he became a member of the Italian Communist Party. Alexander would have been less than thrilled to know that his wife had played a part in the early formation of the socialist novelist and essayist.

A little digging revealed that the Mrs Kay-Shuttleworth named in the Missionary Board minutes as Julia's collaborator was Janet Elizabeth Kay-Shuttleworth (1843–1914), whose father was the educational reformer Sir James Kay-Shuttleworth (1804–77). Janet Elizabeth ('Jenny' to her friends, 'Puss' to her family, and never a 'Mrs') owned Villa Ponente in San Remo, which she had inherited from her mother, Lady Janet Kay-Shuttleworth (1817–72). Edward Lear's Villa Emily was next door to Lady Janet, who had herself inherited Gawthorpe Hall in Lancashire from her land- and mill-owning father Robert Shuttleworth as his only child. When he died, Janet's mother married Frederick North (Lear's friend), and they had a daughter, Marianne. So Janet's half-sister was the famous biologist and artist Marianne North ('Pop' to Janet Elizabeth's 'Puss'), whose botanical paintings hang at London's Kew Gardens.

When Lady Janet died in 1872, besides bequeathing Villa Ponente to her daughter Janet Elizabeth, she left the stately homes of Gawthorpe Hall and Barbon Manor to her son Ughtred, thereby bypassing her husband James, from whom she had lived apart in San Remo for many years. James Kay-Shuttleworth managed Gawthorpe Hall in his wife's absence. A graduate in medicine from the University of Edinburgh and a Congregationalist lay minister, James Kay added the Shuttleworth name to his when he married Janet. This was a requirement of her father's will in order to retain the family name and keep its fortune intact. Had I not recently visited Gawthorpe Hall, which is now in the care of the National Trust, I would not have known the identity of the 'Mrs. Kay-Shuttleworth' in the Church archives or, subsequently, of her connection to 'Mrs. Clode Braddon'. My visit was quite independent of my family history research, which had just begun.

James Kay-Shuttleworth made a major contribution to the formation of a national system of primary education in England as secretary to the government's Privy Council Committee on Education, which administered grants for public education. In 1923 it could even be claimed that '[t]he policy which he conceived has been the ground plan of English elementary education as we know it today… He was its chief architect… To him… we owe it that England is supplied with schools for the children of her people… and without a breach between Church and State' (Smith, 1974 [1923], p. vii). I vaguely remember his name from my own teacher-training course. When he resigned in 1849 on health grounds, he was made a Baronet and later chaired the board of governors of Giggleswick School, Yorkshire, now an expensive 'public' school, a stone's throw away from where I am writing this, and one of many 'independent' schools in Britain whose charitable status draws tax breaks of £2.5 billion a year (Verkaik, 2018).

Janet Elizabeth looked after her invalid mother for many years in San Remo, and when her mother died she disappointed family expectations by not taking on the same role with her ailing father. A biography of James Kay-Shuttleworth suggests that, in addition to inheriting epilepsy, he may have contracted syphilis, which would account for his many ailments (and perhaps even those of his wife) and his shifting moods. The official story of the couple's separation was that Janet's health required her to live in a warm climate (Selleck, 1995). Besides bequeathing Villa Ponente to her daughter, Lady Janet left her sufficient money to live independently, which she did, mainly in San Remo but with frequent spells in England and Germany. Like Julia, Janet Elizabeth used some of her inheritance to promote 'good works'. Yet when I contacted the Shuttleworth family about her role in setting up a school for girls in San Remo with my great-great-aunt, I drew a blank.

The John Rylands Collection at Manchester University holds papers relating to James Kay-Shuttleworth which chart the breakdown of the couple's marriage, including a doctor's report stating that for health reasons it would be better if he 'kept his distance' from his wife. Janet had moved to the continent shortly after the birth of her fifth child in 1851, eventually settling in San Remo with her eldest child Janet Elizabeth, two youngest sons, and their Polish governess, Rosa Poplawska. A few days after Lady Janet's death on the 15th September 1872, Ughtred writes to tell his father that Janet Elizabeth is now free to care for him. But when his mother's estates in Lancashire are finally settled on him, bypassing his father, Ughtred has a change of heart, from then on acting as a go-between for his sister, with frequent letters to his father saying that she is unwell and 'Dr. Freeman advises her to live a quiet life'. On the 26th May 1877, Sir James's death is announced.

Seventeen months later, in October 1878, Janet Elizabeth's next-door neighbour on the Corso degli Inglesi, Edward Lear, just back from

Switzerland, is in a state of shock. His garden is glorious, he tells a friend, but a 'huge hotel is to be built just below… If it is on the left side it will shut out all my sea view: a calamity as afflicts me' (Uglow, 2017, p. 496). Since moving into the Villa Emily, Lear had talked to Lady Janet and Thomas Hanbury about buying the plot of land below his house, which Lady Janet rented from Hanbury. He hoped that nothing too tall would be built on it. But now, with Lady Janet long dead, the land was being cleared, having been sold to 'a German' whom 'Jenny' (Janet Elizabeth) had introduced to Hanbury, who planned to build a large hotel. By the start of 1879 the racket of land-blasting is driving Lear mad: 'horribly out of humour with the Great Bee Stanbury and the Jenny Shuttlecock Hotel' (ibid., p. 498).

Reading Uglow's book, it came to me that the 'Great Bee Stanbury' who, together with Julia's friend Janet Elizabeth, caused Lear such upset, was the creator of the extraordinary Hanbury Gardens at Mortola near Ventimiglia, which I had visited in September 2012. The visit, which took place long before I began my research into Alexander's life, was the highlight of a holiday in Apricale, a tiny Italian hilltop village in the Côte d'Azur along the coast from Ventimiglia. Reached by bus on a late summer's day, memories of walking with my friend in the beautiful gardens that slope steeply down to the sea remain vivid. Our photographs of panoramic views and close-ups of exotic plants and artful follies can still evoke recollections of fragrant smells and sun-warmed skin. Our diary entry for Thursday 27th September reads, 'Ventimiglia 0850 bus, coffee, bought *torta verde* for lunch. 11.05 bus to Giardini Botanici Hanbury (near French border)… Highlights of garden – dragon fountain with turtles, sea views, palm trees, eucalyptus, agaves.'

A leaflet tucked inside the diary fills in some details about its maker: Sir Thomas Hanbury (1832–1907), a Quaker and philanthropist, was an English tea and silk merchant, director of the first railway line built in China, and a gardener. After winding up his business in China, in 1871 he and his wife moved to Mortola, where he had bought an abandoned villa and where his brother had begun planting a garden, which the garden designer Ludwig Winter then developed. Queen Victoria visited Hanbury Gardens in 1882. Three years before that visit, along the coast in San Remo, Edward Lear was writing a letter to his publisher. It included a statement to the effect that, despite 'a written promise', his life as a celebrated 'artist and writer of nonsense and travel' had been ruined by the building of an immense hotel that shut out the sun from the Villa Emily in winter, destroying his studio's light. He was 'moving to New Zealand' and 'all the Sanremisi were not at all reticent in their remarks on the parties who are about to cause it'. When Wilkie Collins leaked the statement to the press, 'the accused "parties" were easily identifiable as Hanbury and the Kay-Shuttleworths: there were threats of libel action and the Kay-Shuttleworth clan turned their backs' (Uglow, 2017, p. 503). In 1881 Lear moved further down the hill, seeking peace and quiet to get on with his work, 'but all have had to be shunted along of the abominable Shuttleworth Hanbury Hotel' (ibid., p. 507).

Janet Elizabeth, the cause of Lear's misfortune (for introducing Hanbury to the 'German' who built the 'abominable' hotel), travelled widely after her mother's death and translated academic books, including *The Life of Johann Sebastian Bach* by C. H. Bitter, from German to English (Kay-Shuttleworth, 1873). Her talent for translation may well have been owed to Rosa Poplawska, the governess who became her mother's companion and an object of suspicion for Ughtred: 'The distressing ailments of both my parents, coupled with my mother's promotion of a Prussian Pole, who was governess to my sister and myself, to be her inseparable companion, caused... estrangement from my father... rendered permanent by the almost hypnotic influence that this woman... came to exercise' (Smith, 1974 [1923], p. 133). Ughtred's jaundiced opinion contrasts with others' impressions. Elizabeth Gaskell noted Rosa's skills as a governess when she called in at the family home at Gawthorpe Hall. And when Charlotte Brontë visited the hall in March 1850 before the couple's separation, she also took a shine to the young woman; 'a quiet, interesting girl whom I took to at once – and, in my heart, liked better than anything else in the house. She also instinctively took to me... She told me she was homesick, and she looked it' (Selleck, 1995, p. 270). Years later, Rosa was also kind to Edward Lear. In 1871, when newly resident in San Remo, his first cat ran off and his second, 'Potta', also disappeared: 'Miss Poplawska brought over his twin brother, with his cut-off tail. They called him Foss, short for "Adelphos", Greek for "brother"' (Uglow, 2017, p. 454). Foss became Lear's constant companion, dying just before the poet's own death in 1888. When he died in September 1887, 'Foss was seventeen, a grand age for a cat, but Lear thought he was thirty, they had been together so long' (Uglow, 2017, p. 549).

Letters to Lady Janet from Elizabeth Gaskell and Charlotte Brontë, sent before Janet's move to the continent, are held in the Lancashire Municipal Archives in Preston. I read them there in summer 2018. Ten letters (some very long) from Mrs Gaskell, written between May 1850 and November 1853, cover personal topics, news about her publications, health, the growth of 'sisterhoods', and Charlotte Brontë. On the 14th May 1850, she refers to Charlotte's recent visit to Gawthorpe Hall: 'I'd like to hear a great deal more about her… I would like very much to know her.' In the penultimate letter, Elizabeth hopes to see Lady Janet before she becomes a '"fixture" in Germany', adding, 'I hear often from the Brontës and went to stay with them a few days at Haworth' (DDKS/37/2–10).

There is just one letter in the Preston archive from Charlotte Brontë to Lady Janet. Dated the 2nd March 1850, she recalls images from her recent visit to Gawthorpe Hall with her father: 'Your grey, stately hall fills one page of my mental sketch book… and old Pendle swells in every background' (DDKS/37/1). The Kay-Shuttleworths had first visited the Brontës at the parsonage in Haworth in early 1850, and invited Charlotte back to Gawthorpe Hall. In a letter to a friend, Charlotte describes her return visit to Gawthorpe: 'Sir James is a man of polished manners… On the whole I got on very well with him… the dialogues (perhaps I should rather say monologues)… did not too much oppress and exhaust me' (Whitehead, 1963, p. 130).

Janet Kay-Shuttleworth introduced Elizabeth Gaskell to Charlotte Brontë in August 1850 when she invited both writers to the Briery, the family's summer home in the Lake District. They immediately struck up a friendship and Mrs Gaskell became Charlotte Brontë's biographer on her death. In that biography she mentions Charlotte's visit to Gawthorpe Hall, noting that Gawthorpe 'lies… above Haworth, at about a dozen miles… as the crow flies, though much further by the road… On the whole she enjoyed her visit very much, in spite of her shyness' (Gaskell, 2015 [1857], p. 212). Charlotte paid one more visit to Gawthorpe Hall with her husband in January 1855: 'They only remained two or three days, but… she increased her lingering cold, by a long walk over damp ground in thin shoes. Soon after her return, she was attacked by… perpetual nausea, and ever-recurring faintness' (ibid., p. 282). Charlotte died on the 31st March after being terribly sick, probably due to pregnancy. She was thirty-eight.

Jenny Uglow believes that neither writer felt much warmth towards the Kay-Shuttleworths. Elizabeth Gaskell knew James Kay through her husband William, another graduate of a Scottish university (Glasgow) who, newly appointed minister at Cross Street Unitarian Chapel in Manchester, met the young Nonconformist doctor in 1831 when he was appointed to a board of health to prepare for an outbreak of cholera in the city. As a founder of the Manchester Statistical Society, set up in 1833 to gather evidence linking poverty and disease, James was well known to the pair (Uglow, 1993, pp. 88–9). Two decades on, both writers find the 'self-important' (now Sir) James hard to take, especially Charlotte, who confesses that, while respecting his intellect and 'marked kindness', she thinks 'the substratum of his character is hard as flint… he perpetually threatens a visit to Haworth' (ibid., p. 248).

Soon after helping Julia set up the girls' school in San Remo, Janet Elizabeth lived in England for a period with Madeline Daniell (née Carter), a prominent campaigner for women's education. Madeline was born in India in 1832, the daughter of a major in the Bengal native infantry, and educated at the Edinburgh Institution for the Education of Young Ladies. After finishing school in Europe she returned to India and married another army officer, Charles Astell Daniell, whose grandfather was a director of the East India Company, and whose aunt, Maria Elizabeth Daniell, was the wife of Frederick Beckford Long, grandson of the Jamaican slave owner and historian Edward Long (see Chapter 5). Madeline was nineteen when she married Charles, who died at Lahore four years later, leaving her with a young son who later died, another son having already died. It is hard to imagine recovering from such tragedies. Applying herself to a cause, being useful, may have been some consolation. Madeline returned to Edinburgh where she campaigned for higher education for women and was a founder of what became St Leonard's School at St Andrews, where she moved to look after her ailing mother.

As honorary secretary of the Edinburgh Ladies' Educational Association, she hosted its first meeting at her home in 1866. The association provided advanced post-school education for women through lectures on English literature, physics and philosophy that were delivered at Edinburgh University and which, by not seeking entry into the professions, avoided male opposition. It was the perceived socio-economic threat to the male monopoly of the professions that provoked hostility at the time, rather than women's education per se. From the late eighteenth century until the early nineteenth, when Enlightenment ideas were still in vogue, women in Scotland had significant access to university lectures, though not as matriculated students. By the later Victorian period, such access was discouraged, and when in the second half of the nineteenth century women tried to enter the medical profession, they were warned by doctors that their 'uteruses would atrophy and their brains would burst' (Smith, 2000, p. 328). Madeline Daniell's sister, Helen Carter Evans, another widow of an Indian officer (who later married Alexander Russell, editor of *The Scotsman*), joined Sophia Jex-Blake in the attempt to gain admission to medical lectures for women at Edinburgh University (Ewan et al., 2007). Helen was one of the 'Edinburgh Seven', the first group of undergraduate female students to matriculate at a British university. The Seven began studying medicine in 1869 but the Court of Session ruled that they should not have been admitted and could not graduate. Their campaign helped hasten the passing of the 1876 Medical Act, which permitted women to study medicine at university. Helen's daughter, Helen Alexander Russell, one of St Andrews University's first female undergraduates, joined the Women's Social and Political Union in 1908, worked on *The Suffragette* newspaper, campaigned for an Equal Rights Treaty at the League of Nations, and wrote for the *London Times* and *The Scotsman* (Ewan et al., 2018, p. 18).

All of these women were part of a late nineteenth-/early twentieth-century women's movement for social and educational reform. All wealthy, none led seamless married lives, through either contingency or choice. Through birth and inheritance Julia Braddon and Janet Elizabeth were able to live independently. Young widowhood linked Julia and Madeline Daniell, as did a connection to India. Madeline's parents lived at Fort William, Calcutta, at the same time as John Clode Braddon's parents, William Braddon and Hannah Maria Daniels. In addition, Julia, Janet Elizabeth and Madeline escaped the fate of many women of their time: constant childbearing, as experienced by Julia's mother-in-law, who died aged forty-four after bearing twelve children. Madeline's childlessness was, of course, due to the tragic deaths of her two young sons.

I could find no family connection between Julia's first mother-in-law, Hannah Maria Daniels (or Daniell), and Madeline's husband, Charles Astell Daniell, but, remarkably, I discovered that Charles was distantly related to Julia through John Foster Barham (via links to the Long/ Beckford/Palmer/Ellis lineage referred to earlier). Julia was also distantly related to the Shuttleworths. A second cousin once removed, Charlotte Anne Livius, daughter of George Livius and Mary Foster Barham, married Reverend Thomas Shuttleworth Grimshawe, who was from a branch of the Shuttleworth family long settled in Bedford. Julia's choice to live in San

Remo – a fashionable place for rich British people in the late nineteenth century, particularly those with poor health – was undoubtedly linked to these networks.

Julia and Janet Elizabeth probably knew one another before their educational venture together in the town. And when Alexander arrived in San Remo with his invalid wife it is likely that both women would have attended his church services, and may even have helped to raise money for his new Protestant church. Two decades earlier, a proposal for an 'English Church' in San Remo had been the subject of correspondence between Janet Elizabeth's mother and the Archbishop of Canterbury, as I discovered from an obscure reference that led me to Lambeth Palace Library in search of a handwritten letter. I managed to purchase a (barely legible) copy of the letter from the library. Dated the 29th March 1864, Lady Janet solicits the Archbishop's support for the church: 'Hitherto,' she writes, 'there have not been many Protestants here – a few English and even fewer Germans and French, but the climate is so mild, and the scenery so beautiful that there can be no doubt that San Remo will in a few years become quite as important as a health destination for invalids as Menton or even Nice. When living here last winter there was no Protestant service... But since then 3 hotels have been... completed – and a very fair congregation assembles in one of them for English Service... Mr. Aspinall... has bought a piece of land for the site of the English Church' (Lambeth Palace Library, Ref. Tait 137ff. 192–6).

Lady Janet died in 1872, so she did not witness the building of the Protestant church commissioned by Alexander the following decade. But her predictions proved correct: from the mid 1880s, Italy did become the preferred destination for elite tourism, as she had intimated to the Archbishop. Liguria was particularly favoured by the ill and infirm, especially San Remo, which by the end of the nineteenth century hosted consuls or vice-consuls for Russia, Greece, Britain, Germany, Denmark, Holland, Portugal, Spain, Sweden and Norway. Tourism had a modernising effect on the region, with a railway line reaching San Remo in 1874. A particularly large number of Scots in the town in the last three decades of the nineteenth century combined with a significant number of North Americans to form a substantial Presbyterian community as part of a larger Protestant one. Non-Catholic societies grew up for foreigners, and many of their members were involved in various kinds of social and charity work.

To cater for this community, under the auspices of the Scottish UPC Alexander commissioned the celebrated architect Pio Soli to design a church. The Moorish Kiosk, a 'temple with an orientalized style', erected in Hanbury Gardens in 1886, was designed by the same architect. Legal documents for St Andrew's Church, built 'in a Romanesque style with Gothic elements', were signed in May 1885 and are now lodged at the National Library of Scotland, together with title deeds, architect's drawings, and payment books from 1882 until May 1885, all signed off by Alexander. Alongside, a note of sale of a plot of land, registered at San Remo on the 17th May 1883, specifies that the plot may be used 'only for the building of a church with a dwelling house attached for the use of the caretaker'. The land cost 33,033 francs, 70c, 'paid by Mr Robertson with the money of the Church which he represents'. In letters dated the 18th March, 4th April and 12th May 1883, all written in French and sent from Villa Bracco, the home in San Remo that he shared with his wife Helen, Alexander urges the architect to make speed. By then, Helen was mortally ill.

After Helen's death in January 1884 (thus missing the church's consecration by just a few months), Alexander was left on his own to nurture, and pay off the debt on, his newborn church. Constantly engaged in fundraising, including numerous sales of work in Britain, his every effort was reported to UPC Board meetings in Edinburgh. His precarious employment was another constant; a situation captured by the steady flow of letters passing between him and the board, which I consulted in the NLS's Special Collections room. Throughout 1885, the year of Alexander's second marriage, dozens of letters reveal his relentless quest for more stable employment. Did he consider moving back to Scotland? If not, why? Were there too few employment opportunities back home, or was a return to cold and wet weather daunting? Was it because his second marriage was in prospect? Was he perhaps having doubts about such a commitment? Or did the marriage proposal only occur later that year? It is impossible to know. But a handwritten letter addressed to Alexander at the Continental Hotel, San Remo, dated the 27th April 1885, a few months before his marriage to Julia and fifteen months after Helen's death, shows his willingness to move just about anywhere. James Buchanan, secretary of the board in Edinburgh, writes:

The Jewish Committee of the Presbyterian Church of England (with whom we are to co-operate in Jewish Mission work)[1] has abandoned the idea of occupying Hebron, as a German society has already entered there and begun work. They are now speaking of Morocco as a sphere of labour... but in the meantime they are only making enquiries. I shall have much pleasure in mentioning your case to the Foreign Mission Board and I have no doubt they will give it their best consideration.

(NLS, MS 7661)

A month later, Buchanan reports back to Alexander that at the Foreign Mission Board meeting 'various members gave very favourable testimony as to your work' but left the matter in the hands of the Continental and Colonial Board (NLS, MS 7694). A further letter from the secretary, dated the 10th October 1885, addressed to Alexander at the Hotel Ghiffa, Lago Maggiore (probably on honeymoon), congratulates him on his recent marriage but regrets that 'there is no prospect of your having the work at Aix at the time we expected. I must say this is what I expected from our friends: I never thought that they would give up the work... However, something else may turn up perhaps for you' (NLS, MS 7622, f. 154). A marriage announcement had appeared the previous week in the *London Times*. It reads, 'On 30 September at the British Embassy in Bern, the Rev. Alexander Robertson of the Scotch Church, San Remo, to Julia, widow of J. Clode Braddon, and daughter of Alfred Dawson Esq. MA, Christ's Coll. Cam. and Flora Foster.'

When Alexander married for the second time his new wife's lifetime pension must have provided him with a degree of security thus far lacking in his working arrangements. Nonetheless, his mounting frustration about job security did not abate, and can be charted through the increasing number of letters noted in board minutes from May 1885 until 1890, when the couple finally relocated to Venice. Since his work as a minister in San Remo was seasonal, Alexander's main source of income at the time, apart from Julia, was his journalism. *The Scotsman*'s contributors' daybook for 1881–7 attests to this, as the increasing frequency with which Alexander's articles appear during the period keeps pace with that of his pleas for more work – forty in

---

1   Who knew such a committee existed?

all – to the UPC Board; spurred on, I imagine, by his new wife. His *Scotsman* contributions grew from a trickle in 1882, 1883 and 1884 (when his first wife died) to a near torrent in 1885, when fourteen letters and fifteen articles were received. The daybook records the number of words in each article because payment was based on column inches. A similar level of activity was maintained in 1886, with a further acceleration in 1887 when, between late February and the end of March, Alexander submitted seventeen news reports, letters and telegrams – a flurry of concentrated activity that was due to a serious earthquake on the French and Italian Riviera on the 23rd February 1887, which had devastating effects.

At a meeting of the Continental Committee on the 17th January 1887, a few weeks before the earthquake, a letter from Alexander intimates his wish to clear the debt on St Andrew's Church before leaving his post in San Remo. He would like work 'for the circle of the year, at least some plan for spring and autumn employment when not at San Remo, perhaps Sienna (even Egypt or Palestine)?' The board agrees to his reappointment for 1887–8 on the same terms: £200 for six months (later reduced to £160), but this must also 'cover all charges for travelling etc.'. Requests to further extend his appointment in San Remo, 'which would be good for the work and would also enable me to have a home' and pay off the debt on the church before leaving, fall on deaf ears. At the end of 1888 the debt for the church still stands at over £2,000 (Small, 1904, pp. 499–501).

In Chapter 3, I mentioned postcards from the period which show the lovely church on the Corso Imperatrice nestling beside the Hotel de Paris. I bought one online and had it framed in gold to match the glow of the sun. Visits to the church were soon part of the tourist trail, with guidebooks and posters advertising Alexander's services alongside various competing religious offerings in German, French or Italian: 'Services Each Sunday From the middle of November till the middle of April at 11 o'clock in the morning and at 3 o'clock after noon,' reads one of Alexander's notices. 'Prayer meeting every Saturday morning at 11 o'clock, signed, Revd. Alexander Robertson Minister from Scotland,' announces one guidebook.

It is safe to say that one person who would not have attended any of Alexander's church services was Edward Lear. He had withdrawn more and more from San Remo society since arriving in the town in 1871, having developed a fairly jaundiced opinion of his fellow expatriates as well as their leisure activities and religious practices. On the 7th March 1886, just a few months before his death, Lear confesses in a letter to Wilkie Collins that 'of what is called the Colony here I know – I am happy to say – nothing. Neither perpetual church services (high & low – candlestick or cursing) are to my taste, nor are balls & Lawn Tennis among my weaknesses' (Uglow, 2017, p. 546).

In the early decades of the 1900s, by which time Alexander and Julia had moved on to Venice, St Andrew's Church fell victim to the diminishing size of San Remo's Presbyterian community and the growing anti-British feeling generated under Mussolini. It was sold to the Commune of San Remo in 1936, three years after Alexander's death, and subsequently demolished to allow for the widening of the Corso Imperatrice, in line with contemporary fashions in urban planning and so as to accommodate Mussolini's massive fascist rallies. Alexander saw Mussolini's fascist project in missionary terms. The final irony is that the man whom Alexander came to revere as Italy's saviour would put paid to Alexander's own legacy by bulldozing a product of *his* mission in Italy. The one saving grace is that Alexander did not live long enough to see the vandalism visited upon his church just half a century after its creation.

Eight

Venice, Italy:
Venetian Sermons

In January 2017 I arrived by train into a mysterious, eerily silent Venice floating on a sea of fog, and soon found my way to the Robertsons' house, La Casa Struan (or Ca' Struan), standing close by the famous Basilica di Santa Maria della Salute, the subject of so many picture postcards and paintings. Overlooking the canal, on a corner with the Salute Bridge, Ca' Struan can be accessed by boat or by an entrance in a side lane off the lovely street, Catecumeni. The house's address, 23 Calle del Squero, is in the lane, though it fronts onto Catecumeni and no longer bears the name Ca' Struan. Its attractive location in the Dorsoduro district was much favoured by nineteenth-century British and American residents of Venice. The house must have been very damp.

By 1890 Alexander's work in San Remo under the UPC had come to an end. He and Julia transferred to Venice, where he had been conducting services for part of the year since 1887. He initially acted as an independent minister until his chaplaincy in Venice gained recognition from the Church of Scotland at its general assembly on the 28th May 1900. Chaired by the new moderator Norman Macleod, the assembly, on receiving the *Report on Continental Chaplaincies*, wished to make 'a special reference to the gratifying success of the Chaplaincy at Venice under the charge of Dr. Robertson', and it endorsed the nominations committee recommendation that 'the petition of

Mr. Robertson [illegible] asking to be admitted as a licentiate of the Church be granted' (Ref. CH/1/4/83, Scotland Record Office, Register House).

Alexander's petition to the Church of Scotland was a last resort, submitted only after many unsuccessful appeals to the UPC for continuing employment under its auspices. His name vanishes from UPC Board minutes between June 1889 and April 1894, when, finally, a report on his well-attended services in Venice is tabled. In view of his 'success in attracting a large congregation', he asks the board to adopt Venice as its 'station' and to pay him a stipend of £100. He even offers to send that sum annually, taken in collections, to cover his salary. A subcommittee answers with a resounding 'no' and restates its 1889 decision to 'sanction' his work in Venice but 'to undertake no pecuniary responsibility in the matter'. The board then compounds its mean-spiritedness by promising to send on to him any moneys donated in his name by his supporters in Venice, noting that 'Mrs. Nairn and several friends' have just phoned the secretary, 'begging' to help to keep their minister. Earlier appeals to the board to improve Alexander's working conditions and to extend his employment in San Remo had been similarly rebuffed, despite appeals from supporters there too. Alexander's eventual decision to throw in his lot with the Church of Scotland was one he clearly struggled with, holding off until 1900, six years after his final rejection by the UPC Board.

From then until the advent of World War I, Alexander, now a Church of Scotland minister, seasonally attracted large numbers to his services in Venice, which were held in premises owned by an American-supported Protestant church near Piazza San Marco. Dwindling numbers during the war years and throughout the 1920s caused services to be relocated to his home at Ca' Struan, which, being close to the large-domed Salute Church, was easy to find, even without the Union Jack which he raised on Sundays to guide people to it. When he resigned his charge in 1931, Alexander was granted a Church of Scotland pension and the title of honorary chaplain (Law, 1993). Shortly before retiring, he was entered in *Fasti Ecclesiae Scoticanae*, which lists all of the Church's ministers. His entry, under 'Venice, Italy', reads:

ROBERTSON, ALEXANDER, born 30 November, 1846, second son of James R. and Elizabeth Fairley; educated at Free Church Normal School, High School and University of Edinburgh [1866–

9]; ord. to South Ronaldsay U.P. Church 7th December 1875; dem. 18th Oct 1881; min. at San Remo, Liguria, 1882 (where he built a church, obtaining from King Humbert a royal decree regarding it); app. to Venice in 1888; D.D. (McGill College, Montreal) 1894; created Cavaliere of the Order of S.S. Maurizio and Lazzaro in 1898. At the General Assembly, May 1900, he petitioned to have his station at Venice recognized as belonging to the Church of Scotland with himself as its minister, and was admitted. Marr. (1) 15th March, 1875, Helen, daugh. of James Stevenson, Falkirk; (2) 30th Sept. 1885, Julia (died s.p., 7th March 1922, aged 80), daugh. of William Alfred Dawson, M.A., vicar of Flitwick, Bedfordshire.

(Scott, 1928, p. 555)

Alexander was also regularly engaged on speaking tours for the Edinburgh-based Hope Trust, which was devoted to promoting Protestantism and opposing Roman Catholicism. Through such public engagements, his work as a minister and writer, and his marriage to Julia, he had access to an elite social circle, including socialites and doers of good works. One such was Lady Mary Enid Layard, whose diary, *Lady Layard's Journal*, offers gossipy insights into British expatriate life in Venice. Lady Layard (1843–1912) was the wife of the diplomat, art historian and archaeologist Sir Henry Layard (1817–94), who served for a period as the British Under-Secretary for Foreign Affairs. Her intimate portrait of the social life of Venice's expatriate high society and its good works includes several references to Alexander and Julia. On the 4th October 1890 Lady Layard writes from her home, Ca' Capello in Venice:

This being the Empress's last day at Venice I gave up the whole day to her and we went to the Sailors' Institute where we were met by Mr Jamieson and the Revd Alexander and Mrs Robertson the Scotch Minister who had been at S. Remo when H.M. was there.[2] He begged her to go to see Mrs Hammond's *asilo* and she consenting we went to the Cannaregio to a nicely kept house where there were 60 boys in school. We saw their dormitory, their carving shop, printing

---

2   An article in the *New York Times* in February 1888 refers to a 'well-informed correspondent in San Remo' reporting that Queen Victoria would be visiting for a short time. Was Alexander that correspondent?

room and shoe making. The Institution is kept up by subscriptions from England and the children are taught Protestantism wh [sic] is a reason we have generally avoided any connection with the school but I must confess it is admirably arranged and probably does a great deal of good by good education. We went from there to the Palazzo Rezzonico where Mr and Mrs Browning received H.M. and showed her over the house.

A brief entry on the 9th December 1900 recounts another visit to the Sailors' Institute, 'where there was a service at 7pm. The Scotch clergyman Dr Robertson addressed us.' On the 24th April 1902, Lady Layard recounts a day of social engagements:

After spending some time we returned home for tea. Mr Whitaker and General and Mrs Sartoris, also M. Guggenheim [Meyer Guggenheim, grandfather of Peggy Guggenheim who founded the Peggy Guggenheim Collection in Venice; a gallery of European and American twentieth-century art] and Dr and Mrs Robertson came to tea besides Clara and Hilda Montalba, and Elaine and I accompanied them home to their door so as to having the pleasure of being with them and taking the air.

On the 3rd January 1903 Lady Layard writes:

I did not get out of doors till past 6 and then in the cool had a pleasant row[3] – left some cards and went to call on Dr. and Mrs. Robertson – the Scotch Minister and his wife. He is a good old man, she a very capable woman – They bought a property close to the Church of the Salute and have made a small but charming house. I told them about the hospital I am arranging and they at once gave me 50 fcs.

On the 25th August 1908, writing from Castel Savoia, Gressoney St Jean, Lady Layard tells of a motoring excursion with the Queen up the Val d'Aosta to the Petit St Bernard:

---

3   The Venetian equivalent of an evening stroll, perhaps?

The Queen's servants had laid the table for lunch on the grass a little way up the mountain so we climbed up and found all prepared in a most picturesque spot... The Queen was delighted with the spot said it was like a scene described by Boccaccio... As we drove through St Didier we saw two people seated on a bench by the road. The Queen[4] had hardly said, "These are English people" when I recognized Dr and Mrs Robertson of Venice. He is the Scotch Minister there. We did not see them again on our return so I suppose they must be staying at Courmayer.

However, a diary entry on the 15th May 1910 signals a break in Lady Layard's relationship with the Robertsons:

Mr Williamson (the ex priest) came to lunch. He is very upset at a horrid book published by Dr. Robertson against the Roman Catholic Church in Italy and had sent it to me to see. I condoled with him being also horrified – Dr R. is a fanatical Scotch Minister – but living here among Roman Catholics he need not insult their religious beliefs.

There is no further mention of either Alexander or Julia in *Lady Layard's Journal*. Alexander had clearly blotted his copybook. The book that upset Mr Williamson and severed the couple's relationship with Lady Layard may have been *The Roman Catholic Church in Italy*, published by Morgan & Scott in five editions between 1903 and 1905. But the most likely cause of their banishment was *The Papal Conquest: Italy's Warning – Wake Up, John Bull!*, which was published in 1909, just a few months before the 'horrified' diary entry.

Lady Layard received the sting of another writer's pen herself. Frederick Rolfe's novel, *The Desire and Pursuit of the Whole*, in which Alexander has a walk-on role, also contains an unflattering, scarcely disguised portrait of Lady Layard as the do-gooder 'Lady Pash'. Lady Layard founded Venice's English Hospital in 1903. In Rolfe's narrative, 'The British Infirmary is a private hobby... originally founded by a committee of aliens resident in Venice... and later... captured entirely by a certain Lady Pash, who (being willing to pay for her pastimes) contrived to silence the committee and to

---

4   Probably Queen Alexandra, wife of Edward VII, Queen Victoria's son and successor.

oust British medical skill by making the Directress acknowledge her sole sway. Mild old darlings... used to say that as Lady Pash paid the piper she had a right to call the tune; and grumblers... were snubbed, and insulted, and (when possible) ruined' (Rolfe, 2002 [1934], p. 78).

The University of Venice's Institute of Architecture (IUAV) holds a file on the Robertsons' 'small but charming house', Ca' Struan, which Lady Layard visited in January 1903. The file is lodged in an archive covering the work of one of Venice's most renowned architects, Giuseppe Torres. In 1905 Alexander and Julia commissioned Torres to draw up plans for the reconstruction of their house: '*un progetto di ricostruzione di una casa alla Salute per Alexander e Giulia Robertson*'. The plans demonstrate that it was not just to be *any* reconstruction; it was to be done 'in the style of a palace'. The file, *Casa Pastore Robertson – 1905*, contains eight beautifully drawn sketches showing the current state of the house from different angles, with suggestions for its reconstruction. There is also a work plan for 'demolition and reconstruction of the old house', together with a 'draft and final estimate total of 967.40 lire', which seems very cheap. Nevertheless, several letters and postcards, dispatched between May and August 1905, query Torres's estimates, solicit meetings with him, and ask him to reply *subito* (immediately). Julia writes most of the letters. Alexander's missives are limited to a handful of postcards requesting Torres's help regarding a photograph taken by John Ruskin of Campo Santa Margherita, a piazza in the Dorsoduro district of Venice. He believes the photograph to be in the architect's possession, and would like to use it in his own forthcoming book. Then, silence. Ca' Struan's reconstruction never goes ahead – perhaps not surprising, given the frequency and the imperious tone of some of Julia's notes to the eminent architect. The correspondence provides a rare insight into the couple's different characters; Julia's letters displaying a manner perhaps learned from her mother in her dealings with 'staff', and Alexander's equally peremptory but vague and detached notes remaining tightly focused on his own preoccupations.

The house now stands empty, damp, sad-looking and dilapidated; painted green and under a compulsory purchase order, awaiting renovation by the local authority. Standing outside it on a chilly January day, I had mixed emotions: sadness at its current state of disrepair; curiosity about the expatriates who found their way to the 'Church in the House'. I even entertained the fantasy of buying Ca' Struan myself. The moment passed.

Now I wonder at the courage and fortitude of the couple who made a hospitable home together, and pursued their individual and joint projects for so long and with such vigour in a foreign land. Julia was clearly a force behind Alexander, emotional as well as material; the many dedications to her in his books attest to this, and to the strength and endurance of their bond.

J. E. Law concludes his dictionary entry on Alexander by saying that above all else he was a prolific writer, and that 'when the extent and nature of his journalism are better known his career will be better understood' (Law, 1993, p. 723). Alexander supplied copy to several journals and newspapers in the Protestant English-speaking world right up until he died. It was during his time in San Remo (before relocating to Venice in 1890) that he became a well-known writer for *The Scotsman*, covering affairs back home as well as in Italy. To keep his finger on the pulse of Scottish popular opinion, as he saw it, he even subscribed to *The People's Friend*, a weekly magazine published by the Dundee-based firm D. C. Thomson, which celebrated its 150th birthday in 2019. Dispatched every week to Alexander's home in Venice, the magazine's tagline is 'The famous story magazine'. Marketed principally at the 'older woman' and with a bias towards Scottish subjects, each issue contains a mixture of short stories and factual articles. Pets, crafts and family are common themes. The journal was a joke in my family when I was a child. So too, to a lesser degree, was its sister publication *The Sunday Post*, although it and other D. C. Thomson staples, *The Beano* and *The Dandy*, were frequent purchases from our corner 'sweetie shop'.

We know that Alexander kept up his subscription because of a letter dated 13th January 1895 which he sent from Venice to his old professor of Greek at Edinburgh University, William Blackie, which is filed at the NLS. Having just read the professor's article on Fra Paolo Sarpi in *The People's Friend*, 'just arrived,' Alexander writes on 13th January 1895, 'I have read with intense interest and delight your noble eulogy of Fra Paolo Sarpi. It has, what all your writings have, that genuine, liberal, patriotic ring about it that warms a Scotsman's heart. When I think of you the words of the border farmer regarding Mr Gladstone spring to mind. Seeing him on the station platform he gazed at him for a little and then going up to him he said "Are you Mr Gladstone?" Mr Gladstone said he was, then the farmer putting his hand on Mr Gladstone's shoulder said, "Man, you're a richt yin!"' Taking the opportunity to mention the pending publication of the third edition of his own book on the radical friar, Alexander solicits a few of Blackie's 'very characteristic lines about Sarpi' to quote in it. Reminding Blackie of his two years as a student in the professor's Greek class when he was himself president of the Young Men's Evangelical Society in Edinburgh, Alexander signs off, 'Congratulating you on your hale old years, and praying you may be long preserved to Auld Reekie to Scotsmen the world over... I am, My dear Professor, Yours admiringly and affectionately, Alexander Robertson' (NLS MS 2640, f123). The letter's style of address is similar to that of the *Scotsman* story about the boy in the rubble, quoted in Chapter 2. A mawkish Scottishness is on show; an attempt to disarm, which makes me squirm. Yet despite such lapses, Alexander had a facility for words that could be turned to cash. A talent for friendship is also apparent in his letter-writing, which was as prodigious as his journalism. By all accounts he and Julia kept an open house. A minister and a Scot with a marked burr and a tam-o'-shanter who was also a royalist, Alexander must have cut a colourful figure, especially on Sundays when he raised the Union Jack to guide people to Ca' Struan, where he held services after the First World War.

Earlier, whilst still in San Remo, Alexander had responded with courage when a serious earthquake occurred on the 23rd February 1887 in the French and Italian Riviera. His vivid coverage of the tragedy for *The Scotsman* begins with a letter written on the day after the earthquake, in which he reassures a friend in Glasgow that the new St Andrew's Church in San Remo is undamaged. His hastily written letter, published in *The Scotsman* on the 2nd March 1887, reads:

> I have just time amid the confusion and excitement amid which we are, to tell you that the church is not damaged. Almost all the others in San Remo are... [and many] houses uninhabitable. We are houseless. Had to sleep last night in a tent in the open air. All in San Remo did this, only we cannot return to our house. Walls cracked and gaping and ceilings down everywhere... Visitors flying from San Remo... Little damage to life here but many killed in neighbouring villages... Such a ruin to our prosperous season... But all must be well.

In the same edition of the paper, a news report by Alexander dated two days after the earthquake is headed 'The Earthquake in the Riviera: A Visit to Bussana, a Village Destroyed by the Earthquake (From a Scottish

Correspondent)'. Driving to the village, 'high up on a spur on the eastern side of the Seriana Valley', with a delivery of oranges, he reports coming upon a group of men returning from the burial of earthquake victims. They had dug up seventy-four corpses and uncovered a woman and child still alive after being buried for fifty hours. Alexander's first sight of the ruined village is reported in dramatic terms:

> The houses, as is the custom in Italian mountain villages, had been piled one above the other so that now we seemed to be looking on Niagara Falls of stones and mortar, out of which were sticking broken chairs and tables, beds and broken crockery, at one place, a clock with its hands pointing to 6.26, the hour of doom to so many.

Over the next few days, Alexander dispatched a series of reports describing the effects of the earthquake on villages up and down the Riviera, with his name now routinely published under the strapline 'Our Correspondent in Italy'.

Two decades on, he is still sending letters and articles to the newspaper from Venice on a wide range of subjects, from sexual abuse in Catholic schools to Italy's involvement in the First World War. On sexual abuse, replying to a letter to the editor accusing him of 'reckless statements' in lectures he gave in Glasgow and Edinburgh on behalf of the Hope Trust, he is unapologetic. In his reply, posted on the 3rd October 1907, he explains that the talks were about the 'appalling state of matters... in many... schools belonging to the Roman Catholic Church in Italy, the teachers in which are priests and nuns, which... accounts for the great anti-clerical agitation... now moving Italy... Many church schools and colleges have been closed... priests and sisters are in prison... for outrages upon pupils, many of whom were children... It is ludicrous to say that the clerical schools are in a wholesome condition.' More than a century later, revelations about sexual abuse in the Catholic Church and its repeated failure to tackle it have all but destroyed the reputation of the Church in Italy and worldwide.

Covering Italy's involvement in the First World War, Alexander's distaste for Germany comes through in several pieces written during the war years. From Venice on the 20th September 1914, he comments on Italy's preparations for war:

In Italy everyone knows that the much-vaunted Triple Alliance had no foundation in fact – it was only another German fiction. It never had and never could have the approval of the people of Italy. Germany has never shown itself a friend to Italy. Austria has never been anything else but its implacable enemy... Italy... maintains her neutrality, but she finds it difficult to restrain her people from expressing openly their love and admiration for England, France, Belgium and Russia and their hatred and contempt for Austria and Germany.

The same antipathy is apparent in an obituary in *The Scotsman* on the 19th December 1917 for Pasquale Villari, professor of history at the Higher Normal School in Florence. Pitting Villari's educational ideas against what he considers to be German ideals, Alexander claims that at a recent conference in Munich, German teachers 'passed a resolution that "as teachers they had nothing to do with reformation of character"'. For Villari, says Alexander, paraphrasing his old Moray House College rector Maurice Paterson, 'We teachers are not intended to be coaches or crammers... [but] to guide uprising generations of men and women *how to live*'. This remained Alexander's lifelong ideal of education.

An early indication that Alexander would become an inveterate letter writer and a committed self-publicist is evident in a news report in the Aberdeen *Evening Express* on the 23rd November 1894:

The Rev. Dr. Alexander Robertson of Venice, having sent to Mr. Gladstone a copy of the second edition of his last book, *Fra Paolo Sarpi*, has received by return of post the following autograph letter:

'Rev. and Dear Sir,
    Accept my best thanks for your very interesting work on Father Paul, which reached me today, and which I have at once commenced. I have a very strong sympathy with men of his way of thinking... It pleases me to learn that a Sarpi literature has appeared lately at Venice... I would... be glad if you would at any time come and see them in a library with Hostel attached which I am founding here.
    I remain your very faithful
    W. E. Gladstone'

Gladstone's Library still exists. Located in Church Lane, Hawarden, it houses over two hundred thousand volumes of theology and history, including, we now know, works by Alexander Robertson.

A few years later, on the 17th October 1898, a 'Literary Note' in *The Scotsman* reveals that:

> His Majesty King Humbert, in graciously accepting a copy of the Rev. Dr. Alexander Robertson's new work, "The Bible of St Mark, the Altar and Throne of Venice", has sent him through the Minister of the Royal House, General Ponzio Vaglia, a letter of thanks, from which the following is extracted – 'The gift of your new work, the fruit of your great love of art and for the city of Venice, has been most pleasing to our august Sovereign, who has charged me to thank you, in his name, for this affectionate renewal of sympathy given by you to him.'

Alexander's desire for public recognition back home scarcely diminished in later life. He would be pleased by (and may well have been the source of) a news item in the Dundee *Courier* on the 4th November 1930, headed, 'Italian King Honours Scots Minister: Decoration for Dr. Robertson of Venice':

> Dr. Alexander Robertson of Venice has been honoured by King Victor Emmanuel III who has created him Commendatore of the Order of the Crown of Italy. The late King Humbert also conferred a decoration on Dr. Robertson, creating him Cavaliere of S.S. Maurizio and Lazzaro… a unique honour to be conferred upon a foreigner… The Church of Scotland has no representative abroad more beloved than Dr. Robertson, and young people who have been… in Venice for a time revere and love him for the fatherly interest he has taken in them and for the hospitality of his home.

King Humbert had bestowed the earlier title on Alexander in recognition of the relief work done by him and Julia in supplying food and clothes to displaced people during the 1887 earthquake. Julia received no such title, though she did catch the eye of royalty later on, as indicated in a 'Court Notice' in *The Scotsman* on the 12th June 1917:

King Victor Emmanuel III, having been graciously pleased to receive one of the wool articles Mrs. Alexander Robertson of Venice has been knitting for the Italian soldiers during the war, charged to convey the royal thanks, writes, 'His Majesty highly appreciates the kind thought that prompted the gift, and regards it with a sincere benevolence equal to the affectionate care you show for our soldiers.'

On the same day that my great-great-aunt's knitting was news, two other reports in the paper offer reminders of the political volatility of the period: the first concerning Irish Home Rule; the second, the recent Russian Revolution. Alexander held firm views about both. He writes to the editor on the 11th October 1912 in support of Ulster's stand against Home Rule, 'in maintaining the Union and the civil and religious liberties of the loyal Protestant inhabitants of Ireland'. In an earlier letter to the paper in 1889, he had quoted Cavour, hero of Italian unification, against Gladstone's bill: 'Sir, Mr. Gladstone boasts that the civilized world approves of his Irish Home Rule policy... [Yet] In one of his letters [Count Cavour] says, "I stand up at all cost for the maintenance of the Union, in the interest of Ireland first, of England second, and of the future of civilization."'

Alexander's views about the Russian Revolution were equally partisan. In 'Italy: Benevolent and Malevolent Autocracy', published in *The Scotsman* on the 27th October 1920, he spells out his distaste for Bolshevism/socialism and uses the opportunity to indulge in a little name-dropping:

The other day – the revolutionaries (including Bolsheviks, anarchists and socialists) – proclaimed a general strike in favour of Russia... At the bidding of those pro-Russians, the life of Milan and Turin was brought to a standstill. Here in Venice the same happened on a lesser scale. In the good old times of the Most Serene Republic – a name justified by the maintenance of peace and public order by the famous 'Council of Ten' – no revolution could be thought of without that body getting a hint of it. It sent out spy citizens to report back on any plot and the plot was allowed to develop...

Then one conspirator was picked up and lodged in the Doge's Palace. Then another... until all were secured, then tried fairly and justly, convicted and sentenced to death... One by one they were marched to the Piazzetta and beheaded... There was perfect liberty for all in Venice, natives and strangers... Talking of these things to the late Joseph Chamberlain... he said: 'But now the days of benevolent autocracy are over.' He used the term benevolent to characterize the autocracy of the Most Serene Republic... As Mr. Ruskin has said 'Not a man crossed the Bridge of Sighs from prison to execution who did not deserve his fate.'

Had the Elizabethan and Jacobean spymasters William and Robert Cecil known about Alexander, their distant relative-to-be-through-marriage, the views expressed here would have made him a man after their own hearts. Nevertheless, two years after Mussolini's assumption of power on the 31st October 1922 as Italy's youngest ever Prime Minister, Alexander is condemning press censorship. On the 23rd September 1924, in an article entitled, 'Muzzling the Press in Italy: Fascist Treatment of Opposition Journals', he wants to believe that Mussolini is not to blame:

> To the sincere regret, I believe, of Mussolini and the Government, *Fascisti* reprisals... have taken place throughout Italy... it is the Press that has suffered most severely... The muzzling of the Press by recently passed Press Laws give[s] power to Prefects... to sequester any newspaper... which may contain in their opinion articles to incite readers against the Government or other State institutions. Even many of the supporters of the Government believe this is a great mistake [and] the means of turning not a few friends into opponents.

A few months later, on the 3rd January 1925, Mussolini recalled Parliament, which had been in recess for the Christmas break. By then, many parts of Italy were in the grip of a wave of fascist violence, and in what has been described as his 'most brilliant *coup de théâtre*' he told the assembled deputies that Italy needed a firm hand, and that he alone was capable of 'dominating the crisis' and, if Parliament would endorse his personal dictatorship, would put the country to rights. The speech worked. It was now a matter of imposing the full weight of fascism: 'The opposition won't be curbed: well, I'll make them obey!' Across Italy, all organisations deemed 'subversive' were shut down, scores of 'dangerous' people were arrested, and 'the cult of Mussolini took flight' (Moorehead, 2017, pp. 130–2).

By 1929 Alexander was much less squeamish about muzzling the press or any other curtailing of civil liberties. It was now clear that it was Mussolini himself who was the chief censor. In 'A Homogeneous Italy', published in *The Scotsman* on the 26th March 1929, Alexander makes clear his allegiances:

When Mussolini was called to power by King Emmanuel III in October 1922 [he] set about creating a united, homogeneous Italy according to the principle 'All inside the State, no-one outside the State, no-one against the State'... Early on, he had himself invested with dictatorial powers when he abolished all parties and dissensions in Parliament and Press. He next suppressed Freemasonry because secret and supposedly against the State. Trade Unions came next because they worked for their own special interests and set... proletariat against capitalists, hence were hostile to the unity of the State Mussolini sought...

Since 1861 when Count Cavour under King Emmanuel II created the Kingdom of Italy... the Church, the Vatican and Pope have been considered not just outside but against the State... Now, by a Concordat made by Mussolini and the Pope and Vatican in February, all *are* inside the Fascist regime... Mussolini has made over to the Pope a piece of territory including the Vatican and St Peters as a foreign state geographically in Italy but not of it: 'The Vatican City'. It is inscribed in the Concordat that the Pope regards himself only as sovereign of the Church... and recognizes the Kingdom of Italy under the Monarchy... with Rome as its capital. Thus Mussolini has accomplished what he set out to do when called to power by King Emmanuel III in October 1922:

'A homogeneous Italy.
All inside the State
None outside the State
None against the State'

(It was precisely this accommodation with the Church and monarchy that so incensed Italo Calvino's parents.)

Alexander's biography of Mussolini coincided with his change of heart about press censorship. Published in 1929, with a signed photograph of the Duce on the frontispiece, the book was clearly endorsed by the man himself. *Mussolini and the New Italy* certainly flatters the dictator, calling him 'a man of versatile genius', under whom Italy had finally 'realized the true democracy of Christianity'. An earlier biography of Emmanuel III had been equally enthusiastic, painting a picture of the King as the country's salvation by overruling his Ministers and 'calling to power' Mussolini and his fascists: 'But for [the King's] will in 1922, Italy would have been devastated by a prolonged and bloody civil war from the Alps to Sicily' (Robertson, 1925).

This is a reference to the struggle between fascism and socialism/ Bolshevism that dominated politics at the time. Italo Calvino's parents stood on one side of the divide; Alexander on the other. And it serves as a reminder of one of fascism's key features: as an ideology of the radical right, its rise has always been aided and abetted by the collusion of mainstream conservatives. It has only ever come to power in countries where democratic norms and mainstream politics have been in severe crisis, as in Germany and Italy in the interwar years. Mussolini and Hitler did not 'seize' power, as popularly thought. They were *invited* to power by conservative elites who saw them as a means of controlling new political movements (Hassan, 2018). As Alexander insists, King Victor Emmanuel III 'called to power' Mussolini to become Prime Minister.

In Alexander's eyes, fascism's tendency towards violence is a price well worth paying for the suppression of 'Bolshevism' and to prevent Italy from being conquered by Lenin. This is a major theme of *Mussolini and the New Italy*, which welcomes fascism as a chance for Italy's spiritual regeneration and political revival (Robertson, 1929, p. 11). Such views now appear frankly delusional, yet as R. D. Kernohan points out, 'shorn of its rhetorical trimmings, [Alexander's] complacent and complaisant attitude to Mussolini probably reflected the mood of many expatriate and Italophile Protestants before the dictator's quarrel with Britain and France' (Kernohan, 2005, p. 126).

Alexander's biography presents Mussolini's life as a story of two conflicting parts divided by the Great War of 1914–18. In the first period, he writes, Mussolini is the 'ardent socialist promoting class warfare, setting the workman against the employer'; in the second, 'he is the ardent democrat, uniting the workman and the employer… in a common brotherhood'

(Robertson, 1929, p. 8). After qualifying as a teacher (not unlike Alexander) and teaching briefly in an elementary school, Mussolini, the son of a socialist blacksmith father and an adored primary-school teacher mother, founded a weekly socialist newspaper, *La Lotta di Classe*, and later became editor of *Avanti!*, Italy's leading socialist newspaper. All of this changed when Germany and Austria declared war in 1914, and Mussolini sided with the Allies (Britain, France and Russia). Expelled from the Socialist Party for supporting the war, he left *Avanti!* and started another newspaper, *Il Popolo d'Italia*, to campaign against the 'government and its communist allies' for opposing the war. In May 1915, Italy entered the First World War on the side of the Allies, much to Alexander's relief. That year the young Marxist philosopher, journalist and sociologist Antonio Gramsci, who would go on to co-found the Italian Communist Party in 1921 and launch its newspaper, *L'Ordine Nuovo*, joined Turin's local socialist weekly *Il Grido del Popolo* to campaign *against* the war.

Gramsci's journalism and theoretical writing were all of a piece. In 1926, the year Mussolini dubbed '*l'anno Napoleonico*' ('the Napoleonic year') and turned Italy into a fascist dictatorship, Gramsci was sent to prison, where he wrote his *Prison Notebooks*. Mussolini's project to establish a fascist regime included a Special Tribunal for the Defence of the State, to try 'any activity whatsoever capable of damaging national interests'. Any anti-fascist activity of any kind was made illegal and any newspaper not part of the totalitarian state was confiscated. Gramsci, as leader of the Communist Party, was duly arrested on the 8th November 1926 and sentenced to over twenty years for calling for a general strike: 'We must prevent his mind working for at least twenty years,' declared the prosecutor at his trial (Moorehead, 2017, pp. 161–2). Released from prison for health reasons, Gramsci died soon afterwards in 1937, aged just forty-six. His teeth had fallen out and he was unable to digest food. By then he had been marginalised by the Communist Party for deviating from orthodox Stalinism. Nowadays, his famous aphorism, 'pessimism of the intellect, optimism of the will', is frequently quoted, as is his depiction of the 1930s: 'The crisis consists precisely in the fact that the old is dying and the new cannot be born; in this interregnum a great variety of morbid symptoms appear.'

I was given a copy of the *Prison Notebooks* when I was living in Florence in the early 1970s. Smuggled out of prison in the 1930s, but not published until the 1950s, the *Notebooks* were first translated into English in the 1970s by the Scottish poet Hamish Henderson. My copy became for me a key text as a young sociology lecturer during that decade, and remained an influence throughout the 1980s when I worked for the Workers' Educational Association, and, later still, in university adult education. Its central ideas meshed with a guiding principle of the 1970s women's movement; namely that 'The personal is political.' So, too, did Gramsci's key concept of 'hegemony', denoting a kind of political domination that extends beyond parliamentary or state control into the realm of culture and ideas.

For Gramsci it wasn't enough for revolutionaries to wage a 'war of movement', as the Bolsheviks did when they seized the Russian state. They had to wage a 'war of position', involving a long struggle in civil society to change what he called 'common sense'. The role of 'organic intellectuals', rooted in working-class life and struggle, was of great importance in his view, as was lifelong education. In the early 1980s, as adult educators infused with such ideas, we believed in popular education based in and worked up from the 'experiences and social position of excluded majorities… to fashion a real alternative' (Barr, 1999, p. 93).

In the 1970s, the political magazine *Marxism Today*, to which I subscribed and occasionally contributed, analysed the rise of Thatcherism in terms of Gramsci's concept of hegemony. Editor Martin Jacques argued that the 'new right' was engaged in a project to redefine 'common sense' as well as gain electoral power. That issue of *Marxism Today* remains in my overstuffed hall cupboard despite various culling efforts. My heart sank when I learned that the man responsible for the imprisonment and death of a man I so admired was the hero of my great-great-uncle. It sank even further when I discovered the extent to which Alexander not only colluded with but actively supported fascism's 'hegemonic' project.

When the war that Gramsci opposed ended, Italy was close to bankruptcy, crippled by a huge war debt and a massive number of deaths. R. J. B. Bosworth believes that Italy's dictatorship under Mussolini was a direct product of the bankruptcy brought about by the First World War (Bosworth, 2005). Alexander, in contrast, adopted Mussolini's analysis of events as spelled out in his newspaper *Il Popolo d'Italia*, which blamed Italy's 'internal enemies' for the country's unrest and indulged in populist 'Make Italy Great Again' jingoism. According to Alexander's narrative, after the war, 'Avanti Popolo' was being sung everywhere, boys were being christened 'Lenin', and strikes were increasing. Something had to be done.

Something *was* done. Mussolini called for action against the 'Bolshevist enemy' through the creation of a new military organisation whose recruits would be dressed in black to contrast with the red of the enemy. Mussolini's 'war against the enemies within' lasted from March 1919 until October 1922, when he organised the 'March on Rome' after issuing a proclamation of revolution. Prime Minister Luigi Facta wanted the King to put Italy under martial law. Instead, and to Alexander's delight, Victor Emmanuel dismissed Facta and called on Mussolini to form a government. 'What a marvellous thing it is,' writes Alexander, that the 'recognition of a common brotherhood of all classes with which Italy is now blessed, is due to him who, for years, by speech and writing did more than any other man to frustrate it, namely Mussolini!' (Robertson, 1929, p. 58).

Alexander swallowed whole the myth that, after the war, Italy was on the brink of a Bolshevik takeover and only saved by the 'bold and prescient fascists'. When that myth had outlived its usefulness, says Caroline Moorehead, a new, more positive myth was needed. It took the form of the 'corporative' state, the 'totalitarian' nation (the word originated in Italy) in which, as Mussolini put it, 'everything [was] in the state, nothing outside the state, nothing against the state'; words often repeated by Alexander in his journalism. It was now a 'time of myths'. The words of the day became '*Italianità*', '*Romanità*' and '*fascistizzare*', with Rome the centre of the world 'as it had been and would be again, once centuries of decadence were swept away' (Moorehead, 2017, p. 178). A similar strategy would be adopted a few years later when Heinrich Himmler, Reich Commissioner for the Strengthening of Germandom, explained the necessity for myths: 'The one and only thing that matters to us is to have ideas of history that strengthen our people in their necessary national pride. We are only interested in one thing – to project into the dim and distant past the picture of our nation as we envisage it for the future' (quoted in Stonor Saunders, 2021, pp. 79–80). In Alexander's eyes, Mussolini, though vested with dictatorial powers, was the true democrat because his aim was to 'unite all Italian employers and employed, servants and masters, rich and poor, as brothers in a great Italian family, all mutually dependent on each other and all subordinate to the State... realiz[ing] the true Democracy of Christianity'. Above all, asserts Alexander, his project is one of moral renewal modelled on the old Venetian Republic, aiming to 'bring back' from the Middle Ages a time of spiritual, economic and political purity (Robertson, 1929, p. 163).

The sort of idealisation animating my great-great-uncle's infatuation with Mussolini has been called the 'politics of eternity'; the displacement of the real challenges of the world with a myth of a sacred past. A propensity for hero worship is certainly apparent in Alexander's life. Yet, for such a seemingly down-to-earth, hard-working and (according to several witnesses) kind man, Alexander's adulation of a man now regarded as the prototype of twentieth-century charismatic dictators is disappointing and surprising. It is the adulation of a true *believer*. It may be that, in the years following Julia's death, Alexander needed a strong hero to give him some sense of stability. A strong and capable woman, Julia's absence would have left a huge hole in his life. Yet I doubt that Alexander would have gone along with the fascist ideology that dictated procreation as a woman's duty and regarded women as incapable of creativity or leadership. And he would surely have revised his opinion of Mussolini faced with the latter's vaunted ambition to build a vast Italian Empire, with boys growing up into fascist warriors and girls into fascist mothers. Alexander's written will makes it clear that he valued women in their own right. Regarding his nieces and other female inheritors, he is specific: 'I declare that the foresaid provision so far as in favour of females shall be for their own sole and separate use and shall be exclusive of their husbands' rights or the diligence of such husbands' creditors.' Of this, at least, Julia would undoubtedly have approved.

Nine

Death in Venice

How does it work with statues in a city that has so many of them? I must have seen him often before, the tall, stern man in a bronze monk's habit, but I had not yet really noticed him. He stands on a high pedestal close to the Santa Fosca on Strada Nova, and it seems I have always taken him for granted, never looking to see who he actually was... Then there is the fact that his statue is set back a little, so that you have to walk over to it to see who this is. Paolo Sarpi.
(Nooteboom, 2020, p. 140)

I went in search of Alexander's grave on the Venetian island of San Michele one cold February morning two years ago. We disembarked from the vaporetto at the Cimitero stop on the tiny island and followed a small sign to the Protestant section of the cemetery, where many nineteenth- and early twentieth-century British and American expatriates are buried. Looking for Alexander's grave, I came across Ezra Pound's; a simple slab of marble with his name etched into it, the 'U' carved in the form of a Roman 'V'. I soon found my great-great-uncle's grave, not far from Pound's and alongside Julia's. It was marked by a large cross set on a large three-tiered plinth, standing in its own plot. The Protestant section (known, too, as the English Cemetery) is a walled garden sanctuary with tall cypresses growing among the headstones.

Before Julia's death in 1922 Alexander had gentler heroes than the man who, later that year, became Italy's youngest ever Prime Minister. One of them was the founder of the nineteenth-century movement for reform of the Catholic Church in Italy, Count Campello; another was the key historical figure of the sixteenth-century Church reform movement, Fra Paolo Sarpi. These two men were the subjects of his first two books, *Count Campello and Catholic Reform in Italy* (1891) and *Fra Paolo Sarpi: The Greatest of the Venetians* (1893). Both books were published shortly after Alexander's relocation to Venice with Julia, and his lifelong obsession with Church reform in Italy was first given expression in them.

Alexander particularly admired Paolo Sarpi, the Venetian friar whose statue is the object of Nooteboom's scrutiny, and who fought against papal infallibility all his life. 'Inevitably,' says Nooteboom, quoting Alexander's book on Sarpi, 'he was cited before the Inquisition; predictably, he refused to appear' (Nooteboom, 2020, p. 149). The multitalented Dutch writer's *Roads to Berlin* (2012) was my guide on a recent visit to that city. His new book, *Venice: The Lion, the City and the Water*, is packed with equally astute insights and entertaining tales about Venice's social and artistic history and the larger-than-life personalities who lived there, including my great-great-uncle – and one very cunning artist.

The Inquisition was not just a Spanish matter, Nooteboom reminds us. There were inquisitors in Venice, and in 1573 three of them interrogated the artist Paolo Veronese about a painting that the Dominicans had commissioned from him for their refectory. The inquisitors did not like the artist's completed work, thinking it blasphemous. They wanted him to paint over the dwarves, the man with the bloody nose, the black men, the jester with the parrot, the Germans ('code for Protestants'), the dog at Jesus's side, and much else besides. Veronese failed to do as instructed. Instead, he simply renamed the painting. *The Last Supper* became *The Feast in the House of Levi*.

The first time I saw Veronese's huge painting, which now hangs in Venice's Gallerie dell'Accademia, I was ignorant of the story behind the title, which it still bears. If paintings had subtitles, muses Nooteboom, in this case it might be 'or, *Hoodwinking the Inquisition*' (ibid., p. 96). Had Paolo Sarpi (1552–1623) been in his native Venice at the time, rather than in a monastery in Mantua, he would have cheered on the wily painter, for he was soon to earn an international reputation for criticising the Pope and the Inquisition. A friar of the Servite Order, Sarpi was also a philosopher, an expert in canonical law, a mathematician and a scientist. He discovered the circulation of the blood before William Harvey and was a friend of Galileo, for whom he ordered and supplied telescopes from the Netherlands.

Nooteboom explains that he gleaned these facts about Sarpi from Alexander Robertson's book on the friar, which he happened upon in an antiquarian bookshop in Venice. Spotting a tiny parchment book, written in Italian about 'a monk who apparently... had fallen out with the Pope', the travel writer recounts how he next found himself 'standing with another book about the same monk in my hands... in English... from 1894, with a cover of bright-green linen stamped with the golden emblem of Venice... I ran my fingertips over the lion's wings, read the name of the author, written in equally gold letters: Reverend Alex Robertson. The "ander" of Alexander should have followed the "x", but there was just a small golden "R" there now, with a golden dot beneath the miniature "R", which made the book impossible for me to resist' (ibid., pp. 141–2). Naturally, I rushed to find the golden dot on my own copy. There was none. The reason was clear: mine was a third edition, with the author's name printed in full on the cover.

The travel writer's copy was a second edition, inscribed with the names of two previous English owners, the first having bought it in Venice in 1896; the second, 'judging by the more modern handwriting, had much later taken it to Sevenoaks in Kent, and an hour later I had already put my signature in it' (ibid., p. 142). 'In the days that followed,' continues Nooteboom, 'I studied Fra Paolo Sarpi as seen through the Presbyterian eyes of the Reverend Robertson' (ibid. p. 143). Occasionally switching to John Julius Norwich's *A History of Venice* for his 'less subjective account than the anti-papal Robertson', the travel writer nevertheless keeps returning to 'the wonderfully partisan Robertson' for his descriptions of some events, such as a conversation between Sarpi and 'a sort of papal envoy', who had renounced Protestantism: 'I would have liked to see the conversation [as recounted by Alexander Robertson] on stage,' says Nooteboom, 'preferably sung' (ibid. p. 149).

My third edition of *Fra Paolo Sarpi: The Greatest of the Venetians*, the one that came down to me from my mother, was published in 1911 by George Allen & Company Limited, Ruskin House, Rathbone Place, London. It bears the name 'Alexander Robertson, D.D.' stamped in gold on its pale green cover. The honorary doctorate of divinity, now appended to his name, was awarded after the book's original publication in recognition of its achievement. By chance, on a walking trip with friends in Northumberland,

I came across a first edition thanks to one of my companions who spotted it in Barter Books in Alnwick; surely the best (certainly the biggest) second-hand bookshop in England. Published in 1893 and 1894 by Sampson Low, Marston & Company Limited, St Dunstan's House, Fetter Lane, Fleet Street, my copy, like Nooteboom's, is covered in bright green linen. Mine also bears the name of an earlier purchaser inside, but with the added dedication 'with the Kind Regards of the Author Alexander Robertson, Venice April 21 1896' written in Alexander's unmistakable black-ink script. On the title page, 'D.D.' has been added after his name, carefully penned with the same black ink, which I had not noticed until I read Nooteboom's account. Alexander must have made the addition himself when he signed the book for its buyer, and in such a way as to make it look as if it had been printed. I now looked more carefully at both of my editions. Sure enough, as Nooteboom noted and found irresistible, there it was in my first edition: Alexander's name in gold lettering, minus the '–ander' and in its place a small 'R' with a gold dot underneath.

I too found the book irresistible, but for a different reason. I was intrigued by the address of the first edition's publisher: Fetter Lane. Could it be the same address in London where John Wesley established a centre for Moravians and other dissenting Protestants in the eighteenth century, which Julia's ancestors frequented? Notwithstanding such a historical coincidence, 'St Dunstan's House' – 133–7 Fetter Lane, just off Fleet Street – is now prime real estate, converted into modern apartments where a one-bedroomed flat can be had for £1.1 million. The London office of the Dundee-based publisher D. C. Thomson is also located in Fetter Lane; just another coincidence that my friend, asked to recce the street for me, reported back.

In his first book, *Count Campello and Catholic Reform in Italy* (1891), Alexander is at pains to stress that many Italians who renounce Roman Catholicism remain Catholics: 'For just as the Italians have not thrown off religion whilst throwing off the papacy, so neither have they thrown off Catholicism. They have ceased to be Roman Catholics, but they remain Catholics. They are firmly attached to their ecclesiastical history and traditions, to their world-famed cathedrals. Their tastes lead them to desire artistic beauty in their churches, and attractive music in their services.' Alexander ventriloquises such beliefs: '"We do not want to change everything… Clear our National Church of all the evils that worldly ambition... has gathered into it. Bring our Church into harmony with our free constitution... Restore to us our Church as our forefathers knew it..." In short, there is widespread desire for a Reformed Italian Catholic Church' (Robertson, 1891, pp. 197–8).

Similarly, in *Fra Paolo Sarpi*, the friar is presented as a reformer on *Catholic* lines: 'So far as those seeking reform of the Church in Venice aimed to overthrow the temporal power of the Pope, strip the Church of ill-gotten wealth, exclusion from every sphere that touches the prerogatives of kings and governments and the civil rights and liberties of the subject and purging the Church of all Papal abuses and scandals, he fought the same battle. But so far as [they] aimed to set up Lutherans or Calvinists in Venice it's doubtful he was sympathetic.' Alexander shared Sarpi's contempt for the corrupt practice of selling 'indulgences' to absolve sin. But he recognised that insistence on faith alone without hope of absolution through confession might be too much for intelligent Italians of his day, as it was for many Venetians of Sarpi's day. Sarpi wished only for what intelligent Italians wish *today*, insists Alexander: 'a return to the simplicity and purity of the early Church... with the Bible and liturgy in the vulgar tongue, with confession and celibacy voluntary... the Bishop of Rome as bishop but not as infallible Pope' (Robertson, 1893, p. 97). Robert Kernohan does not share Alexander's optimism concerning what 'intelligent Catholics' wished for in his day, pointing out that such 'Old Catholics' made little headway in nineteenth-century Italy. Even their leader, Count Campello, 'returned to the Roman fold', whilst Ugo Janni, another leading figure in the reform movement, left the Catholic Church and 'moved to the Waldensians along with his small congregation in San Remo' (Kernohan, 2005, p. 107).

Nobel prize-winner Marilynne Robinson has emphasised the extraordinary shift of consciousness initiated by the Reformation: 'It rejected "salvation by works"... and anything... undertaken with the thought that it would mitigate sin in God's eyes. In place of all this it insisted on faith alone... grace alone... This was a very profound stirring in the deeps of Western civilization... to do with the structure of society and even of individual consciousness' (Robinson, 2015, p. 32).

By 1600 Italy had few Protestants to speak of, but in Venice there was open confrontation with the papacy whenever its own interests were at stake. The Venetian government tried to keep the Inquisition at arm's length, reluctant to persecute visiting Protestants who might be important for trade. It also resented – and was openly defiant against – the increasing centralisation of the Catholic Church that was emerging from the Council of Trent, which had opened in 1545. As a result, when the Pope placed Venice under an interdict in 1606, the city chose as its consultant Fra Paolo Sarpi, who 'showed alarming interest in Protestant theology' (MacCulloch, 2004, pp. 408–9). The Venetian authorities simply ignored the interdict and it was withdrawn.

The affair was of great interest to King James I of England, who much admired Sarpi's *History of the Council of Trent* for its depiction of the council as a lost opportunity for a Europe-wide Church reform. Henry Wotton, appointed Ambassador to Venice by James in 1610, reported back that there was fertile soil there for a new Protestant alliance. That this was a real historical possibility may seem strange today, says Mary McCarthy in her lively essay on Venice, but the republic was 'swarming with Protestant refugees', and, even more important to Wotton, many *clergy* were ready to make a break with Rome, including 'one of the clearest minds of the age, Paolo Sarpi' (McCarthy, 2006 [1956], p. 215). Wotton had received a warm reception in Venice because England was seen as a potential ally in any conflict with Spain or the Papal States. In addition to helping the Doge resist aggression from the Pope, Sir Henry also acted as an agent for Robert Cecil, King James's chief minister and spymaster, whose father William had overseen the beheading of Mary, Queen of Scots for her involvement in the Babington Plot to free her and return England to the Roman Catholic Church (Alford, 2012). Wotton was indeed 'just what the pope said he was,' says McCarthy: 'a secret agent of Protestantism' (McCarthy, 2006, p. 114). Alexander Robertson was fired by the same religious beliefs that fuelled the Cecils' immense power. He would have been delighted to know (if he did not already) that marriage to Julia joined him (however distantly) to a family that had been so instrumental in the formation of the English – and, later, British – state.

Alexander also shared Robert Cecil's taste for Italian Renaissance art. As well as spying for King James's chief minister in Venice, Wotton supplied him with paintings by Titian, Tintoretto, Veronese and Bellini (Parry, 2014). The collection of seventeenth-century Italian paintings which now hangs at Burghley House in Lincolnshire, the Cecils' family home, is regarded as one of the finest in private ownership, and includes the Burghley *Susanna and the Elders* by Artemisia Gentileschi. In the biblical story of embattled virtue, which was depicted several times by the artist (who was herself raped by her tutor), two elders leer over the naked Susanna. The Burghley House version was for a long time kept in a bedroom. Mary Beard comments tartly, 'I doubt anyone there saw it as an advert for sexual restraint' (Armitstead, 2020, p. 35).

The Protestant conspiracy in Venice failed. Fearful of Spanish arms, 'the expedient Venetian Republic compromised' (McCarthy, 2006, p. 226). Sarpi considered taking refuge in England but remained in Venice, coming close to martyrdom at the hands of the Pope's hired assassins. Returning home to his monastery one evening, he was beaten and left for dead with a dagger through his head. Although he recovered, fifteen stabs with a stiletto – one through his right temple and out between his nose and his cheek – left him scarred for life. All that now remains of Sarpi's monastery is an orphanage. Nearby in the Campo Santa Fosca stands the nondescript statue of the friar referred to above. Looking at it again, the now-enlightened travel writer checks 'whether or not the sculptor applied those wounds to the stern friar's face' (Nooteboom, 2020, p. 153). When I first came across the statue of Sarpi, also by accident, I didn't scrutinise its face for scars but I did wonder whether Alexander had had a hand in its creation. When it was erected in 1892 my great-great-uncle had been living in Venice for two years and his book on Sarpi was to be published the following year. I would guess that at the very least he helped raise funds for the project; an enterprise whose success, he claimed, 'was not fated to attend it, for Papal intrigues were as yet too strong' (Robertson, 1893, p. 173). Sarpi never left the Catholic Church despite its mistreatment of him, which continued even after his death, with his grave being emptied several times before finally ending up in the church of the island of San Michele; the island where Alexander and Julia are buried. Nowadays the friar is scarcely remembered and the kind of militant Protestantism that Alexander embodied is also a thing of the past.

Alexander's first two books about reform of the Catholic Church were followed by two tourism-related publications: a travel guide to the Dolomites, and an art-historical guide to Venice's St Mark's Cathedral, the latter greatly influenced by John Ruskin (1819–1900), a leading art critic and another of Alexander's great heroes. The travel guide, inspired by Alexander's love of the 'Scottish Alps', was made possible by the seasonal nature of his work as a minister, since gaps between tourist seasons gave him ample time to explore Italy. R. D. Kernohan believes that it was because

Venice was so far from his beloved Waldensian valleys that Alexander became a great promoter of the Dolomites, and 'wrote in its time the best English guide to the area' (Kernohan, 2005, p. 126).

The first edition of *Through the Dolomites from Venice to Toblach: A Practical, Historical and Descriptive Guide Book to the Scotland of Italy* (1896) is dedicated to Julia, 'My Fellow Traveller'. It is beautifully illustrated, covered in red vellum and embossed with gold writing, 'with forty-five Full-Page Illustrations and Map'. The preface spells out the guide's purpose: 'Many have lamented the lack of a modern book giving practical information in regard to travelling in that highland region, and also dealing with it historically and descriptively.' Alexander's book aims to fill the gap, combining detailed information about hotels, travel timetables, and distances between places, with descriptions and a selective history of each place. I'd have delighted in his entry on Feltre when I attended an Italian language course in the attractive town decades before reading the guide.

Describing walks in all directions from Belluno, including one to Bolzano, with its 'old houses having wooden outside stairs and balconies overgrown with green gourds, bright with yellow flowers and fruit', Alexander's writing takes on a lyrical, almost playful quality; the didactic, sermonising tone of his later religion-dominated texts having not yet overtaken his taste for vivid description. Thus we learn that at Vena d'Oro there is a 'large hydropathic Establishment; pension with baths 8 fr., omnibus to and from Belluno twice daily... Its enterprising owner told us how 25 years ago he bought the spring of water and 90 metres of land from the Austrian government for 24 lire (19s.2d.). He built a little house and began his Water Cure... added field to field and now owns 300,000 sq. metres of land and has accommodation for 150 people' (Robertson, 1896, p. 41). Again, travelling to Agordo 'by coach and horses', Alexander and Julia take a trip by gondola over a lake in the Cordevole Valley, having heard of submerged villages below: 'The peasants say that in winter when the lake is covered with ice... they can peer down into the roofless houses, and see the doors and broken staircases, and at one place a large palazzo, which was probably the Municipality of the place' (ibid., p. 47). And describing houses in the process of being built 'for working men' in Belluno, Alexander muses, 'I am sure it would have delighted Mr. Ruskin to see Gothic windows with cusps, all made of brick, being put in, such as are only to be found in a few very old houses in Venice' (ibid., p. 51).

Alexander uses every possible opportunity to mention his mentor, with whom he shared the book's publisher, George Allen. His travel guide has four pages of adverts for the critic's books, and his next publication, the art-historical study of St Mark's Cathedral, is explicitly inspired by Ruskin's *The Stones of Venice* (1853). Ruskin viewed Venice and its cathedral through a Protestant lens, interpreting the latter as a Book of Common Prayer open to all. Alexander adopts the same metaphor for his own book, even making this explicit in its title – *The Bible of St Mark: St Mark's Church, the Altar and Throne of Venice* – and bowing to the great man in his preface. Speaking to him on his final visit to Venice, Ruskin, Alexander writes, 'opened my eyes to the meaning of this great city of Venice, and of its unique building – the glorious and imperishable Bible of St Mark' (Robertson, 1898, p. ix).

Alexander's vocation as a minister, and his writings about Venice and its art, are all of a piece. We sense this from someone who heard him preach and wrote about him in his own book, *Beyond the Alps: The Story of the Scottish Church in Italy and Malta* (Mackinnon, 1937). Albert G. Mackinnon, a trainee minister when he first met Alexander in Venice, describes him thus: 'A rugged Scot, from Venice he thundered against the Vatican. In no other part of Italy could he have dared to be so outspoken but Venice had an independent spirit.' Mackinnon's vivid account of Alexander's preaching style encapsulates his debt to Ruskin:

As a student I shared his hospitality and listened to his lecture on St Mark's Church. I hear the words again: 'St Mark's Church is an open illustrated Book… One of the texts held up before those who ignorantly officiate at the altar in St Marks is one which condemns all the claims of the Church of Rome: "I am the Door, by Me if any man enters in he shall be saved." Almost equally striking… are the texts and mottoes carved by old Christian Venetians on the lintels of their doors… In Venice, modern Protestantism is shown to be ancient Catholicism, and the Church of Rome what the Syndic of Venice defined it: "A bundle of worldly ambitions and cupidities."' (ibid., pp. 130–3).

Ruskin's influence was at its height during the great period of self-education from the 1880s until the First World War, when many educationalists embraced his ideals. He taught at the Working Men's College in London and promoted the role of museums and art galleries in the formation of public 'taste' and for 'self-improvement'. For him the aim of education was to nurture 'souls of a good quality'. His belief in the inherent intellectual inequality between people, coupled with his sermonising style and moralistic stance, go against the grain nowadays. Yet his insistence on education as an end in itself and as integral to the development of character is as forceful as ever (Atwood, 2011).

Alexander adopted Ruskin's views on Venice just as enthusiastically as he adhered to his educational ideals. In contrast, Mary McCarthy is abrasively impatient with Ruskin's high-minded regard for old Venice as a pure Christian state: 'a sacred garden tended by humble artisans, supervised by upright doges, and defended by brave captains. There was no division in this mystic city; all classes worked together, oblivious of self in the radiance of a unifying belief... Poor Ruskin... always flying in the face of... recorded history, for the sake of a vision. At the very period which he sought to hold up as a model for later ages – the period of the Crusades – Venetian rapacity was the scandal of the Christian world' (McCarthy, 2006, pp. 189–90). Alexander's view of old Venice *is* Ruskin's Venice: the pure Christian state of all classes working together side by side, united by a singular belief; a view not a million miles away from the position Alexander would later adopt in relation to Mussolini's fascist state.

Ezra Pound (1885–1972), the modernist poet turned propagandist for fascism, was also influenced by Ruskin, says academic David Barnes, who believes Alexander played an intermediary role in this, citing Tony Tanner's *Venice Desired* (1992) to back up his claim. Tanner recounts Pound's visit to Venice in 1908, where, shortly after his arrival, Tanner says, the poet met a 'direct Ruskinian influence': the Reverend Alexander Robertson, minister of the Presbyterian Church, who had 'talked to Ruskin on his last visit to Venice in 1888 and published his own Ruskinian book in 1898' (Barnes, 2009).

Alexander certainly played an intermediary role in Pound's life in another respect: the publication of Pound's first poetry collection, *A Lume Spento* (*With Tapers Quenched*). Pound had first visited Venice in 1898 when he was just thirteen, two years before Ruskin's death. During his longer visit in 1908, thanks to money from home, he was able to pay a Venetian printer to produce 150 copies of the collection. Published letters reveal that Alexander assisted the young poet in practical ways during this period. Newly arrived in Venice in early May and writing home to reassure his parents, Pound refers to 'The Robertsons (Scotch Church Pastor) delightful' (de Rachewiltz et al., 2011, p. 110). His lodgings were close to the Robertsons' home, Ca' Struan, and he stresses his neighbours' helpfulness, writing to his father in June that 'Dr Robertson was very kind about playing post-boy with your letter... but as he is a man of sixty one can hardly have him making 2 Trips on every money order' (ibid., p. 116). Constantly in touch with his father about advertising and sales, Pound writes to him on the 26th May 1908, 'Keep the advertising of "A Lume Spento" in full motion – advance orders to be desired and no vulgarity of publicity need be shunned' (ibid., p. 110). In one letter he mentions that 'Dr Robertson called with your letter and we had a pleasant hour'; in another he writes, 'It is beginning to get hot and I shall be glad to move northwards when McIntosh check gets reported. The Robertsons had it deposited and I have drawn against it thru their kindness... the venture has about paid for itself... and 70 copies left to sell' (ibid., p. 122 and p. 125).

Other items of correspondence reveal that the connection between the poet and the Scottish minister endured. Several letters to Dorothy Shakespear, Pound's wife-to-be, make references to Alexander's sermons. For example, one Sunday in May 1913, Pound expresses mock surprise that 'Sandy preached this morning without damning the pope – either out of respect for Pio's health – or because the Scarlet woman of Babylon is to be furiously castigated this P.M.' (Alexander preached twice on Sundays: morning and afternoon.) In a letter to a friend the previous day Pound had mentioned that 'the Reverend Cavaliere Dottore Alexander Robertson' had given him a pamphlet on 'the evils of the Roman Catholic Church'. This was probably *The Great Harlot on the Seven Hills: The Enemy of Britain* by Albert W. Close (1910), which had an introduction written by Alexander (Pound and Litz, 1985, p. 220).

Pound's memories of Alexander remained undimmed even in his later years. The padre's anti-papal sermons are even recalled in one of Pound's *Pisan Cantos*, penned whilst he was imprisoned in Pisa for treason in the 1940s. In Canto 76, Pound remembers meeting Alexander at the church so many years before:

> *"Dawn't let 'em git you," burred the bearded Dottore*
> *when was the Scottch Kirrrk in Venice*

to warn one against Babylonian intrigue
and there have been since then
very high episcopal vagaries
where he lived
well, my window
looked out on the Squero where Ogni Santi
meets San Trovaso
things have ends and beginnings
(Pound, 1954, pp. 461–2)

Another literary work, Noel Stock's *The Life of Ezra Pound*, refers to the poet witnessing Alexander preach in Venice, 'warning his congregation about contamination by Rome which he was convinced was the Scarlet Woman of the Apocalypse and seemed to be saying that Italy was a land of Protestants suffering under Papal tyranny', because only Protestants could have built those beautiful buildings now in the process of destruction by the 'vandalism' of the Roman Catholic Church (Stock, 1970, p. 59).

Pound recalls Alexander's admiration for Paolo Sarpi in his *Guide to Kulchur*:

I remember the RRivrrinnd CCavallliere DDDottoRRRR
AlexaNNdeRRRRR RRobertson with a Scotch accent as tthickk as
three tweeds and a tartan. And evverry Sunday, under the shadow of
the old Campanile, and while the new was building, he poured out
his admiration of Paolo Sarrrrpi and told the unwary traveller how
the banditti were in pay of the ppppope.
(Pound, 1970 [1938], p. 259)

He also mentions the minister in a letter to Marianne Moore, dated the 1st February 1919, which is noted in Volume 2 of Carroll F. Terrell's *A Companion to the Cantos of Ezra Pound*:

I have seen Savonarola still swinging a crucifix
down from the Sala for the weekend of exhorting
the back-sliders of Venice;
and the Reverend Cavaliere Dottore Alessandro Robertson denouncing the

Babylonian woman
and the Rrroman releegion
with fervor...
(Terrell, 1984, Note 197 on Canto 76)

On reading Pound's affectionate depiction of Reverend Robertson with his thick Scottish brogue, a friend commented, 'I imagine him as a tougher version of I. M. Jolly!' Reverend I. M. Jolly was the creation of Scottish comedian Rikki Fulton, whose comedy special *It's a Jolly Life* and final, hilariously doom-laden *Last Call* television monologue were broadcast on New Year's Eve 1999. Reverend Jolly is still sorely missed by many Scots at Hogmanay for such utterings as 'Last week I officiated over a mixed marriage... he was from Glasgow; she was from Edinburgh.' I am grateful to my friend for offering me a new image of my great-great-uncle!

When I visited the graves of Alexander and Julia on San Michele, I spotted the grave of another poet, Joseph Brodsky, the Russian émigré and Nobel laureate, in the same section of the cemetery as Ezra Pound and my great-great-uncle and -aunt. I had not yet come across Brodsky's quirky book *Watermark: An Essay on Venice* (1992), in which one of his anecdotes tells of an evening spent in Venice with Olga Rudge, Pound's long-time concert pianist mistress. Susan Sontag, like Brodsky in town for the 1977 Biennale, had been invited to Rudge's home in the Salute district, where Rudge had lived with Pound during the last decade of his life when he was released from the mental asylum in his native America into which he had been committed for supporting Mussolini throughout the war. Sontag wanted a companion for her visit. In Brodsky's account, the pianist spent most of the evening denying that Pound was a fascist and an anti-Semite.

Pound's recollections of Alexander in the *Cantos* are warmly affectionate, if gently mocking, which cannot be said of Frederick Rolfe's characterisation of the minister in his semi-autobiographical novel *The Desire and Pursuit of the Whole*. First published in 1934, a year after Alexander's death and long after Rolfe's own death at the age of fifty-three, the novel's treatment of Alexander as a lying, scheming Protestant is unstinting – not surprising, perhaps, from the gay son of a fervently Protestant father, who converted to Catholicism in reaction against his strict Presbyterian upbringing. Rolfe was infatuated with Venice. A visit to the city in 1908, intended to last a month, continued until his death in 1913. The main subject of *The Desire and Pursuit of the Whole* is Venice itself. Wandering through the city in August during the festival of Marymas, Nicholas Crabbe, the novel's main character, treats himself to 'a regular debauch of religious observances that day, going from church to church between dawn and noon... [where] whole parishes could (and did) make communion simultaneously... He understood why polemical acatholic swashbucklers, like the lying prophet of Ca' Struan fought against fact, sinned against light, by alleging that Italy has lost Her faith – that, of her thirty millions, not more than two ever cross a church's threshold' (Rolfe, 2002 [1934], p. 296).

Alexander's prose when writing against the Catholic Church could reach equally hyperbolic heights. He produced a new book every few years. *Authority in Matters of Faith*, published in 1901, was followed in 1902 by *The Roman Catholic Church in Italy*, both books reiterating his deep distaste for the papacy and profound passion for the Protestant faith. A few years later, *Venetian Sermons Drawn from the History, Art and Customs of Venice* (1905) offers the clearest demonstration to date that Alexander's life as a writer, preacher and proselytiser was all of a piece. In the text (named *Venetian Discourses* in some editions), he returns to the themes of his earlier book on St Mark's Church: 'The more I know of the old Venetians... the more... I admire their perseverance, intelligence and wisdom, but also their justice and humanity, their healthy morality, and their manly piety... It was because her rulers and her people practised a lofty morality, the outcome of a vital religious faith, that she... gained... her proud pre-eminence among the nations... Venice... lends itself to... Biblical illustration' (Robertson, 1905, pp. vii–viii). A taste for metaphor permeates *Venetian Sermons*. Much is made of the shifting soil upon which Venice's palaces are built: '[W]e are called upon to have characters and lives polished after the similitude of a palace... it is natural to think of the nature of the soil of the heart on which they are to be raised. This, like the soil of Venice, is most unsuitable... there is an indwelling tendency towards that which is evil... as proclaimed in the Bible from Genesis to Revelation' (ibid., p. 6). 'But,' he continues, 'the old Venetians went... to the forests of the Dolomite mountains... and cut down trees of oak, beech and larch... whose wood is hard and enduring... Of these they formed piles... drove deep down out of sight... By this process... the whole soil of Venice has been changed, and rendered stable... And thus, too... with our poor human nature... we have to... go to the Bible, as the old Venetians went to the forests' (ibid., pp. 9–10). 'All the walls of palaces are built of brick... yet... have stood for centuries... because [built on] great foundations... [I]f Christian principle is the foundation stones and if we recognize... God's providence guiding us in our humble orbits and do the duties allotted to us in these spheres however lowly... because God has called upon us to do them, if we do them... in the name of the Lord Jesus Christ – then our lives will receive... a strength... that nothing can overthrow' (ibid., p. 20).

I have quoted Alexander at some length so as to convey the tone and cadences of his sermons. By now there is an almost compulsive repetitiveness to his rhetoric, going hand in hand with a message about being content with one's allotted station in life. *Venetian Sermons* was the last of his books to be published by George Allen (although his penultimate book would see a return to his old publisher, reincarnated as Allen & Unwin). His next book, published by Morgan & Scott Ltd, a London-based, predominantly Protestant publisher, is, as already mentioned, the most likely candidate for his banishment from Lady Layard's soirées. Its title says it all: *The Papal Conquest: Italy's Warning – "Wake Up, John Bull!"* In it Alexander's contempt is unrestrained: 'Roman Catholicism is thus... an engine of material, mental, and moral degradation' (Robertson, 1909, p. 186). Frederick Rolfe, recently arrived in Venice, is sure to have read the book.

After *The Papal Conquest* Alexander did not have another book published for sixteen years. The fallow period between 1909 and 1925 was difficult for him, spanning as it did the First World War and Julia's death in 1922. Despite Julia's pension and privileged background, money seems to have been a constant preoccupation for the couple. She, of course, gave much of hers away in the service of good causes. The earlier toing and froing between Alexander and his Church employers in Edinburgh about salary, security and expenses became a feature, too, in his dealings with his hitherto main publisher, George Allen. As the First World War approached and progressed, the couple's financial worries increased and sales of Alexander's books decreased. A marked change in Alexander's relationship with George Allen can be charted through the letters that passed between them during this period. These also testify to an astonishing level of book sales when Alexander's public profile was high and there was a large and enthusiastic audience for his work back home. In some of the correspondence, reproduced below, Alexander's injured pride is palpable and at times painful to witness. The hurt is easy to understand in light of the substantial profits that his books procured for George Allen over several years. The University of Reading's Allen & Unwin archive holds around twenty items of correspondence between Alexander and the publisher covering the period 1910–16 (MS 3282 Allen & Unwin First Series, FSC 28/177). It does not cover the period during which most of his books were published by George Allen – before, that is, the publisher changed its name. Most of the letters are about money. As the war approaches, matters worsen. There is pathos in one of the later letters in the series concerning the switch in name from 'George Allen & Co Ltd' to 'George Allen & Unwin'. On the 12th September 1914, Alexander writes:

Dear Mr Morgan,
I have seen lately some books published by 'Geo Allen and Unwin'. Is this the firm of George Allen and Co Ltd, reconstructed? If so, am I to understand that the business will go on as before at Rathbone Place? In your letter to me of April 17 you kindly said you would write to me later in regard to the amounts due to me for sales on my various books. May I expect a statement and remittance soon? Owing to the war and Moratorium in Italy, Church Work is ruined here as all travellers are temporarily in financial straits.

Alexander's uncertainty and sense of insecurity had been building for some time. Earlier correspondence shows that queries about accounts and 'new editions' of publications are going unanswered. A plaintive note enters: 'I am wondering if you get my letters, or if anything is wrong? You used to be so punctual in all business matters. I wish you would kindly write to me one way or another.' A few days later Alexander thanks Mr Allen for a payment of £25 14s 9d for the 1909 account. But all is not well: 'I shall write later about the Dolomites. Meantime I shall write to new hotelkeepers and ask for their advertisements to be inserted in the remaining 500 copies of the present edition.' No new edition of his travel guide to the Dolomites will be published after all, as he had hoped.

On the 2nd October 1914 Alexander again inquires about new editions of two of his other books: 'I have no new book quite ready, but I am anxious to bring out a 7th edition of my *Roman Catholic Church in Italy*. Six Editions of 2000 copies each (12000) were sold but the book has been out of print for some years now… Another book of mine is nearly exhausted, *The Papal*

Conquest or Wake Up, John Bull. The first edition consisted of 5000 copies and the published price was 6/. I was arranging with Mr Wm Allen for these books when the crash came. As all my other books have been issued by the Allen firm perhaps you might kindly consider these. It would be nice to have them altogether.'

Three weeks later, on the 24th October, still hopeful, Alexander writes from Ca' Struan, proposing amendments to a new edition of *The Papal Conquest* and to a seventh edition of *The Roman Catholic Church in Italy*. That his hopes are dashed is clear when, on the 3rd December, he writes, 'Dear Sirs, I have received your letter of Nov 23rd, and I am sorry that you do not see your way to re-issue my books, but, at the same time, although Protestant Societies wish them, the season may not be propitious.' Then, poignantly, a pained tone enters on the 14th June 1915 when Alexander writes from 'Villa Romana, Alassio, Province of Genoa, Italy':

> Dear Sirs,
>
> Many thanks for your kind letter of June 4th enclosing statement of a/c of my books, and cheque for £3.17.7… I am sorry that the demand for certain of my books has almost ceased. Of course it is an abnormal year, which may in part account for it. '*Sarpi*' sold rapidly at first (I mean the first two editions), and I never had any book so well reviewed, for a number of dailies had leading articles on it. I am here away from Venice or I would send you some… About '*Venetian Sermons*' they too are well reviewed. Many many ministers and others who have taken copies are delighted with the books…

On the 23rd August 1915, a postcard from 'Villino Romano, Alassio' acknowledges that Alexander's negotiations with the publisher are coming to an end:

> Dear Sirs,
>
> Your letter of June 25th arrived but I have had a rather prolonged illness and it has remained unanswered. I hope to be able to take a gross of copies of *Fra Paolo Sarpi* and *Venetian Sermons*, but as the price you quote is plus the cost of binding, would you kindly let me know what that cost would be? I suppose very little a sixpence or so! Kindly inform me at your convenience.

Finally, a handful of letters, written between February and June 1916, winds up affairs with the publisher. Alexander's vulnerability and wounded pride are manifest. He and Julia had decamped to the Italian Riviera resort of Alassio on the west coast of Liguria for the duration of the war years. On the 10th May 1916, writing from Villa dei Fiori, Alassio, Alexander's pride is plainly scorched, as he reiterates how popular his books once were, and how critically well received: 'I am sorry and surprised about "*Fra Paolo Sarpi*". It had an instant sale at first – 2 editions going off in a short time. At home I have a vol. of reviews of it, some of them leading articles in London papers. I must send you these cuttings.'

By the following month, he has accepted the situation, and on the 7th June 1916 makes arrangements for Allen & Unwin to send around 150 copies of *Venetian Sermons* to his nephew Tom in Glasgow: 'I enclose a cheque for £22.1.6. What about the cost of carriage? I am afraid it will be heavy. If you can share it with me, in the event of your not being able to pay it all, I shall be glad.' On the 13th June, the last letter in the bundle, Tom writes to notify the publisher that he will 'accept delivery of 156 copies of *Venetian Sermons* on 7th July or after'.

In his later years, following Julia's death, Alexander returns to his earlier praise of turn-of-the-century Italy and its anticlerical attitudes – 'the land where one enjoys the fullest religious liberty' – with his book about Mussolini's Italy (Robertson, 1929). This was preceded by an equally enthusiastic biography of Victor Emmanuel III (published, finally, by Allen & Unwin in 1925), which depicts the King as Italy's saviour for resisting the papacy and bringing Mussolini to power. It seems unlikely that the Order of the Crown of Italy, bestowed on Alexander by Emmanuel in 1930, was unconnected to his fulsome endorsement of both leaders in his writings.

'From time to time,' Alexander observes in his biography of Mussolini, 'I ask visitors their impressions of Italy. They answer me "Why, everything has changed for the better. The trains are punctual, hotel and shop-keepers polite and honest"' (Robertson, 1929, p. 175). Whilst for Alexander fascism inaugurated a religious revival, 'what impressed the hordes of visitors to Italy and made them sympathetic to it was an improved travel experience,' comments David Barnes, who includes in this observation the 'aesthetic whitewashing and authenticising of towns like San Gimignano and Arezzo' (Barnes, 2009, p. 40). Walter Benjamin described fascism as the 'introduction of aesthetics into political life' (Benjamin, 1935). A recent, more cynical commentator argues that the regime's lack of consistent ideas 'gave rise to… "an aesthetic overproduction – a surfeit of Fascist signs, images, slogans, books, and buildings"' to cover up this lack (Stonor Saunders, 2010, p. 177). It was the aesthetic draw of fascism that captivated Ezra Pound, whose *Guide to Kulchur* (1970 [1938]) praised fascist Italy for celebrating the Italian Renaissance and for recognising Venice as a city with a proud imperial past (Barnes, 2015). Alexander was himself attracted to fascism by Mussolini's evocation of a distant Italian past, seeing in it a spiritual and political challenge to modernity, and, like John Ruskin, drawing religious and moral lessons from the medieval city, viewed as an ideal Commonwealth.

R. J. B. Bosworth's biography of Mussolini (2002) and subsequent *Mussolini's Italy* (2005) paint a very different picture: 'From 1922 to 1943 [when King Emmanuel dismissed Mussolini] the Italian people fell under the domination of a vicious and retrograde tyranny [which] banned rival parties… killed from 2,000 to 3,000 of its political opponents… destroyed the free press, liquidated non-Fascist trade unions, infringed the rule of law, sponsored a secret police, tempted Italians to spy on, and inform against, each other and re-affirmed crudely patriarchal practices.' Bosworth continues, 'The Fascist dictatorship is often best described as a "propaganda state", one where nothing was what it was said to be and where everything that mattered lay in words. Along with spin – went a profound cynicism' (Bosworth, 2005, p. 6).

Alexander Robertson, for whom words also meant a great deal, became an outspoken supporter of Mussolini in the last decade of his life. Until recently, most critics have believed that Ezra Pound's fascism came late in his career; possibly in early 1933 when he first met Mussolini. It was a shock for me to learn that letters have come to light which cast doubt on this time frame, showing that as early as 1923 Pound wanted Mussolini to hire him as his director of cultural renovation. This means that Pound's support for Italian fascism may have started much earlier than is normally thought. If this is indeed the case, he might even have talked to Alexander about it – a disturbing thought in light of subsequent events and Pound's repellent political and anti-Semitic outlook. Like Pound, Alexander saw Mussolini as a defender of high culture and civilisation. His adulatory book about the dictator opens with a signed photograph bearing the inscription '*a Alegsander* [sic] *Robertson*', written in the Duce's feathery handwriting.

On the page opposite, Alexander's printed declaration reads, 'Dedicated to the memory of Donna Rosa Maltoni by the permission of her son S.E. Mussolini, Head of the Italian Government and *Duce dei Fascisti* who adored her while living, and who even now feels her influence and seeks to follow her wise and loving counsels in his daily life.'

The biography, initially published in the USA in 1928, is illustrated with photographs produced by the Istituto Luce, the cinematographic institute that was taken over by Mussolini's press office in 1925 and thenceforth run directly by the dictator. Every cinema in Italy was legally compelled to show newsreels produced by the institute, in which Mussolini was their main subject. Photography became a crucial means of humanising Mussolini's image, especially after the murder in 1924 of Giacomo Matteotti, the Venetian socialist politician who was openly critical of the dictator (Dikötter, 2019). Shortly before his murder, Matteotti wrote to the founder of the Italian Socialist Party urging more active resistance to the prevailing 'high-handed' fascist regime: '[E]verything it achieves propels it to new willful acts, to new abuses. That is its essence, its origin, its only strength' (letter to Filippo Turati, 6th April 1924, quoted in Scurati, 2021, p. 671).

At the opening of Parliament the following month, Matteotti delivered a long lecture detailing the fraud and intimidation that had led to the fascists' victory. Libyan War veteran Attilio Teruzzi, vice-president of the National Fascist Party, had to be restrained from attacking Matteotti after his lecture. Eleven days later, on the 10th June, Matteotti was beaten, kidnapped and stabbed to death by three men, his body left in a ditch outside Rome, where it lay until the 16th August, when a police dog started pawing at his shallow grave. The medical examiner found that 'the corpse... must have been forcefully compressed into the superficial pit that was too small... Two gold teeth... confirm that these are the remains of Deputy Matteotti' (Scurati, 2021, p. 737). Matteotti was thirty-nine when he met his grisly end. The day after the murder, Mussolini lied to Parliament: 'My hope is that Deputy Matteotti will soon be able to return to parliament.' Yet the victim's wallet and passport were already in a drawer in Mussolini's office, delivered that day from Amerigo Dumini, fascist leader of the violent abduction (ibid., p. 708). The murder seriously damaged the fascists' public image. Yet by the start of 1925 fascism was back in style, with Mussolini soon assuming full dictatorial powers (de Grazia, 2020).

There was no condemnation of Matteotti's murder from Alexander; not even a mention in the Scottish press. His biography of Mussolini, published just a few years later, is equally forgetful, actively promoting the Duce's project of image management by including in it several of the Luce photographs: fondling a lion cub, playing the violin, threshing wheat, saluting a crowd surrounded by his family, sitting on horseback with his son. The second edition of the biography was published in Britain in 1929, as Mussolini presided over a further savage war (the Second Italo–Senussi War) in the Italian colony of Libya during which, in the coastal region of Cyrenaica, chemical weapons and mass executions exterminated a quarter of the local population. A hundred thousand Bedouins were ousted and their land was given to Italian settlers: 'The horrors of the war were concealed from the public at home by an obedient press which hailed Mussolini for bringing Libya into the fold of civilization after centuries of barbarism' (Dikötter, 2019, p. 20). Alexander was part of that 'obedient press', his journalism totally silent about the war in Libya at the time. His revised 1929 British edition of *Mussolini and the New Italy* was equally mute, containing instead an enlarged chapter on 'Mussolini, the Reformer', concerning the dictator's dealings with the Pope.

He could not, of course, have known about Mussolini's later invasion of Ethiopia (also known as Abyssinia), when, in October 1935 (two years after Alexander's death), the dictator ordered hundreds of tonnes of mustard gas to be sprayed on combatants and civilians alike in the East African country. On the 5th May 1936 the Italians captured Addis Ababa, Emperor Haile Selassie fled into exile, and Victor Emmanuel III took the title of Emperor of Abyssinia: 'Ecstatic crowds in Rome learnt that Italy at last had its empire' (Moorehead, 2017, p. 318). As a harbinger of the horrors to come under Hitler and Stalin, an estimated 250,000 people were killed in the war in Ethiopia between 1935 and 1938 (Dikötter, 2019, p. 22). The League of Nations, having previously threatened to apply economic sanctions against Italy, backed down. As Susan Pedersen would later write in her prize-winning history of the League, 'From the mid-1930s… the successive horrors of Italy's Ethiopia campaign, the Spanish Civil War, and the Nazi regime's brutal anti-Semitism put the claim that Europe acted as the standard-bearer for civilization and progress – a claim on which the rhetoric of trusteeship had been based – under impossible strain' (Pedersen, 2017, p. 293).

Before such horrors, when Mussolini visited Venice in 1923, Alexander's wife had been dead for nearly a year; six months before Mussolini became Prime Minister. It would be a further decade before the Italian leader met Hitler for the first time, in Venice on the 14th June 1934, a year after Alexander's death and shortly after Hitler had come to power in Germany in January 1933. It would be several more years before Mussolini stressed Italians' Aryan origins when, in 1938, his 'Declaration on Race' prevented Jews from teaching in state schools, marrying or employing Aryans, serving in the military, owning more than a hundred hectares of property, or possessing telephones (Stonor Saunders, 2010, p. 288).

In fact many people admired Mussolini well into the mid 1930s, including Neville Chamberlain, Franklin D. Roosevelt and Winston Churchill, who praised him for being able to pull together a divided country and make the trains run on time. From the days of the First World War until he invaded Ethiopia in October 1935, Mussolini 'basked in the approval of the British' and there was virtually no mention of the Italian regime in the British Parliament (ibid., p. 169). What Mary Beard has described as the 'retrojection of ideas, desires, or fantasies into the past' seduced many observers, including the British historian Kenneth Scott, who wrote admiringly in 1932, 'Symbols of the past and its significance for modern Italy are everywhere in Italian life today... Perhaps... the Roman Empire never really died but goes on in the New Italy and its premier' (ibid., p. 177).

It can be forgotten that fascism was a Europe-wide phenomenon after the First World War, with street movements of fascists, often ex-servicemen, beating up opponents on the streets of France and Britain as well as Italy. Margaret MacMillan, stressing fascism's theatrical politics and seductive cult of violence, recently commented on BBC Radio 4, 'It was exciting to beat up the communists.' Bosworth's emphasis on fascism's enduring ideological power spotlights the fact that between the wars fascist Italy paved the first path towards the destruction of Marxism, socialism, communism and liberal democracy, 'mapping a short way to repress any followers of these ideologies who hoped to be the humanist heirs of... Enlightenment' (Bosworth, 2005, p. 10).

'Faith', so important for Alexander, was a key notion in fascism's lexicon, cropping up again and again in the rhetoric of the period. Mussolini's fascism was the first nationalist, totalitarian and populist movement to fully display the characteristics of a political religion. '"Fascism is a religious conception… a spiritual community… the very essence of the soul", is how Mussolini defined his movement' (Stephens, 2015, p. 311). Ezra Pound never abandoned his view of history as leading to a redemptive fascist epoch; nor, it seems, did Alexander, though at least he, unlike Pound, died before Mussolini's fateful meeting with Hitler. Yet he should have known better. Had Julia lived beyond 1922, the year Mussolini came to power, she might have tempered Alexander's infatuation. I cannot see her being susceptible to the Duce's posturing.

Ten

Conclusion: A Reckoning

Britain and the US need a full reckoning with the slavery, imperialism and racial capitalism that made some people in Britain and America uniquely wealthy and powerful and plunged the great majority of the world's population into a brutal struggle against scarcity and indignity.

(Pankaj Mishra, 2020)

When Alexander's great hero Fra Paolo Sarpi was seeking reform of the Roman Catholic Church, Christian expansion of both Reformation *and* Counter-Reformation types was yet to become embroiled in one of the greatest crimes in Western history: the slave trade, 'which good Christians would keep going for centuries because they heard the Bible say that slavery was God-given' (MacCulloch, 2016, p. 9). The Foster side of Julia's family was up to its neck in this greatest of crimes; a fact that clearly impacted on Julia in material ways and perhaps, too, in ways that instilled in her the need to make amends. When Alexander married for the second time, it was into a family whose social and economic progress was largely determined by this fact, and by the seizure of land at home and abroad at its heart. An exploration of this hinterland shifted the focus of my research away from just one man's life, and the more I learned, the more some of my own taken-for-granted assumptions were put under strain.

Well into my research into Julia's family background, immersed in questions around landownership in Britain and its colonies, I decided that I needed a better understanding of my own family background on my father's side. So, in late 2019, months after my discovery of the Foster family's Caribbean interests, I travelled by train and bus to the small town of Turriff near Aberdeen to find out more about my ancestors' lives as tenant farmers in north-east Scotland. I also visited Aberdeen University Library to examine Land Registry materials. It was there I discovered that my great-grandfather Alexander Cruickshank (1819–94) was anything but the poor, exploited crofter of my imaginings. The substantial red-sandstone house standing in its own grounds on the edge of town also told a different story.

Valuation rolls for 1875 and 1885 reveal that the 'family farm', Meikle Colp, with house attached, which came to Alexander Cruickshank in 1864 when he married Helen Morrison, was owned by Garden (not a misprint) Alexander Duff, the Laird of Hatton (1853–1933). My great-grandfather was a tenant farmer on land leased to him by the Laird, who lived in Hatton Castle on the Hatton estate in the parish of Monquhitter, which had belonged to the Duffs since 1729 (Tayler and Tayler, 1914). These Duffs, the 'Duffs of Hatton Castle', were related to the 'Duffs of Duff House', who included the Earls of Fife from whom Queen Victoria leased (and her husband later purchased) Balmoral Castle, which she rebuilt. Balmoral now belongs to Queen Elizabeth II, prompting Andy Wightman, Scotland's land reform champion, to remark, 'Private landownership in Scotland remains a small, inter-related and privileged club which is proud to have the Queen as a member' (Wightman, 2013, p. 152).

General Sir James Duff (1752–1839), the oldest, illegitimate son of the 2nd Earl of Fife and MP for Banffshire, James Duff (1729–1809), was knighted in 1779. He owned a sugar plantation and its 202 enslaved Africans in the Hanover parish of Jamaica, which adjoined Westmoreland parish, where the Foster Barhams' Mesopotamia estate was located (see 'General Sir James Duff', *Legacies of British Slave-Ownership* database). General Sir James was a great-uncle of David Cameron, who, in 2015 as British Prime Minister, made a speech to the Jamaican Parliament in which he made no apology for the colonial era. Instead, he recalled Britain's 'work to wipe slavery off the face of the planet' and urged both countries to 'move on from this painful legacy' (Renton, 2021, p. 316).

Despite his title, the general's father James Duff, 2nd Earl of Fife, was the largest landowner in north-east Scotland, which includes Moray, Banffshire and Aberdeenshire and is some distance from Fife. As Moray's major landowner, he was the first to begin granting long leases of land formerly occupied under joint tenancies to 'particular substantial and intelligent farmers'. This allowed them as sole tenants to reap the benefits of their efforts and to have greater control over what was done on the land. Other owners followed suit and by the 1800s single-tenant 'improved' farms were the norm on Duff's estates (Alston, 2021, p. 216). By the time my great-grandfather was a tenant farmer on land leased to him by the Laird of Hatton, the whole north-east of Scotland was a leasehold area in the 'total grip' of great landowners. By 1840 the major function of this landed property was to generate ground rent for the Laird (Carter, 1979, p. 25).

In the 1871 census, Alexander is described as the 'tenant occupier' of Meikle Colp Farm, employing three men and two boys, farming 148 arable acres and paying an annual rent of £161. The census lists the household as including seven servants (probably including the farmhands). Alexander had married Helen in 1864 when he was forty-five and she twenty-one. She had been her brother's housekeeper when he held the tenancy of Meikle Colp, which transferred to Alexander on marrying her. The 1875 valuation roll lists Alexander as the tenant occupier of Meikle Colp Farm, 'under lease of 19 years and less than 57 years'. By 1885 the farm's rent had risen to £169 2d (worth about £20,000 today); one of the highest rents of the Laird's twenty-five tenancies, since poor peasant crofts still formed the vast majority of holdings in north-east Scotland. Meikle Colp, which had grown to 160 acres by 1881, was thus atypical.

Employing wage labour and selling produce on the market, my great-grandfather, a 'farmer and grain manure agent' according to the census, was a 'capitalist farmer' according to Ian Carter: 'We may assume that any farm of 100 tilled acres or more would rely on hired labour and hence be worked on the capitalist mode of production' (Carter, 1979, p. 28). Representing one farmer in six in north-east Scotland in 1885, Alexander was one of those prosperous leasehold farmers described by Robert Brenner in another context as 'capitalist tenants who could afford to make capital investments' (Brenner, 1985, p. 49). Alexander's father, my great-great-grandfather Adam Cruickshank (1787–1874), leaseholder of the nearby 140-acre Mill Moss Farm, employing four labourers, would have fitted into the same category.

Now I understand why my mother, when angry with my father, would accuse him of belonging to 'the bloody landed aristocracy of the north'.

As if in endorsement of this appellation, two large portraits of my great-grandparents, Alexander Cruickshank (1819–94) and Helen Morrison (1842–1930), are lodged in Turriff Museum on the High Street. Photographs show Meikle Colp House as it was in the nineteenth century, solid and imposing, the family gathered in front, looking proud and prosperous. In one photograph, Alexander is absent, now dead; so too is Adam, my grandfather, off to Glasgow. An earlier photograph has them all: Alexander and Helen seated beside Adam, the other six sons and one daughter standing behind, all dressed in their finest. An impressive granite gravestone, placed in the church graveyard in memory of my great-great-grandparents Adam ('Farmer, Millmoss') and Isabella, marks the burial place of several family members.

In contrast, my maternal grandfather James Montgomery (Alexander Robertson's nephew) came from a long line of agricultural labourers in Midlothian. James's own grandfather Thomas (1818–90), one of eight labouring sons, was a ragged-school teacher who lived a peripatetic life, moving from Midlothian via Gibraltar to Liverpool, where James's father Alexander was born around 1846 and where a ragged school was set up in 1849. James's uncle Robert was born in Gibraltar in 1852 during a period when there was a strong Scottish Presbyterian presence on the island. His aunt Isabella and uncle John were born in 1856 and 1859 in Campbelltown, where there was a ragged school.

From 1859 until 1864 Thomas was master of the Ragged and Industrial School, Rothesay, Isle of Bute, as noted in a typewritten pamphlet compiled on the centenary of the 1872 Education (Scotland) Act by one A. M. Orr, who mistakenly names him 'William Montgomery' (Orr, 1972). Thomas's only sister Agnes worked alongside him as the school's matron. The 1871 census finds Thomas, an 'English teacher', living in the St Cuthbert district of Edinburgh with his wife Isabella, son Alexander (aged twenty-five and a 'clothier salesman') and daughter Isabella (a fifteen-year-old 'Bazzar Cashgirl'). Thomas died in the poorhouse of Inveresk and Musselburgh. His death certificate records him as a 'Pauper, formerly Schoolmaster, married to Isabella Crozier'.

The ragged-school movement, founded in 1818 by a Portsmouth cobbler to give free education to the poorest working-class children, grew between 1844 (with the Ragged School Union's establishment) and 1870 (with the Education Act of England and Wales). The first ragged school in Edinburgh, founded in 1847, provided poor children with meals and clothes as well as instruction in reading, writing, arithmetic, habits of 'industry', and Bible study. Many teachers were volunteers and they came from across class divides, including agricultural labourers like Thomas. Seen by the movement's founders as part of an evangelical 'awakening', the role of the ragged-school teacher was regarded as a 'calling' akin to that of the ministry. This meant that both volunteer and paid teachers were accorded the same status as clergy, mainstream teachers and overseas missionaries (Mair, 2016, p. 187). Perhaps Alexander was inspired by his uncle Thomas's life.

I recently had a light-bulb moment related to my earlier revelation concerning the significance of Robert Cecil's name in my family tree. One weekend in March 2020 I attended a talk on landownership by the writer and campaigner Guy Shrubsole at the Keswick's Words by the Water Literature Festival. The coronavirus outbreak and first lockdown were on the horizon, though none of us in the packed auditorium knew anything about that, and the idea of a 'super-spreader' event had not yet been spun. The talk was about landownership in England, and focused on showing that the hoarding and passing on of land by a small elite of powerful families is not a thing of the past but still impacts on the present in crucial ways. At the end of the talk I bought Shrubsole's book and spoke to him. Only then did it dawn on me that 'the richest MP in the British Parliament', the author's local landowning constituency MP Richard Benyon, to whom he had referred in his talk, was a direct descendant of Robert Cecil, 1st Earl of Salisbury.

Before pursuing this for what it reveals about one family's enduring political influence, I want to sketch in the wider context of landownership in the UK, the significance of which can be missed because it is routinely underestimated and insufficiently understood, even in much orthodox economic thinking: land as a topic has all but disappeared from most economics textbooks, probably because to understand land requires a cross-disciplinary approach, involving history, economics, geography, sociology and law (Ryan-Collins et al., 2017, p. 2).

It is generally recognised that the UK has become an increasingly finance-dominated economy. What is less often acknowledged is that it has also become an increasingly real estate-/rent-dominated economy, fed by the large-scale privatisation of land and property. This huge privatisation project includes the sale of social housing through the Right to Buy scheme. Launched in 1979 by Margaret Thatcher and enshrined in law in 1980, the scheme allowed council-house tenants to buy their house below the market rate (effectively receiving a bonus of 30–50% of the value of their property), without public stock replenishment. The most significant long-term result of the policy was not to lift owner-occupancy rates as Thatcher intended; it was to increase massively the cost of renting. This is, at least, Brett Christophers' conclusion in *The New Enclosure: The Appropriation of Public Land in Neoliberal Britain* (2018). Professor of social and economic geography at the University of Uppsala, Sweden, Christophers reveals the extent of land privatisation in Britain since 1979. He judges that around five million acres of land, worth £400 billion, were sold off by the public sector during the past four decades. He calls this a new 'enclosure', comparable in scale to the private capture of the public commons in previous centuries, when rural families were dispossessed of open land for grazing animals and growing food. The 'new enclosure' involves the hoarding of land by private owners who keep the supply of houses below the level of demand so as to sustain high prices. Christophers quotes Adam Smith (1723–90): 'As soon as the land of any country has all become private property, the landlords… love to reap where they never sowed' (Christophers, 2018, p. 305).

Smith's prescience about what economists would later dub rentier capitalism is clear from a report written more than two centuries after his death: in 2006 the Office for National Statistics (ONS) reported to government on the industries that had contributed most to the UK's economic growth since the beginning of the 1990s. In a withering article in the *Guardian* newspaper on 26th August 2006, money editor Patrick Collinson summed up the report's findings: 'So what has helped our economy grow so wondrously? The answer is the rise of the landlord class… In modern Britain… putting up the rent is somehow regarded as economic growth. The US dominates in technology, Germany makes millions of cars, Japan still makes consumer electronics. Britain produces buy-to-let landlords'.

In his more recent book, *Rentier Capitalism* (2020), Christophers construes rentier capitalism as an economic order organised around income-generating assets, in which economic life is dominated by rentiers, and is fundamentally orientated to 'having' rather than 'doing'. The likes of Serco, the private company to which the UK government contracted out its track-and-trace system early on in the coronavirus pandemic, are not experts in *doing* anything; they are experts in securing government contracts – basically, monopolies on the delivery of public goods, which provide guaranteed income streams (rent) for years to come. These contracts are the assets on which their shareholder value is based. The recent PPE debacle is typical: during the pandemic, Boris Johnson's Conservative administration handed a £252 million contract for personal protective equipment (PPE) – of which fifty million face masks proved unusable – to a company with no experience in the provision of such items, but which was owned by an adviser to the then International Trade Secretary Liz Truss. Rentier capitalism has dominated the UK economy since the 1970s, says Christophers. In the PPE case, the asset is the £252 million contract. In the 1980s and 1990s, when Margaret Thatcher sparked off the privatisation bonanza, the income-generating assets created ranged from former council houses to electricity, telephones and gas.

The council house sell-off has had especially far-reaching consequences. Figures released by the ONS in 2020 reveal that homeownership in Britain has collapsed among adults aged between thirty-five and forty-five. The ONS links this to the Right to Buy policy, the boom in homeownership among older Britons, and the slump in social housing (Partington, 2020). Thatcher aimed to remove the state from the housing sector, not slowly, through more private building, but quickly, by selling off existing council housing cheaply. Those who could afford a mortgage became homeowners at the expense of their fellow citizens who, unable to buy as housing stocks shrank, were effectively excluded from the housing market. This was not a victory for 'the market', but of an ideology, says Susan Pedersen. 'It was a state construct, the result of financial decisions taken at the top, and today's housing crisis, and the social inequalities it so perfectly expresses, are its legacy' (Pedersen, 2020, p. 38). Today, nearly one in five households in Britain relies on housing benefit, whilst the beneficiaries of the current rentier economy include a growing number of ordinary homeowners who have used the wealth in their homes to acquire multiple properties to let out to those excluded from ownership (Ryan-Collins et al., 2017, pp. 106–7). Since the interwar years, it was accepted by all sides that the state had an obligation to facilitate housebuilding for both owners and renters. As long as this was so, property ownership might be an aspiration but would not be a condition of full citizenship. This is where we see the radicalism of

Thatcher's council-house sales, says Pedersen. Besides shifting the balance between owners and renters, the policy marked a decisive break with the commitment to housing as a core social entitlement.

As with selling off council houses, so too with selling off public land. 'Thatcher's genius… was to numb potential opposition to land privatization by making millions of people… its direct individual beneficiaries… The fundamental lie[5] was that more widely distributed ownership would do anything more than scratch the surface of entrenched patterns of inequality, in either financial or property wealth. It has not' (Christophers, 2018, p. 328). And whereas increasing gas and electricity bills and train fares are visible for all to see, most people in Britain are not aware that public land *has* been privatised, despite the massive sell-off post 1970s.

Christophers dubs this sell-off the 'new enclosure', so as to compare and contrast it with the original enclosure project, which involved the extinction of common rights to open fields and wastelands. It was these rights rather than the land's ownership per se that were privatised; a process that began at the start of the seventeenth century, became entrenched by the mid eighteenth, and only slowed down in the latter part of the nineteenth. The impact of enclosure was immense and highly visible in its effects, displacing millions of commoners, often violently, as in the Highland Clearances in Scotland.

Scottish historians have written about a revolution in landownership in the west Highlands and Islands of Scotland in the first half of the nineteenth century; a revolution that coincided with the period when the Highland Clearances reached their peak (from approximately 1810 to 1860) and many thousands were evicted from their homes. This period saw the 'rapid penetration of a new breed of proprietors from outside the region,' says Tom Devine; a 'new elite' fuelled by the area's growing romantic attraction for wealthy Victorians. Recent research qualifies Devine's assertions to an extent. By revealing the degree to which slave-based profits from the Caribbean provided much of the capital that powered this land revolution, the research shows that a substantial minority of the 'new' elite was not new but had existing connections with the area.

A recent discussion paper on land reform in Scotland examines the evidence. Devine suggests that the number of estate sales in the west

5   As with the privatisation of British Telecom and British Gas.

Highlands and Islands doubled in the 1830s, when the market for land in other parts of Britain diminished (Devine, 2006). The authors of the recent paper point out that many of these sales occurred in the decade following 1834, when the capital paid out to Caribbean slave owners, consequent upon slavery compensation legislation being passed by the government, began to enter the British economy (MacKinnon and Mackillop, 2020, p. 5). In addition to the new elite identified by Devine, a significant number of the slavery-enriched landowners in the west Highlands and Islands were inheritors of traditional family land who *married into* families who had benefited from slavery-derived wealth. Combining the land owned by such traditional landowning families with acquisitions by the new elite, researchers estimate that nearly two million acres of the west Highlands and Islands – that is, over half the acreage – has been owned by families that have benefited significantly from slavery (ibid., p. 10). Moreover, by paying compensation money to end slave ownership, the British government altered the nature of the slave owners' capital into a respectable 'public' grant, thereby turning what had by then come to be seen as an immoral form of wealth into a respectable form of capital (ibid., p. 12). The effect of this was to disguise the original link with slavery.

Slavery wealth obtained through marriage enabled traditional landholding families to keep their estates when many of their peers had to sell up. This was true of some of the largest and most infamous Highland elites. William Sutherland, the 18th Earl of Sutherland, married into a family with slavery-derived wealth when he married Mary Maxwell, daughter of William Maxwell of Preston, a Jamaica plantation owner who had left her £5,000 on his death. When their daughter Elizabeth's right to the title of Countess of Sutherland was challenged by other family members, she won the case – assisted, no doubt, by this inheritance. Elizabeth went on to marry George Granville Leveson-Gower, Marquess of Stafford, who thus became the 1st Duke of Sutherland. (I referred to him earlier in connection with Joseph Foster Barham II's marriage to Lady Caroline Tufton.) As owners of much of Sutherland, the Duke and Duchess evicted thousands from their homes in the early nineteenth century.

Whilst the processes connecting such landowners to slavery can be convoluted (as in this case), they illustrate a 'crucial historic phenomenon by which land in the Highlands – and Scotland more generally – has been used to alter the form and respectability of capital. Profits from exploitative, high-return ventures in the international economy can be given a makeover and made culturally respectable, non-threatening, and even "traditional" through being embedded in land ownership' (ibid., p. 14). Such a process can be accurately described as a form of money laundering.

Clearance was part of a wider process of land commodification in which villages with intricate land-management systems were virtually eliminated by landlords who, in order to exploit the marketable commodities of their estates, generally replaced them with single-occupier sheep farms or crofting townships. I have already touched on this process in north-east Scotland with reference to my paternal family, who as tenant farmers generated ground rent for the landowner (see also Alexander, 1992). In 1819 and 1820 alone, the Duke and Duchess of Sutherland cleared some 5,600 people from their land in the west Highlands and Islands (Richards, 2013; Alston, 2021).

The legacies of slavery in transforming the west Highlands and Islands have been profound and enduring. Slave profits were based on massive resource and labour exploitation. Those who secured such wealth tended to see land in similar terms: 'Landed estates were simply an extension of their capital and had to be productive' (MacKinnon and Mackillop, 2020, p. 20). Besides this economic reckoning, land in the Highlands came to be seen as a kind of trophy purchase, part of a new image of the Highlands as a sporting playground. Hundreds of thousands of acres were turned into deer forests, 'ecologically impoverished artificial wildernesses into which privileged elites inserted themselves each summer to kill for sport… [in] stark contrast to the mixed arable and pastoral economies and socially complex communities they replaced' (ibid., p. 21). David Alston has recently posited that there was a 'common mentality of control linking estate management in Scotland and plantation management in the Caribbean. There was, however, no similarity between the treatment of Highland tenants and the brutality of slavery' (Alston, 2021, p. 229). Control of land, wildlife and populations created the impression not of a 'new' imperial elite but of respectable owners and families, unthreatening to the British and Scottish establishments. New wealth could appear as old wealth. The fact that only now is the link between land in the Highlands and Britain's enslavement economies becoming clear 'reveals how successful this "disguising" strategy has been… Capital derived from the enslavement of human beings sustained large-scale, monopoly forms of landownership across the west Highlands and Islands… [embedding] short-term, extraction-based estate economies that were volatile, one dimensional and susceptible to wider external market forces… a pattern that is still… recognisable today' (MacKinnon and Mackillop, 2020, pp. 22–3).

Throughout Britain, enclosure involved the forced consolidation of peasant smallholdings into large farms. As Robert Brenner explains, 'With the peasants' failure to establish essentially freehold control over the land [which they did in France], the landlords were able to engross, consolidate and enclose, to create large farms and to lease them to capitalist tenants who could afford to make capital investments' (Brenner, 1985, p. 49). By the end of the seventeenth century, 'English [sic] landlords controlled an overwhelming proportion of the cultivable land… and capitalist class relations were developing as nowhere else' (ibid., pp. 48–9). Stripped of their rights to the land that sustained them, Britain's dispossessed commoners and peasants were now 'free' to sell their labour to rural gentry and capitalist tenant farmers like my great-grandfather, as well as to the emergent industrial-capitalist class in the growing cities.

Nowadays, owning land, especially in a valuable location, guarantees the owner at least a steady income, from either leasing it out for farming, or building on it and charging tenants rent. The reason is simple: 'Buy land,' said Mark Twain; 'they're not making it anymore'. Renting out land requires little effort, as John Maynard Keynes noted. The owner can obtain rent simply because land is scarce. These references come from Guy Shrubsole's blistering 2019 polemic *Who Owns England?* The book's premise is that land and who owns it lies at the heart of the housing crisis in Britain. It is not bricks and mortar that have suddenly become incredibly expensive. It is the value of the land itself that has gone through the roof. According to the ONS, UK land values have increased *fivefold* since 1995.

This vast increase in the value of land, much of it still held by aristocratic rentiers, is driving a housing crisis in Britain which is at root a land-hoarding crisis, says Shrubsole, who draws on Christophers' analysis in *The New Enclosure* (2018). 'Land hoarding' is the practice of holding back land from development until its price increases – 'a practice that is not the prerogative of a few speculative companies but something *all* landowners are liable to do' (Shrubsole, 2019, p. 202). A case in point is Richard Desmond, former owner of Express Newspapers and Channel 5 television, and founder of a publishing group (now property developers) which published 'adult' titles such as the British edition of *Penthouse* and

Asian Babes. The *Sunday Times* Rich List in 2019 calculated Desmond's net worth as £2.6 billion. A well-honed political lobbyist, Desmond knows that nowadays there is more profit to be had in owning a vacant site with planning permission for hundreds of flats than in owning a newspaper. In 2020 Robert Jenrick, Secretary of State for Housing, Communities and Local Government, accepted that his rushed approval of a £1 billion luxury housing development on the long-unoccupied site of Desmond's defunct printing press in London's Docklands had been 'unlawful by reason of apparent bias'. Desmond made a donation to the Conservative Party after approval was given. Jenrick's attempt to overturn Tower Hamlets Council's rejection of the scheme was timed to save the tycoon from paying a £40 million levy under a new community infrastructure scheme that was about to be introduced by the council. Despite his approval being ultimately ruled unlawful, the Secretary of State kept his job.

Shrubsole's book begins with the deceptively mild observation, 'It's often very difficult to find out who owns land in England', and proceeds to tease out why this is the case. Some basic facts are fairly clear, showing that little has changed in the past millennium: the aristocracy and landed gentry still own at least 30% of England, and since 17% of land is not even registered, this is probably an underestimation. Scotland continues to have the most concentrated pattern of landownership in the developed world, with fewer than five hundred people owning 50% of its privately owned land and most of the country still dominated by large estates, often owned by the same families for centuries (Wightman, 2013).

Very late on in my research I uncovered a connection between the Fosters in Jamaica and the powerful landowning Campbells of Argyll. Margaret Foster (1715–86), Julia Robertson's 'great grandaunt', married Colin Campbell FRS (c. 1706–52) in Jamaica when she reached eighteen – the age at which she came into her £4,000 inheritance, as specified in her father Colonel John Foster's will. Colin's father, Colonel John Campbell of Inveraray in Argyll (1673–1740), a nephew of the Duke of Argyll, was the first of the Campbell clan to settle in Jamaica, having survived the failed Darien expedition of 1696 to start a Scottish colony in Panama. Colin, like Margaret, was born in Jamaica and sent to Europe for his education, where he matriculated in 1720 at Glasgow University, and then at Leiden. Archibald Campbell (1682–1761), Earl of Islay, who became the 3rd Duke of Argyll when his brother John died without a legitimate heir, was in charge of Colin's education. The Earl also assisted Colin's election to the Royal Society in 1730 when the Astronomer Royal Edmond Halley proposed him. Archibald's namesake, the 1st Duke of Argyll, organised the massacre of the MacDonalds at Glencoe in 1692. On his father's death in 1740, Colin Campbell FRS inherited Black River estate in St Elizabeth parish with its 240 male and 220 female slaves, along with other properties in Hanover and Westmoreland parishes. After his own death in 1752, by then resident in London's Hanover Square, he is listed in UCL's *Legacies of British Slave-Ownership* database as owning 3,513 acres in Hanover, sixty in Westmoreland and 7,720 in St Elizabeth. I only learned of the Foster family's connection to the Campbells of Argyll when I happened upon 'The Jamaican Observatories of Colin Campbell FRS and Alexander Macfarlane FRS' by D. J. Bryden, assistant keeper of the Royal Scottish Museum in Edinburgh; a discovery that unfortunately post-dated my construction of the family trees that appear in this book (Bryden, 1970). When Colin returned to Jamaica in 1731, he brought with him the astronomical instruments that he later sold to Macfarlane, who in turn bequeathed them to their alma mater, Glasgow University.

In 2015 the current Duke of Argyll, whose predecessor oversaw the young Colin Campbell's education and career, was the recipient of farm subsidies worth £120,097. The family seat, Inveraray Castle beside Loch Fyne, lies within an estate of around seventy thousand acres, having shrunk from the 175,114 acres owned by the Duke in 1873 (Shrubsole, 2019, p. 307). The landed aristocracy's continuing influence is still highly visible in the vast amount of countryside given over to grouse moors, propped up by publicly funded farm subsidies. Less apparent is the fact that some members of the aristocracy make most of their money from their urban estates. Indeed, where aristocratic estates have lost land, in many cases they have made up for this in soaring property prices, with the most lucrative rental income going to aristocrats who own acreage in central London. At the other end of the scale, for many people, owning a house is a distant dream. Public-sector housebuilding had virtually ceased by the mid 1990s, and while in 1980 an average home cost £25,000, by 2008, the year of the financial crash, the cost of an average home was £175,000. Cheap credit dried up, and in 2013 there was the lowest level of housebuilding in the UK since the 1920s. Meanwhile, landowners have successfully lobbied to protect their privileges. Side by side with their huge, unearned benefits through tax concessions and increased land values, affordable housing, once seen as a right of citizenship, has gone by the wayside and millions of people are stuck in pricey rental properties at the mercy of private landlords.

There is a striking table in *Who Owns England?* It lists the land owned by Britain's twenty-four non-royal Dukes and the farm subsidies they receive, totalling £8 million annually. The Duke of Devonshire, who owned seventy-three thousand acres of land in 2001, received £768,623 in farm subsidies in 2015. £218,856 of this was a 'single area payment' for the area of land being farmed – hence, essentially, a subsidy for landownership. The corresponding figures for the Duke of Bedford were £543,233 and £431,163 respectively (ibid., pp. 306–7). The Duke of Bedford's landed estate, Woburn Estate Company Ltd, one of the top one hundred landowning companies in England and Wales, owned 21,474 acres in 2015 (ibid., p. 299). Originally the monastic land of Woburn Abbey, the estate was given to the Russells (later Dukes of Bedford) by Henry VIII in the sixteenth century.

The Dukes of Devonshire and Bedford are in my family tree (as, I now know, are the Dukes of Argyll). They are in it for the same reason that Robert Cecil, Earl of Salisbury, and other members of the Cecil family and related dynasties such as the Villiers are there: intermarriage between the aristocracy and a small group of exceedingly wealthy Caribbean plantation owners whose wealth, accumulated over two centuries from slavery, helped secure the landed aristocracy's continued existence as a powerful class, through marriage into it (see Appendix, Tables 1, 3 and 5). Just as there is scant public awareness of the tax concessions and subsidies made to this landowning elite, so too is there little knowledge of who owns what land.

Shrubsole explains that the figures quoted in his table of the top one hundred landowning companies came from a Land Registry spreadsheet which was accidentally released in response to an FOI request in May 2015. 'All subsequent attempts to get updated figures have been rejected by the Land Registry' (Shrubsole, 2018, p. 298). In the absence of up-to-date figures, Shrubsole estimates that the aristocracy and gentry still owns at least 30% of England; the largest single landowning category. Limited companies and limited liability partnerships (registered in the UK or overseas/offshore) form the next largest group at 18%, followed by the public sector, the Crown, the Church and conservation charities, taken together at 12.4%. Homeowners' share amounts to just 5% of land (ibid., p. 265). The figures are staggering: less than 1% of the population owns 50% of England.

The issue does not just concern farmland. As already indicated, in central London vast swathes of prime real estate lie in the hands of a few 'great estates', and in some cases have done so for centuries. Retention of the freehold ownership of their land and properties is key to the wealth of London's aristocratic estates. Tenants 'buy' their properties on long leases; so the landlord keeps ultimate control. I referred earlier to the Howard de Walden Estate in Marylebone as just one example of the benefits some families still reap from inherited wealth based on slaveholding in the Caribbean and now invested in parts of London with sky-high property and rental values. The estate's current head, Mary Czernin, the 10th Baroness Howard de Walden, worth an estimated £3.73 billion, is a direct descendant of Charles Rose Ellis, Lord Seaford, the Jamaican slaveholder and leader of the West India Interest who loomed large in Chapter 5 of this book. Far from being consigned to the dustbin of history as many think, the resilience of the British aristocracy is one of the great success stories of recent history, observes Shrubsole.

Moreover, whilst defenders of free markets regard such markets as means for democratising wealth, 'in the case of land, it appears that the old landed aristocracy is simply being joined and partly supplanted by a new plutocracy', aided and abetted by the state in the form of tax breaks and subsidies (ibid., p. 135). One such new entrant to the 1% is Sir James Dyson, inventor of the bagless vacuum cleaner. A Brexiteer and Conservative Party supporter, in recent years he has been buying up thirty-three thousand acres of farmland, in what some observers see as a move to avoid tax. Agricultural land is exempt from inheritance tax, and in 2016 Dyson's 'farms' earned him £1.6 million in farm subsidies. Paul Dacre, the former *Daily Mail* editor, is another influential Brexiteer and beneficiary of generous EU handouts for his farmland in Kent and grouse moor in Scotland. The amount of land now owned by 'new money' – industrialists, oligarchs and city bankers – is estimated to be around 17%, compared with the 30% still owned by old money, i.e. gentry and aristocracy. Such estimates are based on work done by investigative journalists and activists like Guy Shrubsole because of the persisting official secrecy around landownership. In their 2006 BBC documentary *Whose Britain Is It Anyway?*, Dan and Peter Snow reached the same conclusion as Shrubsole: that the aristocracy and old landed families still possess around a third of the UK. Since the Land Registry is required to release data on corporate and commercial landowners, we know who owns about a third of England and Wales. Refusal to reveal who owns the rest means that the wealthy aristocrats and businesspeople who are owners of land, some registered through companies in offshore tax havens, remain largely hidden from view.

Conquest, enclosure and colonialism were important means by which the aristocracy acquired its lands. Inheritance laws are the means by which it retains them. Crucial here is male primogeniture, the custom whereby everything has to be inherited by the eldest son in order to maintain the estate intact. Male primogeniture is still the rule in the English aristocracy. But equally important for the latter's continuation as a select elite is the system of hereditary titles. Currently, there are eight hundred hereditary peers created by the Crown without recourse to Parliament: Dukes, Marquesses, Earls, Viscounts and Barons, in descending order. The present Marquess of Salisbury is one of thirty-four Marquesses. He owes his hereditary title to Elizabeth I and James I for raising his ancestors William and Robert Cecil to the peerage, without having to raise a finger himself.

The richest MP in the British Parliament (at least, until November 2019, when he left the Commons) and biggest landowner in the author's West Berkshire constituency is, as already mentioned, Richard Benyon, inheritor of the twelve-thousand-acre Englefield Estate. He also owns an eight-thousand-acre grouse moor in Scotland. Shrubsole's book includes an account of how Benyon attained his wealth. The Englefield Estate grew to be large and wealthy through enclosure. Its deer park was created two hundred years ago by displacing a village, and its woodland, called 'Benyon's Enclosure', denotes commons that were enclosed by the MP's great-great-grandfather, Conservative Prime Minister Robert Gascoyne-Cecil, 3rd Marquess of Salisbury (1830–1903). The palatial Englefield House has been in Benyon's family since the eighteenth century. Sir Robert, who also served as Secretary of State for India, inherited the Scottish island of Rum (sometimes spelled Rhum). Robert's father, another Tory politician, James Gascoyne-Cecil, 2nd Marquess of Salisbury (1791–1868), bought the island in 1845 and displaced a whole community of crofters to make it an estate for country sports. Viewed from the perspective of an islander from another Scottish island, this was bizarre. In 1950 the mother of a friend of mine arrived on Rum from Orkney to take up a teaching job. By then the island was owned by the trustees of Sir George Bullough, a textile tycoon from Lancashire whose father had bought Rum as his summer residence and shooting estate. Irene Robertson, as she was then, wrote to her soon-to-be husband, 'You know, Rhum is a fraud. It's not really an island like I mean when I say I like islands. It is first and foremost an estate. The people are not islanders, they're estate employees... I read that 200 years ago [the crofters] were evicted to make room for a deer forest... It still remains that, and nobody is allowed on the island without permission of Her Ladyship.'

Shrubsole lists the sources of Benyon's wealth. One tranche is from the East India Company, another from property owned through his Englefield Estate Trust Corporation, and a third derives from farming: in 2017 Benyon received £278,000 in farm subsidies. Even more important than Benyon's wealth per se is the example he provides of the continuing political power and influence of landowners in the UK, especially members of the landed aristocracy. The Englefield Estate Trust Corporation is among the top one hundred landowning companies in England and Wales (12,168 acres), closely followed by another Cecil family company, the Burghley House Preservation Trust, which administers the estate of the Marquess of Exeter in Lincolnshire (9,894 acres).

Another member of the Cecil family, the 7th Marquess of Salisbury, Robert Gascoyne-Cecil, Conservative Leader of the House of Lords in the 1990s, was an early user of tax havens, setting up investment firms in Jersey in the 1970s to register through them his ten-thousand-acre estates at Hatfield and Cranborne. Tax havens were developed by Britain in the 1960s and 1970s specifically to provide secretive, lightly taxed and lightly regulated offshore boltholes for money. Their use is now commonplace among Britain's billionaires. The Marquess was simply following tradition as a member of a family that has been at the heart of political power since William Cecil was Elizabeth I's chief adviser. Hatfield House, once Elizabeth's home and now the Cecil family seat, was given to Robert Cecil by a grateful James I in exchange for Theobalds, the Cecils' home. Opposition to the £50 charge for public access to Hatfield House and its grounds is part of a current campaign for the Right to Roam in Britain as is Richard Benyon's vast Englefield Estate in Berkshire; a right secured in Scotland by its first devolved government's Land Reform (Scotland) Act of 2003, which also extended the right for island communities to buy their islands, and introduced community planning. Lord Richard Benyon, raised to the peerage in 2021, is now minister in charge of access to nature.

In Chapter 1, I referred to Melinda Cooper's argument in *Family Values* that the family remains central to contemporary capitalism's capacity for hoarding and passing on advantage. I also mentioned Thomas Piketty for pinpointing the re-emergence of private inherited wealth as decisive in shaping social class, after a brief relative decline in its influence post-war. Piketty did not specify which owners of what kind of assets have benefited most in terms of income since the 1970s. The answer is surprising. It is not owners of financial assets like stocks and shares; it is landowners. More and more income has been realised in the form of rent, suggesting that landowners are taking an increasing share of the economy. Gains in wealth as distinct from income have also been in land. ONS figures show that since the mid 1990s almost all of the increased wealth in the UK has been in the form of land and property, with land value gains accounting for the lion's share.

Brett Christophers concludes, 'Patterns of private land ownership… seem to be at the heart of growing inequalities in both income and wealth under capitalism' (Christophers, 2018, p. 56). Yet, despite the fact that over half of the UK's wealth is now locked up in land, dwarfing savings, landownership remains our oldest, darkest, best-kept secret and 'one of the clearest cases of a cover-up in English history,' claims Shrubsole (2019, p. 25). The only other cover-up that might possibly rank alongside it is the massive transfer of wealth from the public purse to the private sector incurred by the slavery compensation scheme in 1834, resulting in a debt not fully paid off by British taxpayers until 2015 – a fact only revealed in 2018 as the result of a Freedom of Information request. Whilst it is important to acknowledge that ordinary British people also benefited from slavery, it made some uniquely rich and paved the way for the alliance of powerful interests that still dominates how Britain is run today, in many ways. And whilst the names of people involved in the abolition of slavery, such as William Wilberforce, form part of our collective memory (though the names of black slaves involved in the campaign do not), the names of those who fought vigorously *against* its abolition, such as Joseph Foster Barham and George Hibbert, have fallen into obscurity.

When I decided to find out more about my great-great-uncle Alexander, I discovered a handful of marriages that placed him within a network of privileged families stretching back over generations, whose staying power was based precisely on hoarding and passing on. What they hoarded and passed on was, in the main, land. This is the backdrop to Alexander's extraordinary life. It is what ultimately enabled him to write his books and, in the last years of his life, to give his support to a dismal fascist regime that he believed heralded a new dawn. My exploration of a corner of my family's past has revealed a history of wealth begetting wealth that shows no signs of abating. Contemporary capitalism seems especially adept at providing renewed means to hoard and pass on advantage. To repeat: For 'things to stay as they are, things… have to change'. 'Pulling at the strand' of my great-great-uncle's life, as with opening the chest that sparked off my quest, became a way of unpicking the cover-ups in the history of slavery and Empire, and revealing the often ingenious but absolutely ordinary ways in which a few families renewed, replenished and conserved their wealth. What it also revealed is that there has been collusion right through British society to know/not know where money has come from – right down to the RNLI, the much-loved charity of coastal communities where stories of bravery and lost lives among lifeboat volunteers are what people know and celebrate, while the blood-soaked history of the charity's origins are forgotten or elided.

So, were there to be another Scottish independence referendum, would I change my vote, as I hinted in my first chapter? I feel the same antipathy towards Scottish nationalism – towards any kind of nationalism, in fact – as before, though I am now more inclined to reflect on other nationalisms that are also close to home: British and English nationalism. My research is a reminder that the British imperial state was defined by a form of racial capitalism that made some people uniquely wealthy and powerful and plunged most of the world's population into a struggle against scarcity. The current British state is a virtual free-for-all for privateers and outsourcers that outstrips William Cecil's legalised privateering. Compared with this kind of nationalism, Scottish nationalism is an innocent babe.

In light of my family history research, I find myself reviewing the arguments for 'Yes' that were penned before the 2014 referendum. Those that based their case on the fact that the British state has never thrown off its historical roots in a political compromise between aristocratic landowners and early merchant capitalists now feel particularly compelling (Jackson, 2020, p. 162). There is, of course, no let-out clause for Scotland, whose key role in the colonial exploitation that made Britain the nineteenth century's leading world power is undeniable. As Tom Nairn said in a 1968 edition of

New Left Review, 'Scotland is not a colony, a semi-colony, a pseudo-colony... or any kind of colony of the English. She is a junior but... highly successful partner in the general business enterprise of Anglo-Scots Imperialism' (quoted in Scanlan, 2020, p. 69). It is a profound misconception to view Scotland as a victim of imperialism.

One of the most powerful intellectual statements in the run-up to the referendum was Stephen Maxwell's *Arguing for Independence*, published posthumously in 2012. He did more than anyone else to formulate the now-dominant idea of left-wing nationalism. The core of Maxwell's case was democratic and economic, says Ben Jackson in his own highly original and carefully crafted history of nationalist thought in Scotland: independence would ensure that 'the Scottish people would be ruled by a government supported by the majority of the Scottish electorate'; the Scottish state would be 'a fully liberal democratic one, organised around a written constitution, a proportional electoral system, the full panoply of modern rights protections, and a public culture that would hold executive power to account' (Jackson, 2020, p. 162). Who could possibly disagree?

Yet I remain reluctant to vote 'Yes', in solidarity with all the other people on these islands who are dismayed by the swing to the right in government and the narrow English nationalism that helped secure Brexit. As an instinctive anti-nationalist, even I recognise that Scottish nationalism is more sophisticated than its English cousin, eschewing any hint of ethnic nativism in favour of a pro-immigrant civic nationalism (Kidd, 2021). In the absence of proportional representation, and given the collapse of Labour in Scotland, Britain now faces a Tory government for the foreseeable future, with or without Scotland. Were there to be another referendum explicitly tagged to an independent Scotland within Europe, I might think again. Being independent *and* outside Europe would be very lonely.

Postscript

I recently retrieved from deep inside my walk-in cupboard a rolled-up portrait of myself; the only one ever made, though, for reasons I cannot recall, it has never been completed. The artist, a close friend and colleague, Michael Scott, who became a successful painter, had died a few years earlier. Drawn in charcoal and coloured chalk, the portrait is little more than a sketch; an abstract study in blues and browns. My face is a blur but its shape is well captured, framed by my then longish brown hair, its kink, which I vainly try to straighten, clearly visible. I am sitting on a low antique chair; a gift from my mother but, regrettably, long since given away. Facing left with my hands clasped on my lap, I am wearing a long brown corduroy skirt and a soft blue velvet top, typical of late 1970s fashion. The chair is placed in front of a long rectangular chest. Some of the chest's elegant features are included in the sketch, including one of its gently curved feet, and just a hint of its lovely acanthus-leaf carvings. The portrait was drawn in the late 1970s or, at the latest, early 1980s.

This means that when I wrote the introduction to my account of my great-great-uncle in Chapter 1, I misremembered inheriting the Venetian chest from my mother. It is only now, contemplating the portrait of myself sitting in front of it, that I realise that she must have given it to me a few years after my father's death in 1972. I was living in Italy when he died. My mother moved house a few years later and no longer had enough space for the chest in her new flat, just up the road from the flat in which I spent most of my childhood. When she died in 1989 the chest had been with me for over a decade.

I had the portrait framed recently; around the time I started research on Alexander Robertson. It now hangs on a wall adjacent to where the chest stands. What also strikes me now is that my posture in the portrait – facing left – is almost identical to Helen's in the photograph referred to in Chapter 2, in which she poses with her new husband Alexander. My age in the portrait is not much younger than Helen's when she died.

Appendix

Family Tree Tables

In my tree, Robert Cecil appears as '6th great-grandfather of husband of wife of 2nd cousin 1x removed of wife of 2nd great-uncle'. Spelled out, he is Sir Robert Cecil, 1st Earl of Salisbury (1563–1612) and sixth great-grandfather of George William Frederick Villiers, 4th Earl of Clarendon (1800–70) and second husband of Katherine Grimston (1810–74), daughter of the Earl of Verulam and wife of John Foster Barham (1799–1838), second cousin once removed of Julia Dawson, second wife of Reverend Alexander Robertson, the author's second great-uncle. Robert Cecil appears, too, as 'father-in-law of 5th great-aunt of husband of wife of 2nd cousin 1x removed of wife of 2nd great-uncle'. Spelled out, that makes him the father-in-law of Catherine Howard (1595–1673), daughter of Thomas Howard, 1st Earl of Suffolk and fifth great-aunt of George William Frederick Villiers, 4th Earl of Clarendon and second husband of Katherine Grimston, daughter of the Earl of Verulam and wife of John Foster Barham (1799–1838), second cousin once removed of Julia Dawson, second wife of Reverend Alexander Robertson, the author's second great-uncle.

William Cavendish, 2nd Duke of Devonshire (1672–1729) appears as '2nd cousin 4x removed of husband [George William Frederick Villiers] of wife [Katherine Grimston] of 2nd cousin 1x removed [John Foster Barham] of wife of 2nd great-uncle [Alexander Robertson]'. His grandmother Elizabeth Cecil (1619–89) was the granddaughter of Robert Cecil, 1st Earl of Salisbury (1563–1612). Lady Anne Clifford (1590–1676) is in my tree via Joseph

Foster Barham II MP, Julia's first cousin twice removed. Joseph's wife, Lady Caroline Tufton, was the third great-granddaughter of Lady Anne Clifford. John Foster Barham (Julia's second cousin once removed) was the fourth great-grandson of Lady Anne Clifford. There is also a link via John's wife Katherine Grimston's second husband George William Frederick Villiers (1800–70) to Lady Anne Cecil (1612–37). Robert Boyle FRS (1627–91) is on the same tree with the Cecils and the Cliffords, as the brother of Richard Boyle, 2nd Earl of Cork (1612–97), husband of Robert Cecil's granddaughter Lady Elisabeth Clifford (1613–91).

Family Tree Tables

Table 1: Cecil / Howard / Russell / Cavendish / Villiers / Clifford / Boyle / John Foster Barham Family Tree

Table 2: Braddon / Palmer Family Tree

Table 3: Russell / Villiers Family Tree

Table 4: Robertson / Montgomery / Cruickshank Family Tree

Table 5: Smith / Foster / Barham / Vassall / Livius / Morgan / Luttrell-Olmius Family Tree

Table 6: Clifford / Cecil / Tufton / Sackville / Joseph Foster Barham Family Tree

Table 7: Vassall / Foster / Fox / Ellis / Beckford / Palmer / Hervey Family Tree

Table 1

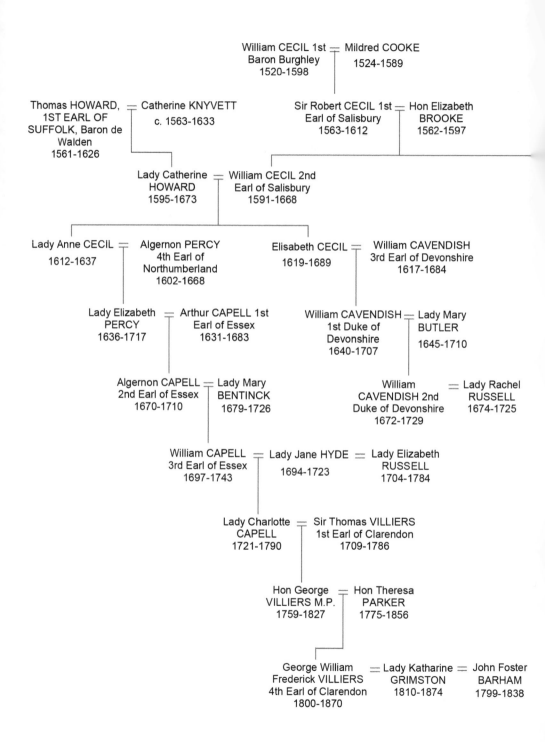

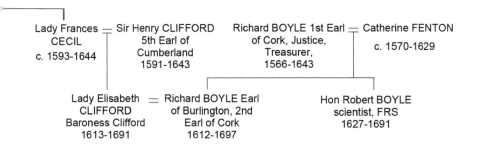

Lady Frances ═ Sir Henry CLIFFORD   Richard BOYLE 1st Earl ═ Catherine FENTON
CECIL   5th Earl of   of Cork, Justice,   c. 1570-1629
c. 1593-1644   Cumberland   Treasurer,
           1591-1643   1566-1643

Lady Elisabeth ═ Richard BOYLE Earl   Hon Robert BOYLE
CLIFFORD   of Burlington, 2nd   scientist, FRS
Baroness Clifford   Earl of Cork   1627-1691
1613-1691   1612-1697

Table 2

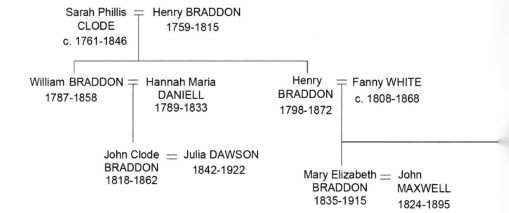

Sarah Phillis CLODE c. 1761-1846 = Henry BRADDON 1759-1815

William BRADDON 1787-1858 = Hannah Maria DANIELL 1789-1833

Henry BRADDON 1798-1872 = Fanny WHITE c. 1808-1868

John Clode BRADDON 1818-1862 = Julia DAWSON 1842-1922

Mary Elizabeth BRADDON 1835-1915 = John MAXWELL 1824-1895

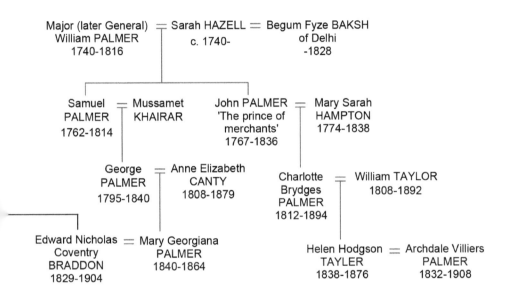

Major (later General) = Sarah HAZELL = Begum Fyze BAKSH
William PALMER   c. 1740-   of Delhi
1740-1816   -1828

Samuel = Mussamet   John PALMER = Mary Sarah
PALMER   KHAIRAR   'The prince of   HAMPTON
1762-1814   merchants'   1774-1838
                         1767-1836

George = Anne Elizabeth
PALMER   CANTY   Charlotte = William TAYLOR
1795-1840   1808-1879   Brydges   1808-1892
                        PALMER
                        1812-1894

Edward Nicholas = Mary Georgiana
Coventry   PALMER   Helen Hodgson = Archdale Villiers
BRADDON   1840-1864   TAYLER   PALMER
1829-1904   1838-1876   1832-1908

Table 3

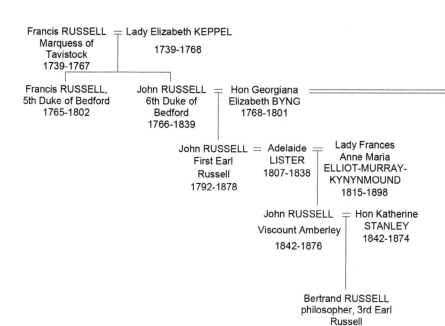

Francis RUSSELL = Lady Elizabeth KEPPEL
Marquess of
Tavistock   1739-1768
1739-1767

Francis RUSSELL,   John RUSSELL = Hon Georgiana
5th Duke of Bedford   6th Duke of   Elizabeth BYNG
1765-1802   Bedford   1768-1801
                      1766-1839

John RUSSELL = Adelaide = Lady Frances
First Earl   LISTER   Anne Maria
Russell   1807-1838   ELLIOT-MURRAY-
1792-1878   KYNYNMOUND
                          1815-1898

John RUSSELL = Hon Katherine
Viscount Amberley   STANLEY
1842-1876   1842-1874

Bertrand RUSSELL
philosopher, 3rd Earl
Russell
1872-1970

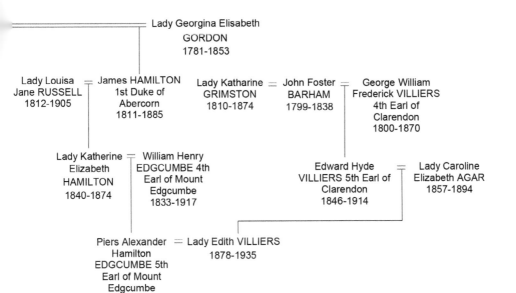

Lady Georgina Elisabeth
GORDON
1781-1853

Lady Louisa = James HAMILTON
Jane RUSSELL   1st Duke of
1812-1905   Abercorn
               1811-1885

Lady Katharine = John Foster = George William
GRIMSTON   BARHAM   Frederick VILLIERS
1810-1874   1799-1838   4th Earl of
                           Clarendon
                           1800-1870

Lady Katherine = William Henry
Elizabeth   EDGCUMBE 4th
HAMILTON   Earl of Mount
1840-1874   Edgcumbe
                1833-1917

Edward Hyde = Lady Caroline
VILLIERS 5th Earl of   Elizabeth AGAR
Clarendon   1857-1894
1846-1914

Piers Alexander = Lady Edith VILLIERS
Hamilton   1878-1935
EDGCUMBE 5th
Earl of Mount
Edgcumbe
1865-1944

Table 4

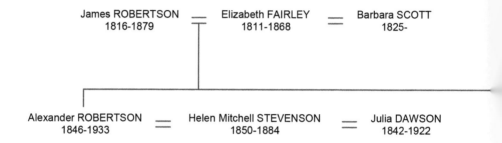

James ROBERTSON   —   Elizabeth FAIRLEY   —   Barbara SCOTT
1816-1879   1811-1868   1825-

Alexander ROBERTSON   —   Helen Mitchell STEVENSON   —   Julia DAWSON
1846-1933   1850-1884   1842-1922

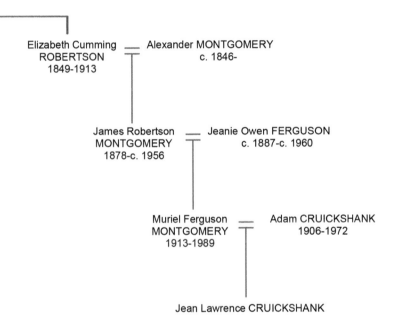

Elizabeth Cumming
ROBERTSON ⎯ Alexander MONTGOMERY
1849-1913   c. 1846-

James Robertson
MONTGOMERY ⎯ Jeanie Owen FERGUSON
1878-c. 1956   c. 1887-c. 1960

Muriel Ferguson
MONTGOMERY ⎯ Adam CRUICKSHANK
1913-1989   1906-1972

Jean Lawrence CRUICKSHANK

Table 5

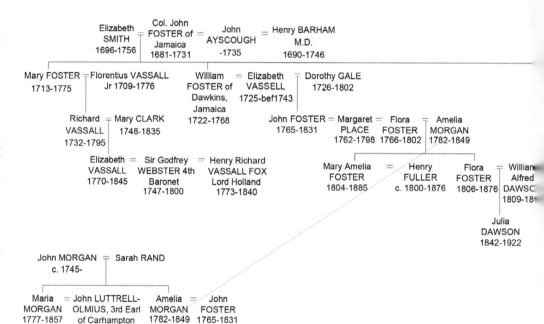

Elizabeth SMITH 1696-1756 = Col. John FOSTER of Jamaica 1681-1731 = John AYSCOUGH -1735 = Henry BARHAM M.D. 1690-1746

Mary FOSTER 1713-1775 = Florentius VASSALL Jr 1709-1776

William FOSTER of Dawkins, Jamaica 1722-1768 = Elizabeth VASSELL 1725-bef1743 = Dorothy GALE 1726-1802

Richard VASSALL 1732-1795 = Mary CLARK 1748-1835

John FOSTER 1765-1831 = Margaret PLACE 1762-1798 = Flora FOSTER 1766-1802 = Amelia MORGAN 1782-1849

Elizabeth VASSALL 1770-1845 = Sir Godfrey WEBSTER 4th Baronet 1747-1800 = Henry Richard VASSALL FOX Lord Holland 1773-1840

Mary Amelia FOSTER 1804-1885 = Henry FULLER c. 1800-1876

Flora FOSTER 1806-1876 = William Alfred DAWSC 1809-18··

Julia DAWSON 1842-1922

John MORGAN c. 1745- = Sarah RAND

Maria MORGAN 1777-1857 = John LUTTRELL-OLMIUS, 3rd Earl of Carhampton 1739-1829

Amelia MORGAN 1782-1849 = John FOSTER 1765-1831

Joseph Foster = Dorothy = Mary (POLE)
BARHAM   VAUGHAN   HILL
1729-1789   1721-1781   1730-1789

Mary   = George Peter   Joseph Foster = Lady Caroline
FOSTER-   LIVIUS   BARHAM MP   TUFTON
BARHAM   1743-1816   1759-1832   1771-1832
1757-1837

John Foster = Lady Katharine = George William
BARHAM   GRIMSTON   Frederick
Charlotte = Thomas   1799-1838   1810-1874   VILLIERS 4th
Anne   Shuttleworth   Earl of Clarendon
LIVIUS   GRIMSHAWE   1800-1870
1791-1851   1777-1850

John Clode = Alexander
=   BRADDON   ROBERTSON
1818-1862   1846-1933

Table 6

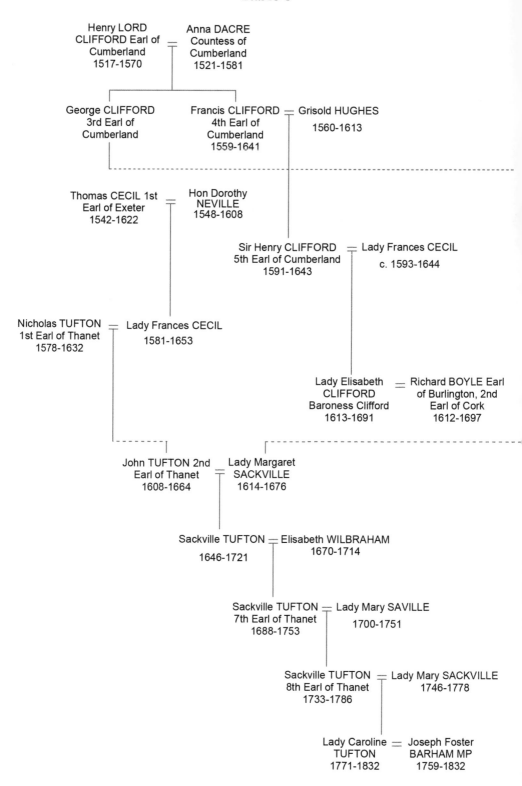

Henry LORD CLIFFORD Earl of Cumberland 1517-1570 = Anna DACRE Countess of Cumberland 1521-1581

George CLIFFORD 3rd Earl of Cumberland

Francis CLIFFORD 4th Earl of Cumberland 1559-1641 = Grisold HUGHES 1560-1613

Thomas CECIL 1st Earl of Exeter 1542-1622 = Hon Dorothy NEVILLE 1548-1608

Sir Henry CLIFFORD 5th Earl of Cumberland 1591-1643 = Lady Frances CECIL c. 1593-1644

Nicholas TUFTON 1st Earl of Thanet 1578-1632 = Lady Frances CECIL 1581-1653

Lady Elisabeth CLIFFORD Baroness Clifford 1613-1691 = Richard BOYLE Earl of Burlington, 2nd Earl of Cork 1612-1697

John TUFTON 2nd Earl of Thanet 1608-1664 = Lady Margaret SACKVILLE 1614-1676

Sackville TUFTON 1646-1721 = Elisabeth WILBRAHAM 1670-1714

Sackville TUFTON 7th Earl of Thanet 1688-1753 = Lady Mary SAVILLE 1700-1751

Sackville TUFTON 8th Earl of Thanet 1733-1786 = Lady Mary SACKVILLE 1746-1778

Lady Caroline TUFTON 1771-1832 = Joseph Foster BARHAM MP 1759-1832

George CLIFFORD
3rd Earl of
Cumberland
1558-1605
=
Lady Margaret
RUSSELL
1560-1616

Richard SACKVILLE = Lady Anne CLIFFORD === Philip HERBERT
3rd Earl of Dorset   Baroness Clifford   Earl of Pembroke
1589-1624   1590-1676   1584-1650

Table 7

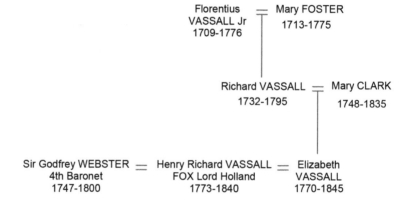

Florentius = Mary FOSTER
VASSALL Jr   1713-1775
1709-1776

Richard VASSALL = Mary CLARK
1732-1795   1748-1835

Sir Godfrey WEBSTER = Henry Richard VASSALL = Elizabeth
4th Baronet   FOX Lord Holland   VASSALL
1747-1800   1773-1840   1770-1845

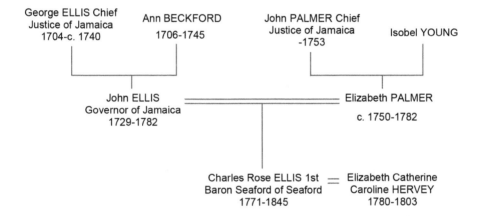

George ELLIS Chief
Justice of Jamaica
1704-c. 1740

Ann BECKFORD
1706-1745

John PALMER Chief
Justice of Jamaica
-1753

Isobel YOUNG

John ELLIS
Governor of Jamaica
1729-1782

Elizabeth PALMER
c. 1750-1782

Charles Rose ELLIS 1st
Baron Seaford of Seaford
1771-1845

Elizabeth Catherine
Caroline HERVEY
1780-1803

Bibliography

Alexander, W. (1992) *Rural Life in Victorian Aberdeenshire*, Edinburgh: Mercat Press

Alford, S. (2008) *Burghley: William Cecil at the Court of Elizabeth I*, New Haven and London: Yale University Press

Alford, S. (2012) *The Watchers: A Secret History of the Reign of Elizabeth I*, London: Penguin Books

Alston, D. (2021) *Slaves and Highlanders: Silenced Histories of Scotland and the Caribbean*, Edinburgh: Edinburgh University Press

Anderson, R. D. (1983) *Education and Opportunity in Victorian Scotland: Schools and Universities*, Oxford: Clarendon Press

Anderson, R. D. (1985) 'Education and Society in Modern Scotland: A Comparative Perspective' in *History of Education Quarterly* (Winter), pp. 458–81

Anderson, R. D. (2018) 'Historical Perspectives' in Bryce, T. G. K., Humes, W. M., Gillies, D. and Kennedy, A. (eds.), *Scottish Education* (Fifth Edition), Edinburgh: Edinburgh University Press, pp. 99–107

Armitstead, C. (2020) 'From fig leaves to pinups: Mary Beard on the evolution of the nude' in *Guardian Review*, 106, pp. 32–5

Atwood, C. D. (2015) 'Five Centuries of Women's Leadership in the Moravian Church', 12th Moravian Women's Conference, Sandy Cove, Maryland, 25–28 June

Atwood, S. (2011) *Ruskin's Educational Ideals*, London: Routledge

Barnes, D. (2009) *'Urbs/Passion/Politics': Venice in Selected Works of Ruskin and Pound*, PhD English thesis, Queen Mary University of London

Barnes, D. (2015) *The Venice Myth: Culture, Literature, Politics, 1800 to the Present*, London: Routledge

Baron, A. (2001) *An Indian Affair: From Riches to Raj*, London: Sidgwick & Jackson

Barr, J. (1999) *Liberating Knowledge: Research, Feminism and Adult Education*, Leicester: National Institute of Adult Continuing Education (NIACE)

Beckles, H. McD. (1985) 'Plantation Production and White "Proto-slavery": White Indentured Servants and the Colonisation of the English West Indies, 1624–1645' in *The Americas*, 41:3, pp. 21–45

Benjamin, W. (1936) 'The Work of Art in the Age of Mechanical Reproduction' in Benjamin, W. (Arendt, H. ed.) (1955) *Illuminations*, London: Fontana, 1973, pp. 219–53

Black, J. (2011) *A Brief History of Slavery: A New Global History*, London: Robinson

Bosworth, R. J. B. (2002) *Mussolini*, London: Bloomsbury Academic

Bosworth, R. J. B. (2005) *Mussolini's Italy: Life Under the Fascist Dictatorship, 1915–1945*, London, Penguin Books

Braddon, M. E. (1998 [1862]) *Lady Audley's Secret*, London: Penguin Classics

Braddon, M. E. (2008 [1864]) *The Doctor's Wife*, Oxford: Oxford World's Classics

Brenner, R. (1985) 'Agrarian Class Structure and Economic Development in Pre-Industrial Europe' in Aston, T. H. and Philpin, C. H. E. (eds.), *The Brenner Debate: Agrarian Class Structure and Economic Development in Pre-Industrial Europe*, Cambridge: Cambridge University Press, pp. 10–61

Brodsky, J. (1992) *Watermark: An Essay on Venice*, London: Penguin Classics

Brown, C. L. (2006) *Moral Capital: Foundations of British Abolitionism*, Chapel Hill and London: University of North Carolina Press

Bryden, D. J. (1970) 'The Jamaican Observatories of Colin Campbell, F.R.S. and Alexander Macfarlane, F.R.S.' in *Notes and Records of the Royal Society of London*, 24:2, pp. 261–72

Burke, B. (1838) *A Genealogical and Heraldic History of the Landed Gentry of Great Britain and Ireland*, London: Henry Colburn

Burke, B. (1891) *A Genealogical and Heraldic History of the Colonial Gentry*, London: Harrison

Busteed, H. E. (1908) *Echoes from Old Calcutta: Being Chiefly Reminiscences of the Days of Warren Hastings, Francis, and Impey*, London: W. Thacker & Company; Calcutta and Simla: Thacker, Spink & Company

Butler, K. M. (1995) *The Economics of Emancipation: Jamaica and Barbados, 1823–1843*, Chapel Hill and London: University of North Carolina Press

Calder, J. (1980) *RLS: A Life Study*, London: Hamish Hamilton

Calvino, I. and McLaughlin, M. (trans.) (2003) 'Political Autobiography of a Young Man' in *Hermit in Paris: Autobiographical Writings*, London: Jonathan Cape, pp. 130–156

Carnell, J. (2000) *The Literary Lives of Mary Elizabeth Braddon: A Study of Her Life and Work*, London: Sensation Press

Carson, P. (2012) *The East India Company and Religion, 1698–1858*, Woodbridge, Suffolk: Boydell & Brewer

Carter, I. (1979) *Farm Life in Northeast Scotland, 1840–1914: The Poor Man's Country*, Edinburgh: John Donald Publishers Ltd

Christophers, B. (2018) *The New Enclosure: The Appropriation of Public Land in Neoliberal Britain*, London: Verso

Christophers, B. (2020) *Rentier Capitalism: Who Owns the Economy, and Who Pays for It?* London: Verso

Clayton, A. (1999) 'Dresden, 1206–1918' in Clayton, A. and Russell, A. (eds.), *Dresden: A City Reborn*, London: Berg Publishers, pp. 9–26

Clifford, A. (Clifford, D. J. H. ed.) (2009) *The Diaries of Lady Anne Clifford*, Stroud, Gloucestershire: The History Press

Cockburn, H. T. (1856) *Memorials of His Time*, Edinburgh: A & C Black

Colley, L. (2007) *The Ordeal of Elizabeth Marsh: A Woman in World History*, London: HarperCollins

Colley, L. (2010) 'Gendering the Globe: The Political and Imperial Thought of Philip Francis' in *Past & Present*, 209, pp. 117–48

Collins, S. (2019) *The Confessions of Frannie Langton*, London: Penguin

Cooper, M. (2017) *Family Values: Between Neoliberalism and the New Social Conservatism*, New York: Zone Books

Crewe, T. (2016) 'The Strange Death of Municipal England' in *London Review of Books*, 38:24, pp. 6–10

Crewe, T. (2017) 'Short Cuts: Labour's Best Cards' in *London Review of Books*, 39:18, pp. 6–7

Cuddy, N. (2000) 'Reinventing a Monarchy: The Changing Structure and Political Function of the Stuart Court, 1603–88' in Cruickshanks, E. (ed.), *The Stuart Courts*, Stroud, Gloucestershire: The History Press, pp. 59–85

Dalrymple, W. (2004 [2002]) *White Mughals: Love and Betrayal in Eighteenth-Century India,* London: Harper Perennial

Dalrymple, W. (2019) *The Anarchy: The Relentless Rise of the East India Company*, London, Oxford, New York, New Delhi, Sydney: Bloomsbury Publishing

Davie, G. E. (1961) *The Democratic Intellect: Scotland and her Universities in the Nineteenth Century*, Edinburgh: Edinburgh University Press

Davies, W. (2018) 'Against Responsibility' in *London Review of Books*, 40:21, pp. 28–30

Dawson, F. (1864) *Princes, Public Men, and Pretty Women: Episodes in Real Life in Two Volumes*, London: Richard Bentley

de Grazia, V. (2020) *The Perfect Fascist: A Story of Love, Power, and Morality in Mussolini's Italy*, Cambridge, Massachusetts and London, England: Harvard University Press

de Rachewiltz, M., Moody, A. D. and Moody, J. (eds.) (2011) *Ezra Pound to his Parents: Letters, 1895-1929*, Oxford: Oxford University Press

Devine, T. M. (2006) *Clearance and Improvement: Land, Power and People in Scotland, 1700-1900*, Edinburgh: John Donald Publishers Ltd

di Lampedusa, G. T. (1960 [1958]) *The Leopard*, London: Collins and Harvill Press

Dick, D. M. (2008) *The Origin and Development of the Native Baptists in Jamaica and the Influence of their Biblical Hermeneutic on the 1865 Native Baptist War*, PhD Caribbean Studies thesis, University of Warwick

Dikötter, F. (2020) *Dictators*, London: Bloomsbury Publishing

Disraeli, B. (1998 [1845]) *Sybil, or the Two Nations*, Oxford: Oxford University Press

Donington, K. (2014) 'Transforming Capital: Slavery, Family, Commerce and the Making of the Hibbert family' in Hall, C., Draper, N., McClelland, K., Donington, K. and Lang, R. (eds.), *Legacies of British Slave-Ownership: Colonial Slavery and the Formation of Victorian Britain*, Cambridge: Cambridge University Press, pp. 203–49

Dresser, M. (2001) *Slavery Obscured: The Social History of the Slave Trade in an English Provincial Port*, London and New York: Continuum

Dunn, R. S. (1972) *Sugar and Slaves: The Rise of the Planter Class in the English West Indies, 1624-1713*, Chapel Hill and London: University of North Carolina Press

Dunn, R. S. (2014) *A Tale of Two Plantations: Slave Life and Labor in Jamaica and Virginia*, Cambridge, Massachusetts and London, England: Harvard University Press

Embree, A. T. (1962) *Charles Grant and British Rule in India*, New York: Columbia University Press

Ewan, E., Innes, S., Reynolds, S. and Pipes, R. (eds.) (2007) *The Biographical*

Dictionary of Scottish Women, Edinburgh: Edinburgh University Press

Ewan, E., Pipes, R., Rendall, J. and Reynolds, S. (eds.) (2018) *The New Biographical Dictionary of Scottish Women,* Edinburgh: Edinburgh University Press

Floud, R. (2019) *An Economic History of the English Garden,* London: Allen Lane

Forster, M. and Smith, S. D. (2011) 'Surviving Slavery: Mortality at Mesopotamia, a Jamaican Sugar Estate, 1762–1832', *Journal of the Royal Statistical Society, Series A (Statistics in Society),* 174:4, October, pp. 907–29

Foster Barham, J. (1768) *Memoir of Br. William Foster who departed this life at Bedford, Oct 31st, 1768. Drawn up by his brother Joseph Foster Barham* (Bedfordshire County Archives: MO 2000/165)

Foster Barham, J. (1807) *Observations on the Agriculture in the North of Bedfordshire,* Bedford: J. Webb

Foster Barham, J. (1824) *Considerations on the Abolition of Negro Slavery and the Means of Practically Effecting It* (Third Edition), London: James Ridgway

Foster, E. (Williams, S. T. and Beach, L. B. eds.) (1938 [1820–3]) *The Journal of Emily Foster,* Oxford: Oxford University Press

Garrard, M. D. (2001) *Artemisia Gentileschi Around 1622: The Shaping and Reshaping of an Artistic Identity,* Berkeley: University of California Press

Gaskell, E. (2015 [1857]) *The Life of Charlotte Brontë* (Complete and Unabridged Edition), CreateSpace Independent Publishing

Gibson, W. and Begiato, J. (2017) *Sex and the Church in the Long Eighteenth Century: Religion, Enlightenment and the Sexual Revolution,* London: I. B. Tauris

Gramsci, A. (Hoare, Q. and Nowell-Smith, G. eds. and trans.) (1971) *Selections from the Prison Notebooks,* London: Lawrence & Wishart

Griffin, C. (1988) *The Moravian Church in Bedford, 1745–1845,* BA dissertation, combined studies (CNAA) degree in British history, third-year special study, Bedford College of Higher Education, 22nd April

Hall, C. (2014) 'Introduction' in Hall, C., Draper, N., McClelland, K., Donington, K. and Lang, R. (eds.), *Legacies of British Slave-Ownership: Colonial Slavery and the Formation of Victorian Britain,* pp. 1–33

Hall, C., Draper, N., McClelland, K., Donington, K. and Lang, R. (eds.) (2014) *Legacies of British Slave-Ownership: Colonial Slavery and the Formation of Victorian Britain,* Cambridge: Cambridge University Press

Hall, C. (2018) 'Persons Outside the Law' in *London Review of Books*, 40:14, pp. 3–5

Hall, C. (2020) 'Mother Country' in *London Review of Books*, 42:2, pp. 11–14

Hall, D. (2003) 'Planters, Farmers and Gardeners in Eighteenth-Century Jamaica' in Moore, B. L., Higman, B. W., Campbell, C. and Bryan, P. (eds.), *Slavery, Freedom and Gender: The Dynamics of Caribbean Society*, Kingston, Jamaica: University of the West Indies Press, pp. 97–114

Hall, S. and Schwarz, B. (2017) *Familiar Stranger: A Life Between Two Islands*, Durham and London: Duke University Press

Hassan, G. (2018) 'Do We Live in an Age of Fascism?' in *Scottish Review*, 31st October

Hassan, G. (2020) 'A Tour Inside Gordon Brown's Britain' in *Scottish Review*, 25th November

Hastings, S. U. and MacLeavy, B. L. (1979) *Seedtime and Harvest: A Brief History of the Moravian Church in Jamaica, 1754–1979*, Bridgetown, Barbados: Moravian Church Corporation/Cedar Press

Hawes, J. (2017) *The Shortest History of Germany*, Devon: Old Street Publishing

Higman, B. W. (1976) *Slave Population and Economy in Jamaica, 1807–1834*, Cambridge: Cambridge University Press

Higman, B. W. (2008) *Plantation Jamaica, 1750–1850: Capital and Control in a Colonial Economy*, Kingston, Jamaica: University of the West Indies Press

Hill, R. (2017) 'One's Self-Washed Drawers' in *London Review of Books*, 39:13, pp. 3–5

Holland, E. (Earl of Ilchester ed.) (1908 [1795]) *The Journal of Elizabeth, Lady Holland, in Two Volumes*, London, New York, Bombay and Calcutta: Longmans, Green and Co

Holmes, R. (2011 [1985]) *Footsteps: Adventures of a Romantic Biographer*, London: Harper Press

Hunt, T. (2014) *Ten Cities that Made an Empire*, London: Allen Lane

Irving, P. M. (1862) *The Life and Letters of Washington Irving*, New York: G. P. Putnam

Irving, P. M. (1864) *The Life and Letters of Washington Irving, 1862–1864*, London: Richard Bentley

Jackson, B. (2020) *The Case for Scottish Independence: A History of Nationalist Political Thought in Modern Scotland*, Cambridge: Cambridge University Press

Jones, B. J. (2011) *Washington Irving: An American Original*, New York: Arcade Publishing

Jordan, M. (2005) *The Great Abolition Sham: The True Story of the End of the British Slave Trade*, Stroud, Gloucestershire: The History Press

Kay-Shuttleworth, J. E. (1873) *The Life of J. Sebastian Bach: An Abridged Translation from the German of C. H. Bitter*, London: Houlston

Kerevan, G. (2008) 'Democratic Intellect or Degree Factory? The Changing Civic and Cultural Place of the University in Scotland' in Bryce, T. G. K. and Humes, W. M. (eds.), *Scottish Education* (Third Edition), Edinburgh: Edinburgh University Press, pp. 681–91

Kernohan, R. D. (2005) *An Alliance Across the Alps: Britain and Italy's Waldensians*, Haddington: The Handsel Press

Kidd, C. (2021) 'New Unions for Old' in *London Review of Books*, 43:5, pp. 13–14

Kime, W. R. (2006 [1977]) *Pierre M. Irving and Washington Irving: A Collaboration in Life and Letters*, Waterloo, Ontario: Wilfrid Laurier Press

Kriegel, A. D. (ed.) (1977) *The Holland House Diaries, 1831–1840: The Diary of Henry Richard Vassall-Fox, Third Lord Holland, with Extracts from the Diary of Dr John Allen*, London: Routledge & Kegan Paul

Kuhn, A. (1995) *Family Secrets: Acts of Memory and Imagination*, London and New York: Verso

Landreth, P. (1876) *The United Presbyterian Divinity Hall: In its Changes and Enlargements for One Hundred and Forty Years*, Edinburgh: William Oliphant and Co

Law, J. E. (1993) 'Alexander Robertson (1846–1933)' in Cameron, N. M. de S. (ed.), *Dictionary of Scottish Church History and Theology*, Edinburgh: T&T Clark, pp. 722–3

Lee, C. (2003) *1603: A Turning Point in British History*, London: Headline

Long, E. (1774) *The History of Jamaica*, London: T. Lowndes

Mabee, B. (2009) 'Pirates, Privateers and the Political Economy of Private Violence' in *Global Change, Peace & Security*, 21:2, pp. 139–52

MacCulloch, D. (2004) *Reformation: Europe's House Divided, 1490–1700*, London: Penguin Books

MacCulloch, D. (2016) *All Things Made New: The Reformation and its Legacy*, Oxford and New York: Oxford University Press

MacKelvie, W. (1873) *Annals and Statistics of the United Presbyterian Church*, Edinburgh: Oliphant and Company

Mackinnon, A. G. (1937) *Beyond the Alps: The Story of the Scottish Church in Italy and Malta*, London and Edinburgh: Oliphants Ltd

MacKinnon, I. and Mackillop, A. (2020) 'Plantation Slavery and Landownership in the West Highlands and Islands: Legacies and Lessons' in *Land and the Common Good: A Discussion Paper Series on Land Reform in Scotland*, Oban, Argyll: Community Land Scotland, pp. 1–23

Mair, L. M. (2016) *'The Only Friend I Have in this World': Ragged School Relationships in England and Scotland, 1844–1870*, PhD philosophy thesis, University of Edinburgh

Major, J. and Murden, S. (2016) *A Right Royal Scandal: Two Marriages that Changed History*, Barnsley, South Yorkshire: Pen and Sword Books

Mantel, H. (2020) *The Mirror & the Light*, London: HarperCollins 4th Estate

Mason, J. C. S. (2001) *The Moravian Church and the Missionary Awakening in England, 1760–1800*, London: Royal Historical Society: The Boydell Press

Maxwell, S. (2012) *Arguing for Independence: Evidence, Risk and the Wicked Issues*, Edinburgh: Luath Press

McCarthy, M. (2006 [1956]) *The Stones of Florence and Venice Observed*, London: Penguin Books

McCulloch, D. (1999) 'Dresden: A Music Metropolis' in Clayton, A. and Russell, A. (eds.), *Dresden: A City Reborn*, pp. 169–94

McFarland, E. W. (1990) *Protestants First: Orangeism in Nineteenth Century Scotland*, Edinburgh: Edinburgh University Press

McPherson, A. (1973) 'Selection and Survivals: A Sociology of the Ancient Scottish Universities' in Brown R. (ed.), *Knowledge, Education and Cultural Change*, London: Tavistock

Mishra, P. (2020) 'Flailing States' in *London Review of Books*, 42:14, pp. 9–14

Mitchell, W. R. (2002) *The Fabulous Cliffords*, Giggleswick: Castleberg

Modjeska, D. (1990) *Poppy*, Carlton, Victoria: McPhee Gribble

Moorehead, C. (2017) *A Bold and Dangerous Family: One Family's Fight Against Italian Fascism*, London: Penguin Vintage

Moorehead, C. (2019) *A House in the Mountains: The Women Who Liberated Italy from Fascism*, London: Chatto & Windus

Morrison, T. (2017) *The Origin of Others*, Harvard: Harvard University Press

Nairn, T. (1988) *The Enchanted Glass: Britain and its Monarchy*, London: Radius

Nooteboom, C. (2012) *Roads to Berlin*, London: Hachette Book Group

Nooteboom, C. (2020) *Venice: The Lion, the City and the Water*, London: MacLehose Press

Olusoga, D. (2015) *Britain's Forgotten Slave Owners*, Episode 2: 'The Price of Freedom', BBC Two, first broadcast 22nd July

Olusoga, D. (2017) *Black and British: A Forgotten History*, London: Pan Books

Orr, A. M. (1972) *The Schools of Bute Chronology*, typewritten pamphlet

Parry, G. (2014) *The Seventeenth Century: The Intellectual and Cultural Context of English Literature, 1603–1700*, London: Routledge

Partington, R. (2020) 'Owning a Home is a dream 20 years out of date' in *Guardian*, 11th February, p. 3

Pedersen, S. (2017) *The Guardians: The League of Nations and the Crisis of Empire*, Oxford: Oxford University Press

Pedersen, S. (2020) 'Shock Cities' in *London Review of Books*, 42:1, pp. 37–39

Pestana, C. G. (2009) *Protestant Empire: Religion and the Making of the British Atlantic World*, Philadelphia: University of Pennsylvania Press

Picken, S. D. B. (1972) *The Soul of an Orkney Parish: Studies in the Life and History of an Ancient Orkney Parish*, Kirkwall: Kirkwall Press

Piketty, T. (2014) *Capital in the Twenty-First Century*, Cambridge, MA: Harvard University Press

Pound, E. (1954) *The Cantos of Ezra Pound*, London: Faber & Faber

Pound, E. (1970 [1938]) *Guide to Kulchur*, London: New Directions

Pound, O. and Walton Litz, A. (eds.) (1985) *Ezra Pound and Dorothy Shakespear: Their Letters, 1909–1914*, London: Faber & Faber

Prince, M. (Pringle, T. ed.) (1831) *The History of Mary Prince, a West Indian Slave. Related by Herself with a Supplement by the Editor, to which is Added the Narrative of Asa-Asa, a Captured African*, London: F. Westley and A. H. Davis

Purver, J. (1999) 'Dresden's Literary and Theatrical Traditions' in Clayton, A. and Russell, A. (eds.), *Dresden: A City Reborn*, pp. 195–222

Rainey, L. (1999) 'Between Mussolini and Me: Lawrence Rainey traces Pound's Fascism to the Palace Hotel, Rimini' in *London Review of Books*, 21:6, pp. 22–25

Reichart, W. A. (1935) 'Washington Irving, the Fosters, and the Forsters' in *Modern Language Notes*, 50:1, pp. 35–9

Rendall, J. (2009) *Steering the Stone Ships: A Story of Orkney Kirks and People*, Edinburgh: Saint Andrew Press

Renton, A. (2021) *Blood Legacy: Reckoning with a Family's Story of Slavery*, Edinburgh: Canongate

Richards, E. (2013) *The Highland Clearances: People, Landlords and Rural Turmoil*, Edinburgh: Birlinn

Robinson, M. (2015) *The Givenness of Things: Essays*, London: Virago Press

Rolfe, F. (1950) *Three Tales of Venice*, London: Corvine Press

Rolfe, F. (2002 [1934]) *The Desire and Pursuit of the Whole: A Romance of Modern Venice*, London: Cassell and Company

Rowbotham, S. (1973) *Hidden from History: 300 Years of Women's Oppression and the Fight Against It*, London: Pluto Press

Rowse, A. L. (1950) *The England of Elizabeth*, London: Macmillan & Co Ltd

Roy, K. (2019) *In Case of Any News*, Glasgow: ICS Books

Russell, A. (1999) 'Dresden's Architectural Traditions and its Surviving Heritage' in Clayton, A. and Russell, A. (eds.), *Dresden: A City Reborn*, pp. 117–43

Russell, G. (2017) *Young & Damned & Fair: The Life and Tragedy of Catherine Howard at the Court of Henry VIII*, London: William Collins

Ryan-Collins, J., Lloyd, T. and Macfarlane, L. (2017) *Rethinking the Economics of Land and Housing*, London: Zed Books Ltd

Ryrie, A. (2017) *Protestants: The Radicals Who Made the Modern World*, London: William Collins

Sanghera, S. (2021) *Empireland: How Imperialism Has Shaped Modern Britain*, London: Penguin Random House

Scanlan, P. X. (2020) *Slave Empire: How Slavery Built Modern Britain*, London: Robinson

Schama, S. (2003) *A History of Britain: At the Edge of the World? 3000 BC – AD 1603*, London: BBC Worldwide Ltd

Scott, H. (1928) *Fasti Ecclesiae Scoticanae: The Succession of Ministers in the Church of Scotland from the Reformation*, Edinburgh: Oliver and Boyd

Scurati, A. and Appel, A. M. (trans.) (2021) *M: Son of the Century*, London: HarperCollins 4th Estate

Selleck, R. J. W. (1995) *James Kay-Shuttleworth: Journey of an Outsider*, London: Routledge

Sher, R. B. (1985) *Church and University in the Scottish Enlightenment: The Moderate Literati of Edinburgh*, Edinburgh: Edinburgh University Press

Sheridan, R. B. (1974) *Sugar and Slavery: An Economic History of the British West Indies, 1623–1775*, Barbados: Caribbean Universities Press

Shrubsole, G. (2019) *Who Owns England? How We Lost Our Green and Pleasant Land and How to Take it Back*, London: William Collins

Small, R. (1904) 'South Ronaldsay (United Session)' in Small, R. *History of the Congregations of the United Presbyterian Church from 1733 to 1900*, Edinburgh: David M. Small, pp. 499–501

Smith, A. (Campbell, R. H. and Skinner, A. S. eds.) (1976 [1776]) *An Inquiry into the Nature and Causes of the Wealth of Nations*, Oxford: Clarendon Press

Smith, F. (1974 [1923]) *The Life and Work of Sir James Kay-Shuttleworth*, New Portway Reprints

Smith, S. D. (2006) *Slavery, Family and Gentry Capitalism in the British Atlantic: The World of the Lascelles, 1648–1834*, Cambridge: Cambridge University Press

Smith, S. J. (2000) 'Retaking the Register: Women's Higher Education in Glasgow and Beyond, c. 1796–1845' in *Gender & History*, 12:2, pp. 310–35

Steele, T. (1997) *The Emergence of Cultural Studies, 1945–65*, London: Lawrence & Wishart

Stephens, P. (2015 [1998]) *The Waldensian Story: A Study in Faith, Intolerance and Survival* (Second Edition), Turin: Claudiana

Stock, N. (1970) *The Life of Ezra Pound*, London: Routledge & Kegan Paul Ltd

Stone, L. (1973) *Family and Fortune: Studies in Aristocratic Finance in the Sixteenth and Seventeenth Centuries*, Oxford: Oxford University Press

Stonor Saunders, F. (2010) *The Woman Who Shot Mussolini*, London: Faber & Faber

Stonor Saunders, F. (2021) *The Suitcase: Six Attempts to Cross a Border*, London: Jonathan Cape

Symons, A. J. A. (1955 [1934]) *The Quest for Corvo: An Experiment in Biography*, London: Cassell and Company

Tanner, T. (1992) *Venice Desired*, Oxford, UK and Cambridge, USA: Wiley-Blackwell

Tayler, A. and Tayler, H. (1914) *The Book of the Duffs* (Volumes 1 and 2), Edinburgh: William Brown

Taylor, M. (2020) *The Interest: How the British Establishment Resisted the Abolition of Slavery*, London: The Bodley Head

Terrell, C. F. (1984) *A Companion to the Cantos of Ezra Pound* (Volume II), Berkeley: University of California Press

Todd, S. (2021) *Snakes and Ladders: The Great British Social Mobility Myth*, London: Chatto & Windus

Trilling, D. (2019) 'I'm Not Racist, But…' in *London Review of Books*, 41:8, pp. 19–22

Turner, M. (1982) *Slaves and Missionaries: The Disintegration of Jamaican Slave Society, 1787–1834*, Chicago: University of Chicago Press

Uglow, J. (1993) *Elizabeth Gaskell: A Habit of Stories*, London and Boston: Faber & Faber

Uglow, J. (2017) *Mr Lear: A Life of Art and Nonsense*, London: Faber & Faber

Verkaik, R. (2018) *Posh Boys: How the English Public Schools Run Britain*, London: Oneworld

Walvin, J. (2007) *The Trader, The Owner, The Slave: Parallel Lives in the Age of Slavery*, London: Jonathan Cape

Ward, J. R. (1988) *British West Indian Slavery, 1750–1834: The Process of Amelioration*, Oxford: Clarendon Press

Welch, E. (ed.) (1989) *The Bedford Moravian Church in the Eighteenth Century: A Selection of Documents* (Volume 68), Bedford, Bedfordshire Historical Records Society, p. vii

Whitehead, P. (1963) *The Brontës Came Here*, Halifax: Fawcett Greenwood and Co Ltd Printer

Wicomb, Z. (2020) *Still Life*, New York: The New Press

Wightman, A. (2013) *The Poor Had No Lawyers: Who Owns Scotland (And How They Got It)*, Edinburgh: Birlinn

Wilkening, A.-C. (2018) 'I Didn't Know That I Was Starving 'Til I Tasted You: 18th Century Moravian Women's Ecstatic Experience of Bridal Mysticism in Communion and Marital Sexuality' in *Lumen et Vita*, 8:2, pp. 40–51

Wolff, R. L. (1979) *Sensational Victorian: The Life and Fiction of Mary Elizabeth Braddon*, New York: Garland Publishing

Books by Alexander Robertson

Robertson, A. (1891) *Count Campello and Catholic Reform in Italy*, London: Sampson Low, Marston & Co

Robertson, A. (1893) *Fra Paolo Sarpi: The Greatest of the Venetians* (First Edition), London: Sampson Low, Marston & Co

Robertson, A. (1894) *Fra Paolo Sarpi: The Greatest of the Venetians* (Second Edition), London; Sampson Low, Marston & Co

Robertson, A. (1896) *Through the Dolomites from Venice to Toblach*, London: George Allen

Robertson, A. (1898) *The Bible of St Mark: St Mark's Church, the Altar and Throne of Venice*, London: George Allen

Robertson, A. (1901) *Authority in Matters of Faith*, London: Society for Promoting Christian Knowledge; New York: E. & J. B. Young and Co

Robertson, A. (1902) *The Roman Catholic Church in Italy*, London: Morgan & Scott

Robertson, A. (1905) *Venetian Discourses Drawn from the History, Art and Customs of Venice*, London: George Allen

Robertson, A. (1909) *The Papal Conquest: Italy's Warning – Wake Up, John Bull!* London: Morgan & Scott

Robertson, A. (1911) *Fra Paolo Sarpi: The Greatest of the Venetians* (Third Edition), London: George Allen

Robertson, A. (1925) *Victor Emmanuel III, King of Italy*, London: Allen & Unwin

Robertson, A. (1929) *Mussolini and the New Italy*, London: Allenson

Index